AT THE SHARP END

ADVICE AND TIPS FROM REAL BUSINESSES

Written by business people,

for business people.

Raising money for Cancer Research UK

OnionCustard
Publishing

To those we all remember with love…

to the survivors,

the carers,

the doctors,

the nurses,

the researchers,

friends and supporters,

this book is dedicated

to every one of you

At The Sharp End

Advice and Tips From Real Businesses

Contributing Authors:
• Steve Abel • Lesley Allart • Sian Bick • Celeste Bolt • Chris Bown • Jeff Boycott • Denis G. Campbell •
• Phil Cheesman • Lady Helen Child Villiers • Dr Michelle Clarke • Carmen Crocker • Nicola Cross •
• Michelle Dalley • Alex Davies • Helen Davies • Elizabeth de Benedictis • Nicola Drummond •
• Brian Fakir • Trish Fulford • Andy Gardner • Picasso Griffiths • Liam Hamilton • Maz Hawes •
• Karen Hensman • Crystal Hinam • Peter Hopkins • Leanne Hugglestone • Kirstine Hughes •
• Emma Jennings • Cat Johnson • Robert Lang • Jacqui Malpass • Nicky Marshall • Rahim Mastafa •
• Peter Maynard • John McAleer • Sibel McColm • Martina Mercer-Phillips • Andrew Miller •
• Mike Morrison • Peter Norrington • Charlotte K. Omillin • Sam O'Sullivan •Rebecca Parsley •
• Jo-Jocelyn Pearce • David Rahman • Lee Rickler • George Savva • Lucy Scott •
• Bob Shepherd • Caroline Skinner • Steve Tasker • Eric Taylor • Phil Terrett • Fran Tyler •
• Jason Vaughan • Barry Watson • Steve White • Sue Worrall • Ann-See Yeoh •

Editor: David Norrington

The chapters covering cancer, and Cancer Research UK
are reproduced with the generous permission of Cancer Research UK.
The individual authors assert copyright to the chapters
that are directly attributed to them, all additional content is
© 2013 Onion Custard Publishing.
All rights reserved.

This book is protected under the copyright laws of the United Kingdom.
Any reproduction or other unauthorised use of the material or artwork herein is prohibited without the express written permission of the relevant author or the publisher. You must not circulate this book in any other binding or cover and you must impose the same condition on any acquirer.

Published in the United Kingdom by
Onion Custard Publishing, Cardiff, UK.
• Web: http://publishing.onioncustard.com • Email: publishing@onioncustard.com •
• Twitter: @OnionCustard • Facebook: www.facebook.com/OnionCustardPublishing •

First Edition, February, 2013
Format: Softback, ISBN: 978-1-909129-34-4

Table of Contents

Disclaimer

The articles in this book are written by a number of contributing authors, and the personal views expressed are entirely their own. *Onion Custard Publishing* accepts no responsibility for any of them.

Also, the views expressed are no replacement for legal advice, and neither the Authors, nor the Publisher accept responsibility for any perceived, actual or consequential losses from readers acting upon any of the advice in this book. Articles are written by specialists, but every reader has individual circumstances which might not be appropriate, and there is no way of guaranteeing that the reader has fully understood and acted on any advice in the manner in which it was intended. Basically, if you're reading this book and take action based on any of these articles – get further advice and do your own research as well, which is just good business sense anyway.

All trademarks are acknowledged, and any perceived slights or offence taken by anyone reading this book are entirely unintentional.

No guarantees of income should be inferred from any of the illustrative figures used in any of the articles in this book.

All links and contact details were checked and found to be correct as of February 2013: things do change so when you read this book they might not be accurate.

Editor's Preface

Like millions of families, mine has been affected by cancer, so my personal story is not that remarkable. It is, however, very relevant to this book because it's the driving force behind assembling a group of business people to help raise money for cancer research. Every author in this book has their own story, their own reasons for contributing their time and energy to writing and promoting this book. But this book not about us, it's about beating cancer, and *Cancer Research UK* is doing great work. Lives are being saved because of them. If this book can in any way contribute to the cause then it's done the job intended.

But there's so much more to this book than just a bunch of people writing something just for the sake of raising money. We're not just printing a book that only we buy. This book is packed with information for small business owners, and people involved in SMEs. More than that, there's a genuine desire to help other small businesses to develop and prosper.

As a small business owner myself, there are several articles in this book that permanently changed the way I think about my own business. More importantly, it's already had a positive effect on the operation of my business on a day-to-day and strategic basis. At a real, practical level, this book has the potential to do the same for your business.

The business people assembled in this book have come together with great enthusiasm and support for the project, and I would like to personally and publicly thank each and every one for hitting the very tight deadlines. I set the challenge of getting this book from launch to publication in just 8 weeks, while trying to involve as many contributors as possible. I hoped for 15-20, I actually received over 60. Why the urgency? For some people the impact of cancer can be that sudden. I wanted to give people a jolt – for them to commit and take action, not to leave it until 'later'. Something this important needs to be done **now**. To those that answered the call, I salute you. It's not been an easy exercise for everyone, and some have certainly found it more challenging than others. Not everyone is necessarily good at getting their thoughts down on paper to a deadline like this, or to schedule the time to write. But everyone in this book clearly did rise to that challenge successfully.

The response I received was phenomenal, I think because everyone involved can see the double value – raising money for charity whilst passing on great advice and experiences to other small business owners. Collaboration, enthusiasm, warmth, and a genuine desire to help others develop – all of these attributes are present in this book, and I hope it shows in the selfless way people are giving their knowledge.

An editorial note must be made that in almost all articles some words were changed, content cut, formatting added or removed, and occasionally new text added, generally without the knowledge of the writers. Due to the tight timescales involved either I, or one of the volunteer proofreaders, will have made some changes for the sake of readability, clarity, or to format the book in a consistent manner. However, I am solely responsible for any of the mistakes in this work, don't think badly about any of the writers as a result of any typos, misplaced punctuation, or poor grammar. Those errors lie at my door. The final word count exceeds 93,000, and you will inevitably find mistakes. I apologise for the minor errors you might discover, but not for publishing it quickly. Yes, in an ideal world it would have been more thorough, but that wasn't what this was about. It was about taking action, today.

I thought long and hard about how to organise the articles in this book, and eventually ended up listing them A-Z by first name. It seemed more appropriate to be this random, than to create contrived headings and force articles together. This book is about the insights and advice that specialists have to offer, and arranging them in the way I have gives you the chance to go on a random journey through the personal world of small business owners. Each chapter offers you something different from the one before, or after, it. The randomness may spark in you a fresh idea, and you might be encouraged to read about topics that you might have otherwise rejected simply by the heading it was under. It only takes one great idea to be spawned from these pages to more than return your investment in the book. It's my fervent hope that you do read every one of the chapters. Each has been crafted with care to give you insights, tips, or advice to help you or your business.

Whatever your reason for buying this book – whether it's to gain some new ideas, or inspiration, for entertainment, or just to contribute to the cause, then on behalf of all the contributors, thank you.

David Norrington, February 2013

Authors & Editorial Team

Contributing Authors

Steve Abel
Lesley Allart
Sian Bick
Celeste Bolt
Chris Bown
Jeff Boycott
Denis G. Campbell
Phil Cheesman
Lady Helen Child Villiers
Dr Michelle Clarke
Carmen Crocker
Nicola Cross
Michelle Dalley
Alex Davies
Helen Davies
Elizabeth de Benedictis
Nicola Drummond
Brian Fakir
Trish Fulford
Andy Gardner
Picasso Griffiths
Liam Hamilton
Maz Hawes
Karen Hensman
Crystal Hinam
Peter Hopkins
Leanne Hugglestone
Kirstine Hughes
Emma Jennings
Cat Johnson
Robert Lang
Jacqui Malpass
Nicky Marshall
Rahim Mastafa
Peter Maynard
John McAleer
Sibel McColm
Martina Mercer-Phillips
Andrew Miller
Mike Morrison
Peter Norrington
Charlotte K. Omillin
Sam O'Sullivan
Rebecca Parsley
Jo-Jocelyn Pearce
David Rahman
Lee Rickler
George Savva
Lucy Scott
Bob Shepherd
Caroline Skinner
Steve Tasker
Eric Taylor
Phil Terrett
Fran Tyler
Jason Vaughan
Barry Watson
Steve White
Sue Worrall
Ann-See Yeoh

Editor & Project Manager
David Norrington

Consultant Editor
Peter Norrington

For their proofreading services, thanks to
Chris Bown
Jeff Boycott
Nicola Drummond

For cover designs and associated artwork, thanks to
Mariusz Paulowski

Cancer Research UK's Support For this Project

Cancer Research UK has been enormously supportive of this project. In spite of the really tight deadlines that were imposed on them they have worked hard to help get this book published as quickly as possible. The inevitable legal issues has been handled swiftly and effectively.

We've been given full permission to reprint all of the details in the chapters about cancer, and about *Cancer Research* UK, which follow.

For complete transparency, here's what we mean when we say we're raising money for *Cancer Research UK*:

- Authors are providing their article without any remuneration whatsoever.
- *Onion Custard Publishing* is providing all editing, design, layout and marketing free of charge.
- Cover design and artwork has been done free of charge.
- Additional proofreading has ben freely provided.
- The only cost that we can't avoid is the production costs incurred by printers, and distribution and handling costs incurred by the sites we are selling the book from, such as *amazon,* or payment fees from *PayPal*, etc. Each format of the book will raise a different amount according to cover price, production and distribution costs, but the important thing to note is that **100% of the royalties** received on any platform will be passed directly to the charity.
- Every pound donated will be used by *Cancer Research UK* to fight the battle against cancer.
- A fundraising page has been established for royalties collected from the sale of this book (and donations, thank you!), where you can track the progress of funds raised. This page will remain live until January 2018.

www.justgiving.com/DavidNorrington

What is Cancer?

Cancer is a disease caused by normal cells changing so that they grow in an uncontrolled way. The uncontrolled growth causes a lump called a tumour to form. If not treated, the tumour can cause problems in one or more of the following ways:

- Spreading into normal tissues nearby
- Causing pressure on other body structures
- Spreading to other parts of the body through the lymphatic system or bloodstream.

There are over 200 different types of cancer because there are over 200 different types of body cells. For example, cells that make up the lungs can cause a lung cancer. There are different cells in the lungs, so these may cause different types of lung cancer.

Normal cells

Your body is made up of billions of tiny cells that can only be seen under a microscope. These cells are grouped together to make up the tissues and organs of our bodies. They are a bit like building blocks. Different types of body tissues are made up of different types of body cells. For example, there are bone cells in bone, and breast cells in the breast.

Genes and cancer

Different types of cells in the body do different jobs, but they are basically similar. They all have a centre called a nucleus. Inside the nucleus are the genes. Genes are really bits of code. The information they carry can be switched on or off. The genes control the cell. They decide when it will reproduce, what it does and even when it will die.

Normally the genes make sure that cells grow and reproduce in an orderly and controlled way. If the system goes wrong for any reason, the usual result is that the cell dies. Rarely, the system goes wrong in a way that allows a cell to keep on dividing until a lump called a 'tumour' is formed.

Benign and malignant tumours

Tumours (lumps) can be benign or malignant. Benign means it is not cancer. Benign tumours

- Usually grow quite slowly
- Do not spread to other parts of the body
- Usually have a covering made up of normal cells.

Benign tumours are made up of cells that are quite similar to normal cells. They will only cause a problem if they:

- Grow very large
- Become uncomfortable or unsightly
- Press on other body organs
- Take up space inside the skull (such as a brain tumour)
- Release hormones that affect how the body works.

Malignant tumours are made up of cancer cells. They:

- Usually grow faster than benign tumours
- Spread into and destroy surrounding tissues
- Spread to other parts of the body.

It is the ability to spread that makes a cancer harmful. If a cancer is not treated, it can spread into the organs near to where it started growing. It can also damage other parts of the body that it spreads to.

Primary and secondary cancer

The place where a cancer begins is called the 'primary cancer'. Cancers may also spread into nearby body tissues. For example, lung cancer can spread to the lining of the chest, the pleura. Ovarian cancer can spread to the lining of the abdomen (the peritoneum). This is called locally advanced cancer.

Cancer cells can break away from the primary tumour and be carried in the blood or lymphatic system to other parts of the body. There they can start to grow into new tumours. Tumours from cancers that have spread are called 'secondary cancers' or 'metastases' (pronounced met-as-tah-seez). A cancer that has spread has 'metastasised'.

The various organs of the body are made up of different types of cells. Any of these cell types can grow into a primary cancer. Different types of cancer behave very differently. The type of cancer affects whether it is:

- Likely to grow quickly or slowly
- Likely to produce chemicals that change the way the body works
- Likely to spread in the blood or lymph system
- Likely to respond well to particular treatments.

Understanding Cancer Statistics

Some cancer statistics can be confusing. Here's an explanation that might help you to understand them a little better.

What incidence statistics mean

Incidence means how many people get a particular type of cancer every year. It is often written as number of cancer cases per 100,000 people in the general population. These calculations are done for every type of cancer. For example, in the UK in 2008 there were:

- 47,693 women diagnosed with breast cancer - about 153 cases per 100,000 women
- 22,846 men diagnosed with lung cancer - about 76 cases per 100,000 men
- 2,138 men diagnosed with testicular cancer - about 7 cases per 100,000 men
- Non melanoma skin cancer is the most commonly diagnosed cancer overall, with at least than 98,000 new cases registered each year. Nearly all these people are cured.

Non melanoma skin cancer is often excluded from cancer incidence statistics because it is usually much less serious than other types of cancer.

Incidence by age

Overall, prostate cancer is the most common cancer in men - 24 out of every 100 male cancers (24%) are prostate cancer. But other cancers are more common in younger age groups. For men aged 25-49, testicular cancer is the most common (15%). Prostate cancer only accounts for 3% of male cancers in this age group.

- If you look at cancers diagnosed in children (under 15 years old) then leukaemia is the most common cancer. 1 in 3 (33%) of cancers in this age group are leukaemia.
- Breast cancer is the most common in women - 31 out of every 100 cancers (31%) diagnosed in women are breast cancer. But in women aged 15-24, melanoma is the most common accounting for 17% of cancers, with only a few women diagnosed with breast cancer in this age group.
- Although there are variations for specific cancers, the number of cancers diagnosed generally increases with age. Nearly two thirds of cancers (63%) are diagnosed in people aged 65 and over.

Incidence by country

This is interesting because it could shed light on the causes of different cancers. Breast cancer incidence is often quoted as an example of this. The incidence of breast cancer in Japan is much lower than in the USA or the UK. But the incidence of breast cancer in Japanese women living in the USA is the same as for the general population of American women. To doctors, this implies that the causes of breast cancer are probably more closely related to life style and the environment than they are to our genetic make up.

Survival statistics

Survival statistics for cancer are usually written as '5 year survival' or '10 year survival'. These statistics probably cause more confusion than any others. What 5 year survival means is that X% of patients were alive 5 years after they were diagnosed. It does not mean that these people lived for exactly 5 years and then died. It doesn't mean they were all cured either. Some of them will be cured. Some will have already had a recurrence of their cancer, but still be alive. Some will get a recurrence after the 5 year period.

5 and 10 year survival statistics

5 year and 10 year time periods are used largely for convenience. Research studies often follow people up for 5 or 10 years. So figures for 5 and 10 years are often available to be quoted. For some types of cancer the chances of the cancer coming back after 5 years is quite small and 5 year survival is sometimes used to mean 'cure' when actually it does not. For almost all types of cancer, the chances of recurrence after 5 years are much lower than they are after 2 years. So the more time passes, the less likely it is that your cancer will come back.

Who is included in 5 year survival?

Everyone who has that particular type of cancer, unless the statistics say otherwise. You may come across 5 year survival figures by stage of cancer. That may be simplified into 'local disease' (cancer that has stayed in the area where is was diagnosed) and 'metastatic disease' (cancer that has spread to another part of the body). For breast cancer, the figures are sometimes divided up by whether the cancer has spread to the lymph nodes or not.

Straight forward 5 year survival figures are very general. They include everyone with that type of cancer, at all stages and grades. If you have an early stage cancer, then the percentage quoted as surviving will be too low. If you have an advanced cancer, then the figures may be a little optimistic. So be wary of taking this type of statistic too literally. The figures quoted are true. But they may not apply to you.

'Disease free' survival

Sometimes disease free survival figures are used. This does mean everyone with that type of cancer who is alive and well (without a recurrence of their cancer) 5 years after diagnosis.

Mortality

Mortality statistics mean the number of people who have died from a particular type of cancer in a year. On their own, these figures don't mean much. They have to be looked at alongside incidence figures and other statistics.

As with incidence statistics, you have to think about what mortality figures actually mean. They don't take account of stage, grade or any specific sub type of a cancer. They are used as a general guide to what is happening in diagnosis and treatment of diseases.

Remember - statistics are general. You may read that 47,693 women were diagnosed with breast cancer in the UK in 2008 and 12,047 women died from it that same year. Don't assume that these are the same women. Almost all of the 12,047 who died would have been diagnosed some years before. In a lot of cases, many years before.

Changes in mortality figures over time are difficult to interpret. The incidence of a cancer may be falling, so less people die from it. Or treatment may be improving so more people are cured. Treatment improvement may not mean cure, but it may mean more people are living longer after they are diagnosed so this will also make the mortality figures fall in the short term.

Cancer risk

The last type of statistics to cover are those about risk of getting any particular type of cancer. This is often written as 'life time risk'. Using the available figures, statisticians work out the risk of any one of us getting a certain type of cancer at some point during our lives.

This is sometimes written as a percentage. And sometimes as 1 in X. For example, the calculated life time risk of lung cancer for a man in the UK is 1 in 14. This means that out of every 14 men in the UK, one will get lung cancer at some point in his life (and 13 won't).

To change this to a percentage, you divide it into 100. 100 divided by 14 equals 7. So the percentage life time risk of lung cancer for a man in the UK is 7%. But this is the overall risk. It will be higher or lower, depending on whether an individual smokes or not. And because it is 'lifetime risk', it is a cumulative risk. This means that the risk adds up as you get older. So the risk for an average 45 year old is not 1 in 14 - it will be much lower.

Again this doesn't mean a lot for any one person. These figures are produced to help people who study the incidence of disease (epidemiologists) and people who work out how much money we need to spend on health care (health economists) do their jobs. They are important because they tell us the most important health problems of our time. And from that, we can work out the areas where we need to concentrate spending on research, screening, treatment and training.

About Cancer Research UK

We've been going since 1902 and along the way we've achieved a long list of firsts. Now we're pushing well into the future – developing newer, kinder treatments, getting closer to cures.

Every step we make towards beating cancer relies on every pound, every hour, every person. And as a collective force we've helped **double survival rates** in the last forty years. But we can't stop there. More than 1 in 3 of us will develop cancer at some point in our lives and with our ageing population, this statistic is getting worse.

We're fighting for a world where no one's life is cut short by cancer. And there is real hope. Each year our scientists get closer to finding cures for cancers – whether through targeted treatment or simply detecting cancers earlier. Genome mapping and new technologies have put us on the brink of major breakthroughs. With the continued help of our supporters we will help turn these breakthroughs into treatments that could save millions of lives and accelerate our progress against this devastating disease.

To save lives; to add years; to make treatments kinder; to inform, prevent; to expel fear and to cure. The only ones fighting over 200 cancers – including the 1 that matters most to you.

Our ambition

Our ambition is to bring forward the day when all cancers are cured. This is our long-term vision. It won't be achieved today or in our lifetime. But one day, it will happen. And if we stand united, cancer doesn't stand a chance. With relentless determination we can push forward more quickly towards a future where cancer doesn't have to be feared.

Every day we are achieving this ambition step by step together. From our volunteers and supporters on the ground to our scientists, doctors and nurses in the hospitals and labs, we're all here to save more lives by preventing, controlling and curing all cancers.

Sooner or later we will find cures for all cancers. Let's make it sooner.

Our work

We fund over half of the UK's cancer research, including the life-saving work of over 4000 scientists, doctors and nurses fighting cancer on all fronts. Every day, our researchers make cutting-edge discoveries in our labs, and our doctors and nurses pioneer new treatments with patients in hospitals. This is why our research is so vital and why we need the public's support to keep forging ahead to create more tomorrows for more people with cancer.

Research isn't the only thing we do. Every year we help millions of people get the information they need to understand the disease. And, together with our supporters, we campaign on key cancer issues including access to cancer drugs, screening and reducing the use of tobacco.

We work in partnership with others to achieve the greatest impact in the global fight against cancer. We provide life-changing information to anyone affected by cancer. We run awareness initiatives so that cancer can be detected early and help people reduce their risk of the disease. And our campaigning and lobbying keeps cancer at the top of the political agenda.

Our progress is your progress

None of this would be possible without our supporters and volunteers. As a result of this amazing support, our work has helped transform the way cancer is prevented, diagnosed and treated today. Here are some of our proudest achievements.

- Our scientists and doctors have contributed to most of the world's top cancer drugs, including:
- Tamoxifen and herceptin – which have saved the lives of thousands of women with breast cancer
- Temozolomide – used worldwide to treat people with the most common type of brain tumour
- Carboplatin – one of the most successful cancer drugs ever developed.
- We pioneered the use of radiotherapy to treat cancer, leading to a dramatic increase in the number of patients whose cancer could be cured.
- We influenced the three national screening programmes for breast, bowel and cervical cancer which save thousands of lives each year. And we were instrumental in bringing in smokefree law in England, which has helped more smokers to quit than ever before and will help prevent an estimated 40,000 deaths by 2018.

How we fundraise

We receive no government funding for our life-saving research so every step we make towards beating cancer relies on every pound donated. With the inspiring generosity and commitment of our supporters we are bringing forward the day when all cancers are cured. With you, we can speed up the progress and create even more tomorrows.

How much money do we raise?

In 2011/12 our supporters raised a staggering £432 million. And, while this is a fantastic figure, every single pound really does count – nine out of ten donations we receive are for £10 or less. Whatever the size of your donation, we promise to spend it wisely and ensure at least 80 per cent is spent on our work to beat cancer.

How your donations are beating cancer

In 2011/12 alone we spent £332 million on research in institutes, hospitals and universities across the country. We also spent £16 million on influencing health policies, and on raising awareness of cancer risks and symptoms by providing information to people affected by cancer.

Around 40 per cent of our annual research activity is on lab studies into the biology of cancer. And we're winning the fight. Every year we're discovering and developing newer, kinder treatments and getting closer to cures.

Why we must do more

Despite all this good news, more than 1 in 3 of us will develop cancer. Every year we receive potentially life-saving research proposals that we simply can't afford to fund. That's why we can't rest. That's why we need to up our fundraising efforts - we must make sure that the day when we cure all cancers is sooner, rather than later.

How you can help

Why not look into how you can get involved with fundraising, or support us in other ways?

Please send all donations to the address below or
call to donate using a credit/ debit card

Phone: 08701 60 20 40

Cancer Research UK | PO BOX 1561 | Oxford | OX4 9GZ

www.cancerresearchuk.org

Please also *Like* and *Follow* us on *Facebook* and *Twitter* for latest news updates

Facebook: www.facebook.com/cancerresearchuk

Twitter: @CR_UK

Alex Davies: Safe As Houses?

Information security, data protection, and legal compliance are three vitally important business components that, if managed incorrectly, can have severe consequences on a company's owners, directors, and staff.

Information Security

Business critical archive records and electronic information are valuable resources within organisations, and appropriate management procedures should be implemented to protect them.

Since the explosion of social media and e-commerce, organisations seem to focus on protecting their electronic information against the risk of data corruption, loss, misuse, or disclosure.

Just as importantly, they should secure their hard copy information against similar threats by implementing records management and retention scheduling procedures. Collectively, these best practice processes are referred to as 'Information Security Management', which can be defined as 'The sharing of information in an appropriate manner, which ensures the information remains protected.'

Risk assessments, continuity planning, and disaster recovery programmes should all be included in an Information Security Management System (ISMS), with the aim of:

- Protecting the accuracy of information
- Protecting processing methods
- Ensuring information is accessible to authorised users only
- Ensuring authorised users can access information when required
- Minimising damage following a data security breach
- Ensuring realistic business continuity plans are tried and tested
- Exploiting business opportunities and maximising return on investments.

Establishing and maintaining an ISMS is a mandatory requirement for any organisation wishing to obtain ISO/IEC 27001:2005 accreditation. Published in 2005, *ISO27001* specifically relates to information security threats, effective control measures, and the necessary management processes that ensure an organisations information security needs are continuously satisfied.

Data Protection

The most recent *Data Protection Act* was passed by the UK Parliament in 1998, and defines UK law on the processing of data relating to identifiable living people. It was enacted to bring the U.K. into line with the *European Union Data Protection Directive* of 1995, and is the main piece of legislation that governs the protection of personal data in the UK. The majority of the Act does not apply to domestic users (e.g., personal address books). However, any entity retaining personal data for other purposes is legally obliged to comply with this Act, albeit subject to some exceptions.

The Act also makes individuals and companies responsible for retaining personal information in a confidential manner. It defines principles relating to the collection, retention, and storage of personal data, which is summarised below. Personal data should be:

- processed fairly and lawfully
- obtained only for specified, lawful purposes
- not processed further in an incompatible manner
- adequate, relevant, and not excessive in relation to the purposes for which they are obtained
- accurate
- up to date
- not be kept for longer than is necessary
- processed in accordance with the rights of data subjects under the Act.

Furthermore, appropriate technical and organisational measures shall be taken to protect personal data against:

- unauthorised or unlawful processing
- accidental loss
- destruction
- damage to data.

The Act also states that personal data should not be transferred to a country or territory outside the European Economic Area, unless that country or territory ensures an adequate level of protection for the rights and freedoms of data subjects in relation to the processing of personal data.

The Information Commissioners Office (ICO) enforces serious breaches of this Act, and their range of enforcement actions includes:

- Monetary Penalty Notices (as of 6th April 2010) up to £500,000.
- Decision Notices relating to the Freedom of Information Act or Environmental Information Regulations.
- Undertakings, which monitor organisations that have committed to a particular course of action to improve compliance.
- Enforcement Notices that can involve the issue of *"stop now"* notices requiring offending businesses to take immediate and specific steps in order to comply.
- Prosecutions that the ICO can initiate, involving criminal proceedings.

Up to the end of 2012, the largest single monetary penalty notice was a £325,000 penalty issued to Brighton and Sussex University Hospitals NHS Trust in June 2012, after sensitive patient details were discovered on hard drives sold through an online auction site.

Regulatory & Legal Compliance

Compliance in general can be defined as: "Demonstrating adherence to a particular standard or regulation." Any organisation wishing to operate in compliance must adhere to all laws, rules, and policies. Regulatory compliance takes into account the staff employed by the organisation, and stipulates that all personnel are aware of relevant laws and regulations, and that they take appropriate action to comply with such legislation.

The extent of regulatory compliance can vary within different countries; the U.K. is one country that is subject to a considerable amount of regulation, some of which is due to E.U. legislation. As there is such a wide variance of regulatory compliance within the U.K., specific bodies such as The Environment Agency, The Information Commissioners Office (ICO), and The Financial Services Authority have been created to police specific regulatory areas.

Legal compliance is a set of processes and procedures that aim to ensure organisations and public bodies abide with relevant laws, regulations, and business rules. The two main requirements that all organisations must satisfy, in order to be legally compliant, are to create corporate policies that are consistent, and with complete respect of the law.

In addition, legal compliance has recently been expanded to include the adherence to ethical codes within certain professions, and encourages organisations to self-monitor the non-governed behaviour that could lead to indiscretions occurring in the workplace.

Having considered the variety of potential pitfalls, it is surprising how many organisations continue to store business critical archive records within a rented room located inside one of the ever growing number of city centre based self-store facilities.

Perhaps more worryingly, however, are the number of organisations that ignore the principles of business continuity, and risk everything by storing data and records onsite at their business premises.

The decision to store on-site or opt for a self-storage unit may be based on a misconception that a fully managed archive service is a more expensive solution for effective document retention.

By analysing the specific costs and previously unconsidered factors, the comparison below shows that a bespoke records management service can actually cost less than you think.

Cost efficiency

- **Self-Store Units**: Stacking archive boxes several layers high in a confined space will damage the boxes and make retrieving documents difficult. When a storage unit is filled to capacity, another entire unit must be rented, thus increasing the monthly storage cost per box.

- **Records Management Service:** Monthly storage costs per standard bankers box can cost less than 1½ pence per day, regardless of how many boxes are stored. Customers only pay for what they need.

Retrieval and collection

- **Self Store Units:** Sending company staff to retrieve documents will incur wages, liability insurance, mileage allowance, and lost office productivity. With multiple staff accessing the unit, accurately returning files to storage is not guaranteed due to shared accountability.
- **Records Management Service**: With a simple email, any number of files or boxes can be delivered to your office or desk within hours. Files are tracked on the supplier's database, and returned to their correct location by trained archivists. Some suppliers even provide a 'fully inclusive service', which means that all handlings, local deliveries, and collections are conducted free of charge.

Security Methods

- **Self-Store Units**: Unsupervised access is often allowed, a constant throughput of unknown people pose a potential threat to your records. The types of materials stored within neighbouring units are unknown, and potentially hazardous.
- **Records Management Service:** Some suppliers ensure only fully trained and CRB checked staff has access to customer archive records. Some storage facilities are protected 24/7 by manned security and CCTV coverage.

So, should you be concerned about your existing information security or business continuity arrangements, then relieve some of the burden by engaging the services of a professional records management company.

Alex Davies is Sales and Marketing Manager at The Maltings Limited, offering bespoke records management services and tailored office solutions in Cardiff, South Wales.

02920 462045
alex.davies@themaltings.co.uk
www.themaltings.co.uk

Andrew Miller: Life Isn't Perfect

I have spent over 16 years working as an Insolvency Practitioner, dealing with numerous companies that went bust. Consequently, I have seen how it can affect directors and business owners as they see their enterprise collapse before their eyes.

If you click onto the business book section of Amazon, or any similar book-based emporium, you will find hundreds of titles along the lines of *How to Make a Million Dollars in 10 Days, The Pathway to Success* or *The Ten Things You Need to Rule the Business World*. The trouble is, they are all written by multi-millionaires with several global businesses who spend their time wandering the Earth, telling people how great you can be as long as you work hard and subscribe to their next DVD. They are perceived by general society as being 'successes'.

And that's fine. You should read those books. Copying successful people is, they say, the best way to succeed and these guys know how to do it well. However...

Life isn't perfect and things don't always go to plan. Sometimes they go spectacularly wrong. And this is something that most business books don't discuss. They may have a section on how to carry on when things don't work first time, most of them avoid the full-on 'negative' angle.

Now, that's all very well if you are in the corporate rainforest trying to climb as high up the tree as you possibly can. But what if you've just fallen off your tree and landed in a pit of quicksand? Who would you rather get help from in that situation? The guy perched at the top of the highest tree who can tell you how to avoid the quicksand? Or the person stood nearby with bleeding fingers because they've just clawed their own way out?

From the many people I have met, once the dust has settled and they have got back on their feet again, every single person said the same thing. "It was one of the worst periods of my life... but I learnt so much as a result."

As someone whose business is based on helping people in such difficulties, the natural next step was to find out precisely what they had learnt and to pass those lessons on.

So, I started talking to as many people as I could that had been through a corporate insolvency. I spoke to a wide range of directors, men and women, in many types of business: from large international exporters to coastal town souvenir shops and manufacturing enterprises to service industries. It included people who had seen their marriages torn apart; been threatened in the street by angry creditors; hidden behind closed curtains waiting for the bailiffs to go away; and sunk into the depths of depression, causing them to hide from the world for months on end.

Naturally, there were many issues specific to individual situations but, quite quickly, some common themes started to emerge. Ultimately, I was able to develop a book that detailed these key themes and drew out the learning points arising from those interviews.

However, whilst the book was focussed on what happens in the worst-case scenario, the key learning points that came out of it were sound business concepts that every business owner can apply. From a start up, to an established business, through to a failing enterprise. Keep these in mind, and your chances of getting to the top of the tree will be greatly increased.

Be really clear about what you want

Have a very clear image about what you, as an individual, want from life. Which things are important, both materially and emotionally.

Understand that where you are headed is the most important thing and what happens to you on the way is just stuff that happens. It may shape you, but it does not define you. When you know why you do what you do, you can choose the right battles to fight.

Separate the person from the business

Be aware that the two can exist independently, so don't confuse the performance of one with the other. Be clear about when you are wearing your business hat and when you are wearing your personal hat, especially when it comes to employees and major stakeholders such as the bank. Both elements need to be worked on and supported.

In terms of yourself, recognise and understand your emotional behaviour. Be honest with yourself. Otherwise, how can you improve?

Raise your awareness levels

In terms of your business, make sure you know what the wider market is doing. Be very clear about what measures you need to have in place to flag up early warning signs within the business.

You can't do everything

Don't be afraid to ask for help. Be good at what you do, so give your brain time to relax so that you can stay on top form. Bring in experts to deal with the bits that you're not so good at. There are always options available to you. You just might not be able to see them. Get into the habit of talking to others, even in the good times.

Act now

This is not a kid's game. There are no prizes for the one that keeps quiet the longest. Even if it is the smallest of steps, such as talking to a friend or emailing a business contact, just get the ball rolling.

- What's the worst that could happen if you did?
- What's the worst that could happen if you didn't?

Afterthought: changing a culture

There are two main conundrums that I, and many others, seek a solution for. Firstly, how do you get people in difficulty to ask for help earlier? Secondly, how do you ensure that, if the business does fail, the entrepreneur at the top gets back on their feet quickly.

Solving these issues will be a huge boost to our national economy. More successful businesses and fully active entrepreneurs can only be a good thing.

There is a common perception that the United States seems to have a better handle on the matter. The list of hugely successful individuals that have a string of business disasters behind them is much longer than in the UK. Their ability to bounce back and move on appears to be much greater. It is my opinion that this is principally a cultural thing.

There are two main elements where the USA seems to approach things differently to the UK that I think make a massive difference. First of all, there is a big distinction between business failure and personal failure. Businesses are perceived as tools; as ventures; things to try out. Some work and some don't and when they don't work you move on and give something else a go. The vision lies within the person, not within the corporation. So if you lose the latter it doesn't matter. In the UK, when the business goes down, there is a much greater chance that it will drag the individual with it. Secondly, American culture is much more open to asking for help. There is a greater demand and acceptance over there for psychiatrists, coaches, mentors and so on. This seems to apply at any and every stage of life or business.

If we in the UK were in the habit of talking to people about our issues at every stage of our lives, then we would have no problem at all in asking for help when things got really difficult. Taken together, I think these two approaches to life make a huge impact. How you intentionally change a nation's culture in such a drastic way, I don't yet know. Hopefully, this book will help a few people to move in that direction.

Andrew Miller is author of Hope Won't Pay the Wages*, available on amazon.*

Twitter: @armcoaching
www.hopewontpaythewages.co.uk

Andy Gardner: The Business of Doing Business

Growing up, especially while in school or college, I tried lots of different part time jobs. The experiences gained and skills learnt, have stood me in good stead throughout my adult life. In my early twenties I took these skills and ventured into the world of the self-employed. While I believe many values are intrinsic to being both employed and self-employed, the hostile environment I stepped into meant it was a steep learning curve. Being the first in my family to be self-employed, only exacerbated the sharpness of the learning experience.

Finding myself in a competitive, dynamic and all too often greedy industry meant the information and practices adopted by many, would-be role models, were confusing and baffling at best. With the wisdom and experience that ten years brings, together with that of the history books, those early observations now confirm to me how short-sighted, flawed and negative many of the practices I observed were. In this situation, learning and remaining true to a sound set of principles, coupled with the pressure to succeed and make money, was not easy; which brings me on to the purpose of this chapter.

It has become apparent to me that many of the common fundamental principles that are required to be successful both in business and in life are often lost in the 'noise' that is propagated by so many. Negative media reports, flawed management, gossip, and a fear of past mistakes all revel in the glory of hype and hyperbole that frequently lead to individuals feeling lost and confused as to what to do for the best. It is with this in mind that I will set out what I believe from a set of universal principles that are crucial to success, both in the present and future.

Listen and learn

Engaging and being interested in both the people and places you spend time around, I believe to be crucial. I have found that showing a genuine and enthusiastic interest culminates in reaping huge benefits. Often taking the time to ask questions and learn a little about people I have met, has given me countless insights and knowledge I would otherwise not have had. *So* valuable I believe such casual exchanges to be, that I would now say they are integral to both me, and my business. In the same way as having an understanding of the community or area you are working in can only help you in your ability to find and facilitate business.

A secondary, and equally important benefit of engaging with the people and environment you find yourself in, is that such practices provide you with the opportunity to build personal relationships. Such platforms where understanding and trust can be fostered, allows business to be done with a level of ease and certainty otherwise unachievable.

Answer your phone

Many people in business claim to be actively seeking new leads and business. However all too common, it is these same people who fail to answer calls, emails and post, with many of these very same people failing to get back to people at all. Failure to follow such a simple principle denies not only the opportunity to do business at that point, but also inhibits the development of future business.

I am not advocating being available 24/7; in fact I believe it is absolutely essential to have defined periods of leisure time. Although it makes logical sense that by being available, answering the phone and getting back to new and existing prospects gives you the best possible chance of converting leads into new business.

There are several well-respected business authors who advocate the strategy of making yourself difficult to get hold of by ignoring calls and messages, and even by cancelling meetings to free up your time. There are many theories you can subscribe to, but answering the phone and actively trying to complete and create new deals is just common sense. If meetings are not important enough they should not have been arranged in the first place.

A perfect example is the one described by the producer of the TV show, *The Apprentice*. While the show was still in development he was in New York, and on a whim, phoned through to *Trump Towers* with the idea of pitching the concept of the show to Donald Trump. He thought at best he might get Donald's secretary or his secretary's secretary. However, as Donald wasn't busy and his phone was on, it rang straight through and the man himself answered. Liking what he heard the producer was invited for meeting that afternoon and later that day the deal was done. Good for both sides. Keeping all personal opinions of Mr. Trump aside, surely what this example illustrates is simplicity itself. Essentially, that is what I believe being in business is all about. Be the best possible middle man you can, make it as simple and as straightforward to do business with you as you can.

Be concise

Knowing your purpose, and not forgetting what role you are there to perform, is often key to encouraging people to want to deal with you again. Going round the houses, massaging one's ego and talking about what you had for dinner last night has no place in a business transaction. Treat the time both you and the person you're dealing with, with respect. Even if the people you're dealing with are not. Be focused on the task in hand and how to successfully deliver the goal you are setting out to achieve.

Be consistent

Approaching people and tasks with a calm, assured and articulate demeanour can only help lay the foundations of success. Being careful not to panic, gossip, get carried away with things, or fuel the short-lived amusement, which such behaviour often produces, takes effort. Adopting a more mature and stable approach makes you more approachable and thus breeds respect.

Urgency

Showing a level of urgency and importance to a task or person demonstrates that you are there to do business. Being too casual or laid back can prevent progress from being made. With all such things a balance must be sought. Although in most situations it must seem like an opportunity or lead is important to you or it may not end up being there at all.

Be honest

This applies both to oneself, to others and even the task in hand. Getting to the bare truth of the matter, and understanding what went well and what didn't, is absolutely crucial to long-term success. Only by fostering reliable and honest feedback can an accurate and objective assessment be carried out. To do this oneself, a level of care and respect, coupled with an understanding of the people and task in hand is required.

Genuine and thorough assessments are rare to come by, as the courage required to ask difficult questions of oneself, others and the situation is all too often lacking. Having the willingness to improve, be brave, be fair and be honest, I believe, are absolutely crucial to being successful.

Being able to generate and supply such information should allow you the certainty to know if progress is being made and allow people your doing business with to know you are trustworthy.

Be positive

While I do not believe in 'blue sky' thinking, seeing new challenges as opportunities not obstacles and by greeting each day with a level of enthusiasm and fun, allows you to make the most of varying conditions we are all faced with.

It is harder to do business with people who are negative and forlorn. Such attributes present less of an attractive opportunity to potential new clients.

Throwing enough energy and enthusiasm at every opportunity that arises, provides you with the certainty and peace of mind needed to know you did everything to capitalise on that situation, allowing you to move on without wondering "What if?", or "What else could I have done?"

Appearance

While I do not believe in strict dress codes, looking like you are there to do business is important. What you wear, and when you wear it, has as much to do with what you do, as who you are dealing with.

You should be able to express yourself with your appearance as ultimately it is with you that people are doing business with... and your personality matters. But to me, your appearance should also make it as easy to do business with you as possible, and this too is an expression of your personality.

Adapt

The willingness to adapt and learn is essential. Having a sound set of principles, like the ones I'm suggesting, are the building blocks. Meeting challenges head on and developing new skills to get things done are the tools of business. The ability to be flexible, and to negotiate, are also valuable skills which can allow one to nurture business where perhaps otherwise there would be none.

Be determined

Having the conviction and steely appetite to be determined is crucial. While it is only natural that you will have an awareness of what your colleagues or your competitors are doing, by being determined, disciplined and focused you will give yourself every opportunity in achieving your goals.

Having the conviction and the self-awareness to understand who you are and what you are there to achieve can propel your opportunities you hadn't potentially considered, and thus you become the catalyst for your own continual improvement.

Belief and vision

If you are conducting yourself in a good way and challenging yourself to be a success, both in business and in life, you have every right to believe in yourself. To be true to yourself, and manage such high principles is not always easy, but the self-worth it generates is priceless. This cannot be underestimated for your future success and happiness. I do not like to get too caught up with having a single inspiring vision or plan, as this, in my opinion, can detract from the opportunities and pathways that may occur day to day. However if you take the self-worth and belief that you are generating, by working hard and being honest, it is possible to envisage just how great things can be.

Last points

Too many successful people you read and hear about in media will not be operating under such a set of values or principles. This I feel very sad about. However what I propose to you is an opportunity, not just to be successful, but also to earn, own and achieve success.

To Nan

Andy Gardner is a Mortgage & Financial Adviser and partner at C A Mortgage Services Ltd with over 10 years' experience in the Financial Services Industry. A former professional rugby player, Andy now specialises in offering independent advice across a range of financial areas.

07859 043580
andy@camsltd.com
www.camsltd.com

Ann-See Yeoh: Remaining True to Yourself

All too often, the Western mindset of success is one of achievement through strife. There is a gentler way of living with ourselves and our world. A way of navigating our way along the river to success. Our lives are a gift to others and we need to stand up, and give ourselves permission to be us, and live a life that you love. It is about being happy in moment. It is about simply living and living simply. It is about time.

In yoga, there is a term *Jivamukti* which translates to mean "liberated being". Whilst many paths lead us towards personal transformation, I personally connect with the concept of being liberated. It implies that the process of coming alive is not about becoming, rather it is about uncovering what has always been there.

Who you are what you are meant to be has always been there. Life, through its mysterious weavings, has draped years of expectations and shaped you into someone you no longer recognise. Our work lies in removing these layers and reclaiming our ability to see ourselves clearly. As the legendary Miles Davis put it: "Sometimes you have to play a long time to be able to play like yourself".

The Mindful Success Path

We have all chosen the path we are on. Through life, we are presented with choices all the time. Just because you have always walked a particular path, does not mean that you need to stay on that path.

Everything changes and is changing, including your life. You are on a journey. It may seem that today is very much like yesterday. It is not. It is different. Nothing is the same and you need to realise that this is the illusion.

All successful people have chosen to walk the road less travelled. They have created the vision they hold that is true for them, what lies in their heart. There is no running in place, treading water in life. Everything is in motion and time waits for no one. If you walk long enough, you will get somewhere but is that where you truly want to be?

The Mindful Success Path is designed to help you get on track to a better life, whatever a better life means for you. This path is neither a guarantee of wealth, fame, nor one of eternal happiness. It is simply a plan to help guide you to becoming a better version of you and revitalise your life.

R • E • P • A • C • [K]

Reflect

At the start of any inward journey and before you can decide what you want for your life, you must first understand who you are and what brought you to this point in your life. You need to spend time on reflection so that you can move forwards.

Evaluate and envisage

If you seek a better life then you have to decide what you want from your life, and create a vision of what that is. This means you have to look at your dreams and aspirations, evaluate your talents and strengths to go about creating a realistic vision for you and your loved ones.

Plan

Only when you have created your vision are you in a position to formulate a plan that will consider the different aspects of your life. On your journey, you need to remain mindful as to how steering a different course can affect your life as you know it.

Action

Nothing is going to happen until you take action. Too often people dream, create goals and draw out their plan only to not succeed. People who succeed get up and get on with their plan so in order to be successful – you have to just do it!

Commit

When the going gets tough, the tough get going. You can envisage a fantastic life and make all the plans in the world but you will require more than just taking action. You have to truly commit to undertaking the journey and pledging your time and energy to the pursuit of your vision.

Keep faith

This is an extra step. Even the most dedicated person will hit roadblocks as life has the tendency to throw us curve balls. When such times hit, keep the faith and know that you are always meant to be where you are.

There are no rehearsals in life. We have one shot at it. So I invite you to step on the mindful path to success and you will any area of your life on track to where you wish it to be. Whatever success is, it is personal to you, and a genuinely successful life means your health, your relationships, your career, your finances, your sense of fulfillment and your legacy. Realise that all it takes in one step at a time, and to own the fact that you are at the heart of your own personal success.

Ann-See Yeoh is a trainer, mentor, author and an entrepreneur involved in several businesses, including Mindful Success, which offers online and offline personal leadership events. Ann-See has over 20 years' experience as a trainer globally, and is a yoga practitioner.

www.mindfulsuccess.co.uk

Barry Watson: Making Facebook Business Pages Work

Let's assume that you've made the decision that social media is important to your business, and that *Facebook* is just too good a marketing opportunity to miss. How do you go about maximising your effort on this platform? There are some common mistakes that the newcomer, and even some seasoned users, fall foul of. These mistakes are generally the result of onc of four situations:

- Lack of understanding of, and compliance with, *Facebook* policies. Nothing gets your page banned quicker than complaints against their rules.
- Lack of understanding of traditional marketing principles – many of the 'offline' rules apply as equally online. It's just another form of communication, after all.
- Lack of understanding of how *Facebook* users use the platform. You have to work your way into a *Facebook* profile – it's pretty hard to just smash right in there.
- Lack of understanding of the full range of features and tools available to *Facebook* page developers. Many business owners have no idea about the additional functionality that can be added to a page.

The following checklist is your way of making sure you understand and access some key features of your *Facebook* business page. So, let's crack on with an overview of ten things you need to be doing.

Cover photo

Regularly changing your cover photo shows clients you're an active company, involved with your visitors and updating your page with new and relevant content. Choose dynamic images, sometimes humorous ones, and at certain times of year seasonal images. You can use your cover image to lead people to what you are trying to promote at any given time – without breaking *Facebook* rules, of course.

Choose your images with some care – if viewed as a gallery of images, how would they look? Would they be a consistent set of images, giving the same overall view of your company, or do they give mixed or confusing messages? Your cover photo has the potential to be a real attention-grabber or a damp squib – the choice is yours.

Opt-in

Offer a free mini-product to your customers to give them a taste of your service, and to build a mailing list. When this simple free giveaway is linked to building your list, you have a powerful way of growing a fantastic business asset. What's the point of having tens, hundreds or even thousands of people liking and interacting on your page unless you take the next step to converting them into customers? If you don't ask them to join, they can't do it for themselves, so make it as easy as possible for visitors to become real prospects and then into actual customers.

Respond to comments

Interaction is one of the most important factors in social media marketing. If you don't respond to comments, clients will stop doing it and you'll lose your following. If someone takes the trouble to comment, respond in some way, even if it's only to 'Like' it. Regularly, and promptly, commenting on other people's comments shows that you care about your page and are taking it seriously. Thanking people for their nice comments and responding to more critical ones will build trust that visitors are being listened to.

Think about your *Facebook* business page as a 24/7 customer service agent for your business, always there to take questions and comments. Be polite, informative and responsive. Irrespective of who is tasked with responding to comments, you should strive to handle everyone with the same standard of professionalism that you would show if someone called your company.

Update regularly

Frequently update your page and posts with shareable, appropriate, quality content. By doing this, you provide the clients with content to share on their wall. This will then increase the number of "people talking about this", which will in turn spread your name.

You might be sharing things you've found, announcing new products or services or perhaps sharing new ways that customers are using your products or services. For some businesses, the priority might be to become a trusted source of news or advice, particularly where high-priced services are offered. This is a longer-term strategy and requires sustained, concentrated activity, lots of quality content and a thorough knowledge of your area of expertise. You become the go-to company when you post quality, rather than quantity. One of the objections many people have to social media is the banal nature of much of its content. If your page content is high quality, you'll get a better quality of followers in turn, and build a more loyal tribe of supporters.

Freshness of content is everything on the internet. The big players – *Facebook* and *Google* in particular – love sites that update regularly with new content (even if that content is actually shared from elsewhere). It shows that the site is being used and that it is current. Updating your page on a regular, perhaps even daily, basis is one of the most important factors in keeping your page fresh. This will also improve your *Insights* as it's a form of engagement with your clients. If someone sees your page not being updated regularly, they're going to get bored quickly and you could end up losing the 'Likes' you have accumulated. By updating your page regularly, you're giving your clients something to see, something they might not have seen before that they find engaging, interesting or entertaining, something that they may end up sharing from your page. This is exactly what you want to happen as it will boost the chances of your business page becoming more widely recognised .

Variety is also essential – don't just post links to your website from your *Facebook* page or just information about your products or services. Post rich content in a variety of formats – text, links, images, video, articles, news stories, press releases, product launches, seasonal items, etc.

Use of graphics

Make sure your graphics are sized correctly, sharp and attractive. If your graphics are incorrectly sized, they will appear blocky, pixelated, stretched, blurry or otherwise ugly. This will, in turn, make your company seem unprofessional.

If you don't understand the technical aspects, then get someone who does to sort out your images. Nothing screams at visitors faster and louder that a page isn't worth looking at than bad graphics.

The flip-side to this, however, is that nothing says to a visitor that a company is professional, well managed informative and worth dealing with, than strong branding and clean images.

Mind your language

Use grammar correctly, avoiding text-speak, slang and jargon. Using incorrect grammar is a common mistake for people attempting to use social media marketing. This makes your company look unprofessional and therefore will make clients less inclined to take an interest. Social media doesn't mean that you have to reduce everything to abbreviations, emoticons, text-speak and street-slang.

Avoid technical jargon - you may use it every day, but not all of your visitors will understand it and that will switch them off as fast as using too many LOLs or ROFLs (whatever that means ☺!).

Good manners

'Like' back when people 'Like" your page. This is a simple matter of courtesy and respect. If someone takes the time out to 'Like' your page, the least you can do is spend ten seconds liking theirs in return. It will also increase the possibility of others connected with the page finding *your* page.

Interaction

Post on other people's pages, not just your own. Posting on your own page is obviously good. Going onto other's pages as well is great! It shows that you're not just connected with them so they can 'Like' your posts, but also to allow you to interact with them on their wall. By doing this, you also reassure your visitors that you're not just on *Facebook* purely to advertise your business, but also to engage with people. This will appeal to many people as it shows that you run a selfless company that cares about their clients and what they have to say. By showing your clients that you are interested in what they have to say, you are also creating a deeper relationship with them.

Furthermore, you might just get involved in some conversations where you can legitimately provide some solutions for other people. Avoid looking only for conversations that allow you to slip in adverts and if you do decide to do this, only do it sparingly and appropriately.

Transparency

By giving your full company details on your page, you are allowing customers to see that you are a genuine company and if they need to, research a bit about you. This is likely to form a sense of business-client trust. Give visitors reassurance that you are not trying to keep information from them and that you, as a company, are willing to answer questions if necessary.

Not only does it reassure clients that you're reliable, it also gives them the knowledge of where to go if they have any issues with anything that your company does for them.

If you were to purchase an item from someone, would you prefer to buy the item from someone you met in the pub, not knowing who they are or how to contact them if you need to? Or would you prefer to buy it from a friend that you know personally and know how to get in contact with? I know which one I'd choose!

Understand Insights

Insights is what *Facebook* calls the analytics part of your page. They are very useful in determining the overall success of your *Facebook* page – you can see how many 'Likes' you have gained and how many people are 'talking about' you – a truer measure of interaction.

You can track the success of specific marketing initiatives, even specific news items, by the increases in 'Likes', and importantly the number of people talking about your page.

For example, if a post of yours goes truly viral, you'll see an upward spike of activity and you can hopefully retain interest by following up swiftly. Just posting for the sake of it in a routine and disinterested way won't allow you to respond to surges of interest in your page. If a news item you post garners lots of interest, what better opportunity is there to slip in a product/service related post to your new audience?

This is not an exhaustive list by any means, there are many more essential things you can be doing on *Facebook*, and some serious mistakes to avoid.

Barry Watson is the Managing Director of Club Social Junction, which offers clients a wide range of social and video marketing tools, advice and support. He's also author of Facebook 20/13: 20 Ways to Grow Your Business, 13 Common Mistakes to Avoid*, available on amazon.*

01291 622091
Twitter: @ClubSocialJct
www.facebook.com/ClubSocialJunction

Bob Shepherd: Shiny Things In Business

Do you need a web site that is all singing and dancing? Does your business have a social media presence on *Twitter, LinkedIn, Facebook* and *Pinterest*? What about blogs? What about networking?

Just what *do* you need to do to present your business to the outside world? What about that business plan, a break-even measurement, credit control and a top of the range dashboard on everything from the cost of your tea breaks to the quality of your customers' credit references?

Do you need all this?

I have seen all of these punted as 'must haves' with many more besides. It is quite possible to get caught up in the excitement and find you are investing time, money and effort in something that triggers a nagging doubt in you saying it might be a waste of time. Time is the biggest resource for any small business and it is the one often most abused.

The truth and the practical point is that all of them can and should be useful with a cap on the time and the expense involved. If your business is well put together and working together, the time you invest in these things and indeed anything should be proportionate to the need. You should not be giving too much emphasis and focus to anything. It is true that dis-economies of scale kick in for small businesses. The cut-down and cheaper version may be quite adequate for an acceptable smaller expectation of output.

Networking and the online presence

Some networking is a good idea and you should pick your groups, meetings or events carefully. There is no standard to measure the effectiveness of these things. What may be good for one business may not be for another and that may simply be down to personalities.

For a start-up business you are faced with a hundred options all of which promise to be the answer to all your needs for new business opportunities. Do work out a way of assessing the importance and the relevance to you of the meetings you attend.

You cannot attend them all or you are in danger of networking and not working. Some will operate at a senior level only which often means that senior executives, solicitors and accountants gather together and will only talk to you if you are shown to be worthy of their clique. This is not real networking though it does operate on a certain level. Others appear to have caught the eye only of new micro businesses desperate for business or to get you to sell their products for them. Some are expensive, some are not, and some are free events. Any gathering of business folk is an opportunity to network in fact, and you should have contact cards in your pocket at all times with a pen and small pad to jot down reminders.

There are less obvious networks centred around Church, Golf, Masons, Round Tables or some other groups, all of which can be highly effective.

Go where you feel comfortable, that is within your budget and seems to be supplying you with good leads and contacts. If you miss one event, never fear, there will be another along in a minute!

Social media and the strategies to go with it are relatively new and, depending on the audience you need, can be very effective. At the very least for a small business it will show engagement with young fresh ideas if you are careful what you write. How much time you spend is a matter of discipline. Bearing in mind the earlier comment about resources you should keep it in line with the desired result. Little and often is best.

Blogs are one way of publishing your activities easily and creating your own business flavour. Be careful not to libel anyone in any of your on-line publishing but you have the chance to make your views known more now than ever before. Make sure it works in your favour and not against your interests. What should you blog about? Once you become used to the idea it will become obvious. Start with a little lesson for everyone on some aspect of your business world that everyone seems to get wrong. Give some advice on how to deal with that situation effectively and guidance on what you can do for them on a professional level. Tweets on *Twitter*, postings on *Facebook*, *LinkedIn* or anywhere else are really just blogs of a certain size.

A business plan IS essential but it does not necessarily need to be written down in great detail according to some imposing template. The important words are 'business' and 'plan' which should tell you that a little forethought and organisation will go a long way. If you have a framework to work within it is better. Consciously review it often with an open mind.

Controls over costs and the performance of your business are vital but should be useful and not get in the way. Any business needs to spend some money on promotional activity in some form. For the small business it is a matter of directing these funds in the most efficient and purposeful way.

The picture is better in focus

The point with all of it is that it needs to be in proportion with your business, its targets of costs and market and have a purpose that has some sort of return for you in creating your business profile, your shop front and your reputation.

Your approach to this can be serviced in large part by a coherent mixture of personal presence (networking at events), on-line presence, and communication with the audience you attract. Each channel of communication links and supports the others and it all needs to be balanced and effective in getting your message across.

How you do that is a mixture of chit chat, responding to situations and queries, and selective broadcasting of offers, service, knowledge and the general impression you are giving to any observer. What you can do with a little care is to establish a web of communication across a number of 'platforms', which is the modern business speak for getting your message out.

Always remember that the message you are giving is your message. Whatever you think you are saying the necessary result is that someone else receives it. They are subject to all their background, their prejudices, their education, their standards of English, their level of creative interest and a host of other interpretations that you will probably never know. Consider for a moment the successful comedians, who play to thousands of people in an audience against those unsuccessful comedians we have all come across sometimes that hit the wrong note and make us cringe for them. They all have this same problem and a few of the best manage to master the absolute art of commenting upon a subject in a uniquely personal way that engages with a huge audience and engenders a similar response in most of them. Wonderful stuff! Those same people will appear on a panel show and not manage to carry it off so well.

Is it complicated? Not really. You are taught the principles of these things from your first day at nursery. How you answer the phone is as important as any slogan or strap line. What you say in a throw away tweet is as important as a carefully constructed article. How you conduct yourself is as important as the look of your web site. It all needs coordination and presentation with a consistent message of quality, manners and authority.

Simple!

Bob Shepherd runs a business-building consultancy in South Wales. His background in finance has helped many SMEs to develop quickly, and save money while establishing a sound foundation for growth. Bob has 12 years as a consultant, with an extensive corporate career before that.

07747 758596
mail@BobShepherdassociates.co.uk
www.BobShepherdAssociates.co.uk

Brian Fakir: Staying Afloat when the Ship is Holed

OK, so now you're a business owner, romantic isn't it? All the hard work you've put in: the months of research into your market, your competitors etc. You've launched your baby, but then something dramatic happens, and it's all about to be undone. It doesn't matter if you are a micro home-based business, an SME, or a multinational; the following principles apply to all business types.

Planning

You've probably already been through this bit. The banks, institutions, and business angels and the dragons all want you to pitch your business plan to them before they've parted with any money for your idea.

See, the clue is in the word *plan*. For most of us, an unwelcome exercise, which may have prompted, shall we say, some economical use of the truth, particularly when asking for financial support. Our forecasts may have been on the generous side, and our recognition of the downside somewhat muted. After all, you're going to be successful at what you do, right?

Insurance: a necessary evil, or something more useful?

Have you had a good look at you insurance policy lately, the one you had to buy in order to be in business? You know the paragraph that says, "We will not insure you for Acts of God, pestilence, whirlwind..."? If you are smart, you'll have a clause like that, one which actually covers you adequately for business interruption if your broker is pie hot.

The Wikipedia definition for *business interruption insurance* is:

Business interruption insurance *(also known as* business income insurance*) covers the loss of income that a business suffers after a disaster while its facility is either closed because of the disaster or in the process of being rebuilt after it.*

A property insurance only covers the physical damage to the business, while the additional coverage allotted by the business interruption policy covers the profits that would have been earned.

This extra policy provision is applicable to all types of businesses, as it is designed to put a business in the same financial position it would have been in if no loss had occurred.

For the insurance companies this is a finger in the wind figure, based on the unknown certainty information provided by you. This estimated figure could sometimes add a significant amount to your premium. Plus, your estimates will probably be downgraded by the insurer to limit their payout.

Continuity planning

You can alter this scenario by putting another plan in place: a *Continuity Plan*. Continuity plans have been around a long time. Under *The Civil Contingencies Act 2004* hospitals, care homes, prisons, etc. must have continuity plans.

They became more widespread after the Twin Towers 9/11 terrorist attack in New York. Large multinationals became very nervous and felt another terrorist attack was imminent, so they put extensive plans into immediate effect. These were large-scale mobilisation plans for huge amounts of data and staff, and at a huge cost too. That's fine for the big companies, but what about SME's?

Therefore, we come back to *your* business. What would the cost be to you if some unplanned event happened? Your insurance policy is fine for some of the loss, but the claim is going to take time to process, and probably won't cover everything you lost. What really happens is that your business loses credibility, your reputation is shot to pieces, and your competitors gain another.

This can be easily overcome by planning. It involves you thinking about your business, not in a logical manner, but in an out-of-the-box way. "What if?" becomes your most frequently asked question, and the wilder the better, because this will prepare you more thoroughly. Now the unexpected becomes expected.

There are many companies that offer BCP (Business Continuity Planning), and they often rely on large-scale infrastructure and logistical mobilisation in an almost military manner. There are other consultants that work on a more basic level, asking you about your business and how portable it is. You really don't need an over-engineered solution to a simple process.

The first thing to ask yourself

Can I continue trading after a major incident to my premises? The fact is that *90% of SME's don't survive after a major incident* because they haven't planned for it. However, if you plan for it, the more encouraging statistic holds that 90% of the time you will carry on trading.

Say you work from home. In the event of a fire, for example, what's the worst that can happen, and how would your business survive?

Now, thanks to intelligent cloud based software, you can easily back up all your data, and access it from anywhere: your smartphone, tablet, or even someone else's home or office. The data are no longer physically stored in just one place, because the cloud has backups at other physical locations, in case *they* burn down.

So now your recovery plan means that you can simply pop to a shop, replace your fried laptop, run over to your nan's house, plug it into her broadband connection, and be back up and running in just a few hours.

Remember that bad news travels faster than good. So make sure that you tell your customers, before anyone else does, that this event hasn't affected the business, or your ability to deliver on their deadline for their project. You have now given your customers *wow* customer service.

There are more things you can do which are simple and effective. You may just have to think out-of-the-box a bit, and perhaps you may get a bit of advice so you are in the 10% that survive in the event of an emergency, instead of going under like the other 90% do.

Brian Fakir is the Owner of MB Fire Consultants, offering Fire Risk Assessments, Health and Safety consultancy, advice on fire regulations, Business continuity, and recovery support, and all aspects of fire safety training. He's been involved in the industry for over 20 years, and self-employed since 2003.

07985 999748
Twitter: @mbfireconsultan

Carmen Crocker: Developing Your Marketing Toolkit

Imagine driving along the motorway on a lovely sunny day when, suddenly, clouds thicken and the light starts to fade. What do you do? Hopefully, you put your headlights on so that others can see you clearly. And then it starts to rain. What do you do? Push the brake to slow down? Put on your windscreen wipers?

What you're actually doing is using a range of tools at your disposal, in order to arrive safely at your destination. This is how you should consider your marketing toolkit (commonly known as the *4Ps* - product, price, place and promote - or the *marketing mix*). Don't think of them as marketing speak, jargon or that *"marketing is not for me"* - think of them as a range of tools that you can flex as necessary to achieve your business objectives. So what are these tools and what should (or can) we do with them?

Product: what's at the heart of your business?

Product is at the very core of your business and of your marketing mix. It may be a tangible, physical thing, or an intangible service. Your product is the reason that your customer will give their money to you rather than a competitor. You can think about it on a number of levels[1]:

- **Core**: What is the actual thing they're buying?
- **Expected**: What will they also expect to come with the product?
- **Augmented**: What would make the product even more valuable to them?

For example, if you are buying a bargain flight to Spain your expectations might be:

- **Core**: a flight to Spain
- **Expected**: online check-in, 20kg in the hold, safe aircraft, ability to buy refreshments on-board
- **Augmented**: choice of flight times, choice of airports, no fees for printing tickets, complimentary refreshments onboard, friendly staff, airport transfers from home.

Map out your product with your customer in mind, making sure that what you're offering meets their core expectations as a minimum. Ideally it needs to have the potential to exceed their expectations.

If you haven't already profiled your customers, do so *before* you map your product out, as you should be doing the former with them in mind. What will your customer value? This will put you in a good position to identify exactly what your main offering and bolt-on extras will look like, and whether some will be integral to the offering, or whether some will be paid for.

1 adapted from T Levitt's Total Product Concept

Price: what will you charge, rather than what will they pay?

Price is the only revenue earner in your marketing toolkit – all of the other elements are costs, so it's crucial to get this right. Many entrepreneurs and small businesses build their pricing strategy based on a price that they think the customer will pay. If the customer won't pay a fair price for your product or service, don't sell it to them! Don't do what most do and immediately lower your price. After all, you're not in business to do them a favour – you are creating a livelihood! Pricing can be developed using three different bases:

- **Cost:** How much it costs to make and deliver the product (including constituents and time)?
- **Competitors:** How much competitors are charging for similar products or services?
- **Value:** What price customers are prepared to pay?

These three elements shouldn't be considered in isolation. Think holistically about your product, your customers and your market. As long as you cover your costs, and keep your profitability objectives in mind, there is really no right or wrong way to set your price. Remember that price should also reflect whether you are providing a premium or budget product, and also whether you are looking to enter the market place. For example, Apple adopt a skimming strategy setting high prices for new products knowing that those techies who just have to have the latest gadget *now* will happily pay high prices. Then they reduce prices over time for those who need a little persuasion to buy. Other companies may set their entry prices on products that are new to the world very low in order to penetrate the market and create a level of demand that enables them to put prices up later.

Place or distribution: getting your product or service to the customer

Getting your product or service into an appropriate distribution channel is essential in order to give your customers access to whatever it is you're selling. For services, this is usually quite straightforward. This is often accomplished directly through you, or through an agent. For businesses selling physical products distribution may be more complex than that. Distribution chains may have one or more of the following links:

- **Direct to the consumer**: Either in person or online.
- **Through retailers**: They will sell your products on to the general public. They may impose packaging, pricing, quantity and sale or return requirements on you, but will be able to help you sell a higher volume as they have a wider, established customer reach.
- **Wholesalers**: Wholesalers will buy large quantities of supplies from producers and sell them on in smaller quantities. For example, a corner shop might go to a wholesaler to buy their products. These guys will signpost smaller retailers to your product.
- **Local agents**: Appropriate if you're selling into another country.

Each additional link in your distribution chain will mean an increase in price to the end customer, or a reduction in revenue to you, so weigh up each channel carefully. Decide what the most effective distribution method is for your business and then how widely you want to make the product or service available.

The market

- Who are your customers?
- Are they all in one geographical area?
- Where might they buy?

Geography

The physical distribution of goods costs money. Are you planning to send low value products over some distance? What impact will this have on the price to the end-consumer?

Competitors

What distribution systems do they have in place? Remember that the further afield you reach, the greater the logistical implications in terms of cost (both financial and time). Make sure that you take this into account and don't let your customers down. Aim to deliver excellence through your chosen method of distribution.

How are you going to promote it?

Here's the big one. This is the tool with which most mistakes are made and most money is spent (and wasted). There are six elements to promoting your product or service:

- **Advertising**: Paid-for non personal communication via TV, radio, outdoor (buses, tubes, and billboards), cinema, magazines, newspapers. It can be national, regional or sector specific.
- **Personal Selling**: One to one meetings can be very effective as they offer the ability to respond immediately to queries and otherwise unseen body language.
- **Direct Marketing**: The individual targeting of customers most likely to respond which is hidden from your competitors
- **Public Relations (PR)**: Often wrongly considered by advertisers to be their poor relation! PR holds more credibility than advertising as it isn't paid for (so it's similar to word of mouth recommendations). But when it comes to editorial there is no control.
- **Sales Promotion**: BOGOF offers (buy one, get one free), daily deals, coupons, etc. These are great for a quick sales boost, but can cause damage to your brand or pricing policy if used too often.
- **Internet and E-Marketing**: A huge potential customer reach with the added potential of tracking exactly where the customer originates.

So which do you choose? There are four questions to ask yourself.

Resources vs. cost

- **What's your budget?** An advertising campaign could cost £thousands or more. Is this realistic or are you going to have to examine other elements of the promotional mix? If you're looking at other promotional elements don't forget to factor in time. Social media is often considered inexpensive (or free), but it actually takes a significant time investment to return on the investment of time successfully.
- **What are the number and location of potential customers?** If your customers are geographically concentrated you may be able to use personal selling. However, if they are spread across a larger geographical area an alternative will need to be considered.
- **How much information does your customer need?** If you are selling a technical product or service (whether a piece of machinery, widgets or an insurance policy), an advert or email may not be enough. Something direct (telesales or brochure), or personal selling will allow you to get to the finer details that are likely to be required.
- **Who are you selling to?** If you're selling to retailers or wholesalers (pushing your product to market) then the personal touch, or promotions, may be appropriate. If you're selling to consumers (creating a market pull by having them ask retailers for your product) then something generic with a wider reach is more appropriate such as advertising.

Golden rules of promotional plans

Plan your campaigns upfront. Set your budget and stick to it. A "not to be missed" opportunity will always come along – so keep 10% unallocated, or stick to your budget and just say "no". Get help from a designer. You might know your product and have some great straplines in your head, but my experience tells me that they'll be ineffective - let the designer do their job. Give them the facts and let them come up with the creative stuff. Plan your activity on a Gantt chart, print it out and put it on your wall. Update your chart every month and colour code it. Green means an activity done. Orange means an activity is happening, but a bit late. Red means not done. Print it out and keep it on your wall as a visual reminder. Measure the effectiveness of your campaigns quarterly and if it's not working then stop and review it. If it is working – well done! Whoever said running a successful business was easy? Great ideas are the easy bit – making a success of them is slightly more difficult. Your marketing toolkit will help to ensure that you get the right products, in the right place and the right time. Just like driving from A to B.

For Marius Gray. Always loved. x

Carmen Crocker is the Owner of Heath Marketing Ltd, offering outsourced planning, implementation, training and marketing consultancy. She has worked in advertising and marketing for over 17 years.

carmen.crocker@heathmarketing.co.uk
Twitter: @heathmarketing
www.heathmarketing.co.uk

Caroline Skinner: Seven Ways to Stay Safe

Effective health and safety management makes good business sense. A safely run business wastes less time and money on covering staff absences, accident investigation, replacing damaged equipment, repairing a damaged reputation etc. The benefits include business efficiency, lower insurance premiums, improved staff morale, greater client satisfaction, and less involvement with compensation claims and enforcement bodies.

Does your company have a health & safety policy?

This document outlines who has overall responsibility for managing health and safety in your business, any delegated responsibilities, and gives an outline of your company's general commitment to organising your work in a way that prevents accidents and ill-health.

A written health and safety policy is compulsory if you have 5 or more employees. However, even if you have fewer staff, a health and safety policy can often help you to secure contracts etc. It can also be used to good effect as an induction training tool to secure staff commitment to maintaining safe working practices.

When did you and your staff last look at your risk assessments?

Written risk assessments are also compulsory if you have 5 or more employees, but they are a good idea even if you have less staff as they should be working documents to help you with your health and safety management. Have you covered all work activities, any staff at particular risk, e.g. young people, disabled staff, pregnant workers, and considered any visitors or customers who might be affected by your work activities?

Check periodically to make sure that the control measures you have introduced are working, and make sure that any changes you make to work activities do not introduce additional hazards. Review your risk assessments at least annually, or if there are any indications that it may no longer be relevant, e.g. after an incident or accident, or a change to your work practices.

What hazardous substances are you using, and do you know how to control them effectively to prevent injury or ill-health?

Doing your COSHH (Control of Substances Hazardous to Health) assessments will help you and your staff to use them safely and prevent health problems such as burns, blindness, someone ingesting chemicals etc. Where possible you should consider replacing the most hazardous products with less hazardous ones, or use them in a less hazardous form, e.g. tablets instead of liquid etc. For remaining hazardous substances, can you reduce the amount you store and use? Do you have a spillage procedure and suitable First Aid provision? Can you reduce the number of staff who use it and/or the length of time they are exposed to it? Is your storage suitable? Where relevant, can you enclose a process or provide extraction to remove fumes? Do you need to provide appropriate personal protective equipment? For some hazardous substances, you will need to provide health surveillance for your staff. Have you also considered other risks involved in using hazardous substances, e.g. manual handling injuries, work at height, fire etc?

Check your accident records and statistics, and look for patterns that might indicate a problem.

A string of minor incidents might not be due to an accident-prone worker – do you need to improve working methods, machinery guarding, maintenance schedules or supervision levels? Are there any particular types of injury that seem to happen frequently, or any specific piece of work equipment that causes injuries? Do your employees report all incidents and near misses, including those that involve clients and visitors, however minor they might be? Are there any near misses that could have resulted in serious injury? Someone might not be so lucky next time.

A stitch in time

Dealing with all these issues promptly will reduce the time you spend dealing with lost work time, replacing workers, and processing insurance claims. Speak to your staff regularly about health and safety issues that affect them – do they have any concerns about hazards at work? You should consult them about any matters that affect their health and safety, including changes to their work, and there are a number of ways you can do this – meetings, noticeboards, safety bulletins etc. Most importantly, you can use your staff's experience to help you to develop your risk and COSHH assessments, and their knowledge can save you time and money in helping you to find sensible solutions to health and safety problems.

Have your staff been properly trained since you employed them? You can't rely solely on health and safety training provided by their employers in a previous job. You need to ensure that staff definitely know how YOU want them to work. For instance, if you employ a trained and certificated forklift driver, they don't need to re-sit their forklift truck driving test, but you will need to ensure that they are familiar with the forklift trucks you use, and the layout of your premises, including any particular hazards or requirements etc.

Make sure that you keep training records so that you know when to arrange refresher training to keep staff skills up to date.

Have you got access to competent health and safety advice?

You should have access to suitably experienced and qualified assistance when you need it. This can either be someone in your workplace who has sufficient expertise to act as your health and safety manager or you can use a consultant to advise you on more technical, legal or specialised health and safety issues. A competent health and safety advisor should enable you keep up to date with any changes to industry working practices or health and safety legislation that apply to your business.

These general health and safety tips apply to all types of businesses, and they cover the basics that are needed to ensure that you run your business safely and legally. For higher risk or specialised businesses, there will be some industry-specific issues that need to be addressed in more detail than can be covered here.

For all those who weren't as fortunate as I've been.

Caroline Skinner is Director at XHSE Ltd and Skinner Safety Services Ltd, offering practical health and safety services and training. She has many years' experience in assisting a wide range of industries, including 12 years as a Health and Safety Inspector with the Health and Safety Executive.

01737 289187
www.xhse.co.uk
www.skinnersafetyservices.co.uk

Cat Johnson: Top Telecoms Tips

It's that time of year again... your mobile phone contract is due for renewal. Where do you start? There are so many handset and platform choices these days that it's hard to make an informed decision. There seems to be a new handset being released every time you turn the TV on. They all claim to be the best performing, and offer something that the others don't, so where do you look first? Do you choose *iOS, Android, Windows* or *BB10*?

Firstly, as an SME, do you have a business or domestic contract? We see a fair few SME's that are using a domestic contract for business purposes, when as a business customer on some networks (such as *Orange, T-Mobile* and *EE*), the business tariffs come with 24 hour faulty replacement on some handsets included at little or no additional cost. The customer service departments are a lot easier to deal with on business tariffs too.

Don't rush to take the advice of friends just because you need a new handset, as their needs and yours might be very different You need to feel comfortable with the handset choice you make, as this might have to last you for two years, so take your time. Everyone has a preference of handsets, platform and network provider, so if you have a preference, find a provider who will listen to you, rather than badger you into what they want you to have. You have to be comfortable with the choice as you'll be together for a while!

Then, there are also those oh-so 'friendly' staff at your local high street phone shops. They will try to sell you what they think is right, but they don't generally want to build a long-term business relationship with you, just grab the commission bonus that will be awaiting them. It's funny how they always seem to offer you something just over your budget. They are trying to maximise their short-term sales figures, not help your business long-term.

Here's a short troubleshooting guide to help you choose the correct handset for you, and your employees, needs.

- **What main functionality do you need from a handset?** Think what its main uses will be...calls, emails, video conferencing, social media, SMS messaging, business applications, using it as a tethering device.
- **What is your preferred platform?** If you're happy with one platform, ensure the latest handset that supports that platform and can do everything the older version of that handset can. Seriously, I've done some comparisons on handsets and at times the older handsets have more functions – *new* isn't always the same as *best*.
- **Are employees using your handsets?** If you are choosing handsets for employees, do you want them to be restricted from using some functions? You can block them from having access to functions such as adding and removing apps, *facetime*, *siri*, etc.

- **Do you need it to be durable due to working conditions?** Especially relevant if you're in the construction industry, you might want to either get a shock-proof model, or see if a case can be purchased to wrap around the handset you've chosen.
- **Do you need a good camera to take pictures for work purposes?** Not all camera-phones are created equal, and the resolution alone isn't always the best guide for the quality and versatility of the camera. Test out the models before you buy to make sure they will do what you expect in the field.
- **Does it need to sync with your office email provider?** If you're out and about a lot, then connecting to your email might be crucial. Don't assume that all handsets work with all email providers though.
- **Does style matter?** The rest is down to your preference of styling and extra functions.

Getting the handset insured

The biggest insurance claims or problems we see are usually down to water damage, yet funnily enough this is one item that the networks or many other main mobile phone insurers won't let you claim for. Just be wary and check the terms and conditions before you sign up for any insurance policy and also check the 'get out' clause too. Most high street banks now offer 'free' mobile phone insurance these days, which seems too good to be true...because it usually is. 'Free' usually means that if there's a problem, they will send the handset off for repair and return it to you within 6-8 weeks.

Choosing your tariff

Once you've chosen the handset, make sure you choose the correct tariff for you. Don't just have the tariff because it means the handset is 'free' as this may mean you pay out a lot more over the course of 2 years, than you would if you made a small payment upfront. Check your last two bills, read them and analyse them. Are you going over your monthly tariff, if so why? Make sure you get a tariff which covers what you're using but isn't excessive. You can always move 'up' a tariff as many times as you wish over the course of your contract but can only ever move down one tariff; and only after the first six months of the contract.

Ensure your handset is compatible with your IT infrastructure

This is sometimes an area that is overlooked. As the technology on the handset is so advanced, there shouldn't be a problem linking your new mobile to your emails and calendar...right? Some handsets are hard to link to your emails and calendars and will only sync correctly with certain email software. Check first to ensure the choice of handset won't cause you further issues or costs down the line.

Getting your handset up and running

It can be a stressful, long and drawn out process getting a new handset up and running. Years ago the mobiles used to come with an encyclopedia type instruction booklet, now they come with very little apart from how to put your SIM card in and switch it on. Make sure you get some sound advice, help or knowledge beforehand. Here are some quick tips to avoid further problems.

- Make sure everything you need on the handset is backed up onto the appropriate desktop software for that platform.
- Ensure there is a simple way to transfer your contacts from the old handset to the new one. Try something like *www.Zootta.com* which will save all your contacts forever, so whenever you change handsets, you can swap them over safely.
- Ensure any media (photographs, music etc) are stored safely before you start transferring it all to your new mobile.
- Also make sure if you are trading in or selling you old handset, restore it to factory settings, so all your apps, passwords, photos and music are removed from the device.

Avoiding bill shock

This probably seems like 'teaching granny to suck eggs', but sometimes the simple things are the easiest to miss and result in high bills.

- Ensure your wi-fi is always switched on. You'd be surprised at the amount of people who switch it off and do then forget to switch it back on.
- Try not to download software updates when you're not connected to wi-fi as this can result in extreme data usage or the handset crashing if you lose 3G / 4G connection.
- Always check the prices of apps and read terms and conditions as there are some that will stream constantly in the background (usually music apps) and result in bill shock for data usage.
- There are now some seriously good free apps out there these days if you are prepared to search a little.
- Always close the apps down once you've used them.
- Beware of location services, especially when abroad, as most social media apps tend to use these to show the location you are posting from.
- Always contact your network provider before going abroad as the tariffs are now very competitive and they do offer some great data roaming bundles. Just ensure you turn off data roaming on your handsets until you need to use it. Just in case!
- Beware that when abroad if you receive a picture message, this could switch your data roaming back on without your knowledge.
- Download a data manager app onto your handset. We use *My Data Manager* which is free. This allows you to set up a bespoke plan outlining your billing date and data allowance for the month. The package then advises you when you've reached limits, how much data you used, location and whether it's wi-fi, 3G or roaming data used. This knowledge is crucial, especially when you or your employees are out in the field

using the handsets and downloading data.

- Another one to watch is the online or email competitions. Some of these generate premium rate texts to your handset that can be charged anything from £1.50 per text.

These are just a few hints and tips on how to make sure you get the best from your mobile contracts and devices. Your mobile is probably one of your most-used and most valuable business tools. Invest in this technology thoughtfully and carefully. The alternative is being locked in to a long contract using an impractical handset, on a tariff that's too expensive for your needs.

For my amazing children Sam & Conor, who are my life and my purpose and for my dad, whom I still miss every day. Thank you for being my motivation and inspiration. I love you x

Cat Johnson is a Director of i-Com Solutions, offering a complete range of telecoms services to businesses.

01495 760511
Twitter: @icom_solutions
www.i-comsolutions.co.uk

Charlotte K. Omillin: Live Green, Work Green

Most green practices use what we already have, but use them more efficiently. Greater efficiencies translate into reduced costs. You don't need to start a new business to go green, just improve what you already have. If you are the owner of a small business, then you'll be eager to learn how 'working green' can reduce your monthly bills. But it's "all about the customer", you will say. That's right. Once you are convinced about the benefits of operating your business in an environmentally conscious way, you'll attract customers who are already living green, and new customers willing to become more ecologically-minded.

Recycling in the business and reducing waste are both simple, effective ways to create a green workplace. Other practices, like seeking out energy-efficient and recycled products, can also move you towards a greener business. At the top of the list we find ink and toner cartridges, followed by paper products, cleaning chemicals, lighting and electronics.

An easy first step towards making your business more environmentally friendly is reducing your energy consumption. Take a moment and look at the numbers on your monthly energy bill. How much are you paying? Too much? Let's take a look at a few tips that will help reduce these costs.

- Replace incandescent light bulbs with compact fluorescents. A 25-Watt compact fluorescent bulb produces about as much light as a 100-Watt conventional incandescent bulb, but uses a quarter of the electricity. The price of these bulbs has diminished over the last few years. Many pay for themselves in energy savings in the first few months.
- Turn off the lights. If you are planning on leaving a room for more than just two minutes, it's more economical to turn the light off than to leave it on. The idea that leaving energy efficient lights on all the time is cheaper; actually it's a myth.
- Program your computer to sleep automatically when not being used.
- Unplug the battery chargers and adapters when not in use – even when plugged in and switched off, they still draw electricity.
- Consider a programmable thermostat. To reduce energy output overnight, lower the thermostat in the winter and make it higher by a few degrees in the summer. For every degree reduced in the winter, you might save three percent in total energy use.
- Change your boiler. Most people wouldn't consider getting rid of a working boiler. But as they get older they become less and less efficient. An older boiler, for example with a pilot light, is spending five percent of the annual bill just keeping that tiny flame alight. Modern boilers don't need a pilot any more, thus making an instant saving.

- Manage your blinds. If you keep them open in the winter this reduces the need for artificial light. In the summer, keep them closed on warm days to reduce the load on your air-conditioning.

These are only a few ideas to reduce your energy consumption. When you realise you are saving money, you will want to know more about how to manage your business in a healthier way.

Here are a few examples of ways to remind your employees how to save water in the workplace:

- Display water conservation posters and other materials at your business
- Fix leaks and dripping taps
- Install appropriate plumbing.
- But let's move on to your main concern.

How could my business gain more customers by having green credentials?

By changing your marketing strategy to green marketing. This means showing your customers you are environmentally friendly. But how?

Be authentic, and be an example of what you say in your marketing campaigns. Be sure that the rest of your business policies are consistent with whatever you are doing that's environmentally friendly. Both must be met for your business to establish the kind of environmental credentials that allow a green marketing campaign to succeed.

Tell your customers why it matters to be green. Most people are uninformed, or misinformed, on the importance of respecting the environment. Explain to your customers why it is important not only for them, but for future generations. You, the business owner, are the expert now. There's no need to be preachy about it, be a role model instead... and lead by example.

Involve your customers in personalising the benefits of your environmentally friendly actions. For example, a shop owner switches from plastic bags to paper bags. Explain why your company took this decision. Or the business owner could ask customers to bring their own recycled bags for shopping.

- Be creative, and reinvent your business every day
- Adapt or change the logo of your company and give it a green touch
- Celebrate Earth Day on April 22nd every year – build that date into your marketing strategy, and promotional activity
- Give a special or free Earth Day gift to your clients
- Offer treats to the kids (your future clients), who will remember Earth Day
- Make posters representing your business celebrating Earth Day
- Connect with other green businesses or green organisations
- Advertise together by creating a monthly newsletter that lists all the green businesses and their eco-news
- Contact official organisations that support green businesses

- Organise a green event
- Sponsor green activities

It's also important to find out which green practices and events are going on in other countries. You need new ideas to increase sales and to catch the interest of new customers. Don't hesitate to read magazines or surf the internet for green websites and news.

Managing a green business is gratifying. You target a growing market and you have the chance to contribute to make the world a better place with your employees and customers at your side.

Charlotte K. Omillin is a Belgium-based writer and illustrator of children's books. She is author of The Adventures of Zeppi *series. A lover of nature and the environment, she interweaves ecological themes in her books.*

www.amazon.co.uk/C.K.-Omillin/e/B0094S162A
Facebook: www.facebook.com/TheAdventuresOfZeppi
LinkedIn: www.be.linkedin.com/in/ckomillin

Celeste Bolt: Getting the Best from Your Web Designer

The digital world of web design is quite a confusing place. How do you know what to look for when you start to think about marketing your business online? When you're self-employed, choosing a web designer is a crucial decision, as a good website can bring you more business – but a bad one can drive away prospective customers.

I recommend that you do your homework when looking for a designer. The relationship between designer and client is an important one and not to be underestimated. Getting it right at the start ensures for a solid foundation on which to build one of the most important aspects of your company.

Get to know your designer and form a good working relationship

Choose the person with the 'right fit' for your business. It is important that your designer fits in well with the company, and understands you and your products. Pay attention to how much they ask you about you and your business. They should want to get to know you and your business intimately. How else can they design a site that reflects your values, unless they spend this time to get to know you? You are asking them to create your shop window in which you are to sell your products and services to the world. They must be able to demonstrate their understanding of what you actually do in your company, its values and how it runs.

Your designer should be someone you enjoy speaking to. Ask yourself if you click with their personality and mindset. Are they giving you insight and ideas that you'd not thought of before? Are you excited to work with them? If so, you are on the right track.

Never separate the design and coding of your website

You want one person or company conceptualising, designing and implementing your website. Splitting this is never a good idea and you will never get as good a product as you will if everything is done by one person. This is such an important part of the design criteria. If you are working with multiple designers, ideas often get lost in translation. The process becomes like a game of Chinese whispers and the workflow suffers as a result. Be sure that your designer has control of your project from start to finish.

Get a recommendation from a trusted source

Who do you know that has recently had a new website? Take the time to see if there is anyone that your colleagues recommend. Do some homework and search the internet to see what websites particularly stand out. Find out who the leading designers are in your area.

It is also worth being specific about the type of person that you want to build your site. Are you looking for an established agency with a proven track record? Or is it more important to find someone that is very creative? Would you prefer to work with a highly technical designer? The more homework you do, and the time spent researching the designer who will market your company, the better fit you will get. The majority of people who are unhappy went with the first web designer they happened to see. This never works.

Be sure you know your website requirements

Do you want a Volvo or a Ferrari? These are completely different cars with different looks, speeds and specifications. Both work for the person driving them from A to B, but there are lots of differences that make them not both just 'cars'. Your website is exactly the same, and the price will be reflected accordingly. Not all sites perform the same jobs, look the same, or have the same features.

How do you need to drive sales and raise awareness? Be aware of whether you need something that is completely bespoke and written exclusively for you. Often there are other solutions that may fit your requirements.

Be sure to do your research as best as you can to give your designer a better understanding of what you want. If you can speak their language you'll get more of what you want. A good designer will be able to talk to you without trying to baffle you.

Remember that nobody knows your company and business like you do. If you are able to go in with a plan your designer should advise you accordingly with a good strategy. So be sure to think about whether you want a static basic site, or something that you can edit. Look at all the options and get advice.

Understand the goal of your website and how to achieve them

What is it that you need your website to do? It's very important to understand the commercial purpose of your site so that your designer can design effectively.

Are you trying to attract leads? In which case you need to be sure that your message is prominent in the design. If you have a strong marketing message to get across, be sure to get it in the top fold of your site design.

Are you a creative business? If you are, then possibly you need to have something that looks quirky to showcase your skills. Visual portfolio websites can often be the best representation of your talents.

Are you a start up business? If so the goal of your site might simply be to show a professional presence to potential clients. Have you thought about how you will expand your site in a year's time? The majority of our clients wish to further expand their services and we design for that accordingly.

Perhaps you have a current site and realise that you are not fitting in to your target market. In that case it is important to understand what your rivals are doing more effectively. Often there are designers who specialise in a business sector. Don't underestimate talking to a designer who designs exclusively for your industry, as they will already have an in-depth knowledge of your field.

Future-proof your design

When we design for our clients we think about the future. You need to do exactly the same, after all there is no point spending time and energy on a site that you will need to redo in a few months time. With the advance of technology, the design of websites is constantly evolving. Take the time to be sure that your site will be just as effective and that it will work just as well for your company in five years time.

With mobile use quickly out-stripping access via desktop or laptop, it may be important to you that your website is accessible on mobile devices. There are several ways that this can be achieved. While responsive site design ensures that your site is displayed to a consistent standard across all platforms, and devices, it is not always necessary to have a responsive web design, to display your website across mobile platforms.

How beneficial to you is it to be able to edit your site? This is also something that needs to be considered before your site build begins. Are you planning on updating your products and services regularly? If so, this is another type of build, with it's own set of considerations. Or do you just need to have a blog integrated into your site?

Do you need to have the facility to sell products online? What about taking payments? This is important for any website designer to know before they get started. You cannot save this information and throw it out as an "Oh by the way..." once they have already started building your site.

Plan your content right from the start

Start with the elevator speech. If someone asks you what you do, whilst riding in an elevator, you only have a few seconds to tell them. What do you say? You don't need to have every word accounted for, but you should have an idea of how you want your company represented. Think about translating that into your pages and layout.

Speak to your designer about having a copy writer to write the contents of your site. Most designers will recommend someone who will assist you with this. Good copy often makes a good site, as it is a very effective way to drive sales. Ask to work with a copy writer who has a proven success rate on *Google*.

Also be sure to look at your images. This is another very important factor for the success of your website design. Fabulous images that showcase your products are essential. Try not to use stock images as they often end up all over the web and are over-used. If you are a smaller company why not get some head shots? These can be used for your social media campaigns as well as your website. Have a think about how you can use your images, and copy for other means of marketing your company.

Look at your existing materials

Do you have any existing brands, designs, or promotional materials? Do you already have company colours? A logo? If so, how have they worked for you in the past? Take them to your designer and see what recommendations they have based on what you are currently using. If there are any issues or tweaks required, *now* is the time to make them! Be sure that your designer is aware of any brand strategies that are currently in place and before you start any design or concept work.

If you don't have anything in place start from scratch. Have an idea or what colours and combinations you think best reflect you and your organisation. The best place to start is the web. Go and have a look at what is available out there. Make a list of links to show your designer of what you like, and more importantly what you hate! Take in samples and colours to your design meetings and give your designer a great head start.

Have Realistic Expectations.

Set a workable time frame, and be sure to let your designer know in advance of any deadlines. However, don't expect your designer to be able to keep on track with your project if you are not keeping to your end of the bargain. Always answer your emails, have content ready for them upfront, and make important decisions quickly. All these factors help speed the process along and it makes for a good working relationship.

Be realistic about price. If you are asking your designer for a top of the range *Ferrari*, don't expect to pay *Volvo* prices! Understand that the more complicated the process is, the longer it takes to get done. Set the goal posts at the start and don't move them or throw in complications. A good designer will brief you at each stage of the project and make you aware of time scales and issues in the project. Always be sure that you and the designer stick to the brief.

Think about your hosting and maintenance plan

Who is going to look after and maintain your site when you are ready to unleash it on to the world? Costs of hosting and maintaining your site vary with each design company. Some offer free services for a year while others provide the same services for a minimal fee. Although the hosting of your site is not an immediate consideration to the design. It will be an ongoing factor.

Domain names are also an important factor and it is worth talking to your designer and asking their advice. These should be secured straight away and it is also good practice to own all *.co.uk* and *.com* domains that relate to your service, area, product and company name.

Don't get taken in by false promises

Don't choose a designer that promises to get you right to the top of *Google*. Ignore those bogus emails that promise to get you to number one in a day. It's not the job of your designer to get you to number one. It's the job of the Search Engine Optimisation (SEO) expert, and this is a completely different field. Be sure to go though this with your designer. If your design company provide this service in house, then look at the listings for the sites that they currently have and speak to those clients. Are they as good as they say they are?

Having proper design is just the first step. It is a solid commitment to dominate *Google* and to get your site a decent amount of steady traffic. It is an ongoing process from your team for a time long after your designer finishes their work before you'll see big results. It is well worth talking through all the options with your designer's SEO expert.

Have a good marketing plan.

What are you going to do with your site once it is up and running? Again I may be biased, but I never think it is a good idea to let your design agency do things like implement your *Google Adwords* campaign or create social media campaigns for you. There are agencies that specialise in that, and if you have the right web product, the right marketing team can really make it work for you. Again, be sure to talk options through with an SEO expert.

The majority of our clients don't think about what they are going to do with their site afterwards. If you had a shop on the high street and nobody ever walked past, who is going to buy your product? You have dressed your shop window and hung the open sign up on the door, but with no footfall your business will not survive. Be sure you know what actions you are going to take to market your site to your chosen audience. Have this plan in place and discuss it with your designer right from the start.

Conclusion

Think of your designer as an essential part of your marketing team, and treat them as such. Be prepared for meetings, ask them to come up with several options and costs if necessary. If you are unsure, ask! Remember that you are hiring them to market you and your company. Therefore, the more ground work you do in the beginning, the better your site will work for you. A strong relationship between you and your designer should never be underestimated.

If you just take the time to follow these suggestions to take the guess work away from your web designer, they will love you! They will look forward to working with you and their proposal price will reflect that. You will also benefit by getting exactly what you want out of your web designer, and therefore, exactly what you want out of your website.

For my mum and mother-in-law, both brave enough to fight the battle and win!

Celeste Bolt is the Creative Director and Owner of Cherry Cube Design, a web design company specialising in interactive website design and development, branding, graphics and print. Celeste's speciality is interactive media and web design, utilising installation, video, mobile and online technologies in unusual ways.

07969 868822

celeste.bolt@cherrycubedesign.co.uk

www.cherrycubedesign.co.uk

Chris Bown: Searching Like a Pro

The internet is a great source of valuable information. Aside from doing some shopping, and finding directions, it's a great way to learn about your business sector, what's new, and what your peers and rivals are doing and discussing. As a business journalist and researcher who started work before the internet was available, I relish the opportunity to have such easy, instant access to so much information. The world at your fingertips, what could be better? Trouble is, there's so much information, how do you find what you really need? Searching can so often throw up a bewildering display of websites, but none of them appear to solve your problem. Here are a few tips and tricks, to help you get more out of Googling, and to get the information you need more quickly.

Rubbish in, rubbish out

When using a search engine such as *Google*, think about what you want to know. What documents or websites might be likely to hold the information you seek? And what are the key words that will be within that website or document, which will allow you to track the right information down?

Unique words:

Think about any rare or unique words, which are likely to be within the material you are seeking; does an author or someone mentioned have an unusual name, for example? Enter these to sharpen the results you receive.

Ask a question:

If you're seeking an answer to a question, then enter the whole phrase; chances are, someone else could have asked it before (on a forum, for example) and so you will quickly find the answers they received.

Think of alternatives:

Your turn of phrase might not be the same as that of others. Think about other ways to say something, or alternative words that others might use (e.g. children, rather than kids; physical education rather than sports lessons). Academic words are more likely to deliver more academic information.

Spelling:

If there's a word that's hard to spell correctly, try entering it incorrectly (though sometimes *Google* will try and automatically correct you). You might find the answer from a website put together by someone who is knowledgeable, but not a great speller.

Fact, fiction or hearsay?

So you've asked *Google* a question, and a string of websites have been suggested, with the first ten listed in front of you. A website can look visually very believable – that's how spoof shopping websites get people to part with their credit card details in December. So an initial scan can mean it's difficult to see which sites are reputable and likely to deliver correct information.

How can you quickly see which websites look more likely to deliver your answer? Start by taking a look at the website addresses – there are some quick giveaways:

- A site with an address ending *.gov* is a government or local authority website
- Anything with .ac near the end will be a webpage from an educational institution
- A web address with *blogspot, wordpress* or *tumblr* within its title string is likely to be a blog website, more likely to contain comment and opinion, rather than hard facts

If you are looking for information about a specific topic, then a *Wikipedia* page can often be a very useful place to start. *Wikipedia* pages are generally checked for accuracy, and will often provide useful links to other information sources. Look for these lower down the page, and click to open them in new screens to see if they have better information for you.

Look for links

When reading a website, or seeking information about a topic, always look out for links to other sources. These may be highlighted with a hyperlink, or it may be that another website, or an author, may be mentioned. If so, open up a fresh search window on your computer, and start Googling those details.

Most browsers keep a track of your viewing history, so it is easy to go back, should you get sidetracked to a website that's not very helpful. But it is often helpful to open each link in a fresh tab, or a new window.

Foreign languages

It's natural to search in your own language. After all, English will give you access to sites around the world, from the US, Australia and a string of other English-speaking territories, as well as UK sites.

But if the information you are after covers a topic that is more prevalent in another country (for example, bullfighting may well be better covered on Spanish websites) then it may be sensible to find out one or two relevant foreign words, and search for them instead. This could open you up to another whole raft of information sources.

Don't worry about not being able to understand the foreign language source: most modern web browsers will help translate web pages into English for you (and *Google Chrome* is very good at this). You may also find you get a much better perspective on a topic – rather than a purely British viewpoint.

Latest news

A search engine such as *Google* will deliver what it believes are the most relevant information sources on the web, for the search terms you enter. If you want up to the minute information, news and views, then you'll need to search in a different way.

News can be searched using *Google News* – accessed via a tab within *Google*, or by going to *news.google.com* before entering your search terms. This will bring up the latest media reports on a subject area. *Google News* has several settings so you can define whether you want a global, regional or UK focus to the news sites you are offered.

Social media also offers a great view of what's current. Platforms such as *Twitter* and *Pinterest* provide good search abilities, enabling you to track relevant words and terms – and see what people are saying about them, in real time.

Don't miss out on video

Search engines are great at ranking documentation, and analysing the words on the webpage. But there's an increasingly valuable range of information, help and advice available to you via other media, and in particular video.

YouTube is not the only video storage site on the internet, but it is by far the largest. And as it now belongs to *Google*, the ability to accurately search for suitable video content is being honed all the time.

So, if you are looking to find out how to do something, or to solve a tricky problem, and the answer could be demonstrated to you, then think about looking for a video. Everything from how to set up your smartphone, to advice on fashion, DIY or cookery, is now increasingly available as a video. Tips on how to amend Word documents, set up fiendishly complicated equipment, demonstrations of how to use all sorts of kit, these are often ready to guide you.

The chances are, if someone has worked out a solution to a problem, they'll make a quick video to help out others. As every smartphone has a video camera within it, and *YouTube* accounts are free, it's really very simple to create quick videos and share them.

A selection of videos is frequently offered to you if you do a *Google* search, but the best route is to head to youtube.com and use the search function on that page. Use the same discipline as with *Google*, when deciding on what keywords to use in the search box.

What's that number?

Many of us have inclusive minutes packages on our mobile phones or home landlines, but get charged extra for calling numbers starting with 084 or 087 – non-geographic numbers to use their technical name. Banks and other large organisations love using these numbers, as it enables them to manage calls more easily. Some also like them because, while you are being kept on hold, they earn a few pence from you.

You can often find an alternative by visiting a handy website, *www.saynoto0870.com*, which lists geographic numbers for accessing many major companies and organisations; offering a number that won't cost you anything to call it. The site lets you put in the 087 or 084 number, and will present a selection of alternatives for you, depending on which part of the corporation you want to reach. The site's free to use – and your phone call will be free, rather than chargeable, as a result.

Second, here's a way to find out someone's mobile phone number. Say you're trying to reach a person – perhaps a senior person in a corporate role – but they won't make their mobile number available, and their personal assistant has been told not to give it out to anyone but close associates. It may still be possible to find that number, using the internet.

Simply type their name and 07 into Google (for example, type in "Roger Fleetfoot 07") and, if their name and mobile phone appears somewhere, you'll find it. The success of this relies on the person's name and number being published anywhere – such as a village cricket club newsletter, for example. This is not guaranteed to work – but it does sometimes, and it's quick, and free.

Chris Bown is a business journalist, editor and researcher with almost thirty years of experience. A deputy editor of two niche business newsletters covering hotels and planning issues, his output is published every day online.

www.mrcontent.co.uk

Crystal Hinam: Looking Good Online

Keep it simple. Simplify your website content.

First impressions are hugely important. When people visit your web site, you have seconds to convince them to stay and explore. On your homepage, keep it simple, explain what you do and what makes your business different from your competitors. Showcase the most important thing(s) you want to tell the user when they visit each web page. If a web site has too much information on a page, it can often be too confusing to take it all in. Additionally, search engines often prefer separate topics on each page, as it sees this as more relevant to the user.

Keeping a structured, simple page allows you to visually highlight important calls to action, including action buttons or contact details such as your telephone number and email address. You may want to highlight them using colour, fonts or icons. These elements need to stand out in order get your website users to *do something*.

Get personal and show you're human

There are a number of ways to create a personal connection with your website users and potential clients. Use photographs of yourself and any employees, with a (very brief) biography, and testimonials from happy clients to build trust and familiarity. Make sure your business address and phone numbers are displayed on your contact page, users like to know where you are located, and contact you easily.

Using words like 'you', 'we' and 'us' can help engage clients and make them feel valued. For example, 'we are very pleased to share this exclusive offer with you: receive 20% off your next purchase'.

Add videos or photographs to your website/blog to showcase what you and your company get up to. Let users see that you are a part of the community and that you are someone that they can relate to. Post a range of images or videos from various community and business events you and your company attend or are involved in. For example; take photos at your networking event, group outing, charity event or presentation, and post them on your website/blog, *Pinterest*, *Instagram*, *Twitter* and *Facebook*.

Write a blog and build trust with your potential clients as a thought leader in your industry. Writing a blog takes time but the results can be amazing. Ensure you research the topics your audience is interested in and keep the content simple so all users can understand (try to avoid using industry abbreviations and acronyms). Share your personal story as it relates to how you got involved in the business, industry trends, company news and address any FAQ's that your clients often ask about etc. And don't forget to share your blog posts via your chosen social media platforms.

Colour is key

Colour is very important when it comes to designing a website, it isn't used simply for aesthetic reasons; it has meaning. Whether a subtle hint or a bright patterned background, the right colour scheme can really catch a user's attention. Every colour evokes a different feeling or mood and therefore can result in a different reaction when seeing it.

For example, if you have a call to action on your web page, you will want it to stand out. For larger buttons, choose a colour that is less prominent (relative to surrounding elements/background) and for smaller buttons you may want to choose a brighter colour. But whatever colour you choose, make sure the design of the button is noticeable without interfering with the overall design.

If you're designing your website/blog yourself, be careful when setting text and background colours. For web usability it is extremely important that readability is preserved. Many page designers are tempted to use light colours on light backgrounds or dark colours on dark backgrounds. For example, grey text on a black background might look fabulous on your monitor, but if the gamma value varies on another person's monitor, it can be unreadable. What you see on your monitor is not what everyone else sees, and you cannot account for how everyone sets up the brightness and colours on their own screens.

To avoid colour contrast problems, white and black are reliable, and red is common for highlighting items and 'call to action' elements. The best colour combination in terms of contrast is yellow and black, but this would give your website users a headache!

Another aspect of colour and usability to consider is the variation of visual capabilities in web users. Human colour perception varies hugely, users with vision that is somewhat colour-deficient are often unable to differentiate between colours of similar hue when those colours are of the same lightness and saturation. Someone with the most common colour deficiency, red-green colour blindness, would have trouble seeing the difference between red and green when the red and green are close in saturation and lightness. This can be a problem on the web if links are similar in hue, lightness, and saturation. So, in this example, it would be difficult for a user with colour blindness to determine which links have been visited and which have not. If colour is being used to highlight a web page element, try to use an alternative that indicates importance, perhaps using a bold font, a larger font or capital letters.

When does free cost you money?

You can search online and find a wealth of sites that offer "royalty free images". There's a big difference between free from cost and the freedom to use. You must clearly understand this difference if you are to avoid potential legal wrangles over image use. You may find images which have no cost, but require attribution, but then again you can also find images which cost money and still require attribution.

Image is everything

Many people use images found on *Google* and other websites for their own website or blog, in many cases, they may be breaking the law due to copywriting restrictions. However, it is very easy to find free and cost effective options to avoid getting into trouble.

- Take your own photos. There's absolutely no disputing copyright if you know the photograph is your own.
- Request Press images if you are using them from an organised event
- Contact PR agencies or designers who have their own collections and may want the promotion.
- Stock Images. There are many stock photography websites, offering literally millions of royalty-free stock photos, illustrations, and vector graphics at various sizes and resolutions. My preferences are shutterstock.com and istockphoto.com. You can find some fantastic quality photos, and many have the option to download them in high quality for use in printed materials.
- Use public domain images. Although they are often very old, their copyright may have expired, or they have no copyright at all and are useable by any of us quite freely. *Flickr* has a fantastic project, *The Commons*. Under this scheme cultural institutions that have reasonably concluded that a photograph is free of copyright restrictions are invited to share these photographs under their new usage guideline called 'no known copyright restrictions'.
- Creative Commons. Many *Flickr* users have chosen to offer their work under a Creative Commons licence.[2] But be careful, not all photos on *Flickr* are free to use. Some of them are marked 'All Rights Reserved' and you still need to obtain permission to use them, even though they may be free of charge. The ones marked 'Some Rights Reserved' are usually under the Creative Commons licence. There are a few licensing options under the Creative Commons licence to become accustomed with.
    - **Attribution 2.0 Generic**: Share (use), alter, crop the images, and you must credit the photographer.
    - **Attribution-Noncommercial 2.0 Generic**: Share (use) remix, alter, crop the images, and you must credit the photographer, and you cannot use these for commercial purposes.
    - **Attribution-No Derivative Works 2.0 Generic**: Share (use) the photos but you cannot alter, crop or write on them. You must credit the photographer.
    - **Attribution-Noncommercial-No Derivative Works 2.0 Generic**: Share (use) the photos but you cannot alter, crop or write on them. You must credit the photographer. You cannot use these for commercial purposes.

[2] *www.flickr.com/creativecommons*

This may sound confusing at first, but *Flickr* makes it very easy. Each image has a copyright description and *Flickr* provides a description of each licence, and an example of how attribution should be handled, so you can be sure you are using the images correctly.

What's in a font?

Your corporate logo may use a particular font that was chosen by your designer. Just like images, not all fonts are created equal either. There are a vast number of fonts available which are free – and free in both senses of the word. But there are also premium fonts that require attributing to their creator, and/or must be paid for. A trip to a site like *www.dafont.com,* will give you plenty of example of both.

So, when you had your beautiful new logo designed, did you ask what font was used, so you could match it across printed, and online, materials? If you didn't, matching fonts exactly can be a challenge.

The next challenge is transferring your custom fonts onto the internet. Because browsers are limited in what they can handle, you'll find very few sites that are able to consistently display anything other than the standard set of web fonts. If you want a block of text in something more fancy, you'll probably have to resort to turning them into images. By doing so, search engines will find it harder to locate the actual words you use, so you may not come up in web searches.

When it comes to using fonts, it's generally the case that you'll have to dumb it down to the lowest common denominator (i.e. the simplest fonts), if you want it to actually be readable on as many screens as possible.

Getting your website to look good is a combination of the words you use, the colour scheme, the layout and your use of images. Done well, it can make your site look stunning. Done badly, it can turn visitors away in seconds. So, consider how your website looks and navigates with care – and make the most of your investment in your website to deliver what you want it to.

Crystal Hinam is a Director/Graphic Designer at Little Birdie Studio, offering a wide range of web design solutions to local businesses. Crystal has over 6 years experience in the design industry working at various graphic and web design companies in and around Cardiff.

crystal@littlebirdiestudio.co.uk
Twitter: @crysalini
www.littlebirdiestudio.co.uk

David Rahman: Food for Thought

What you think about all day takes on the identity of who you are. These thoughts affect your body, your relationships, your business or job, your friendships and your dreams. What the human mind can do in exquisite fashion is to create the life that you are thinking about. It's funny how experiences in life shape the person who you become and the reality that you therefore experience...

When *Apple* founder Steve Jobs was a boy, one day his dad asked him to paint the fence around the house. The fence was painted white and it seemed a pretty easy job to Steve, as painting is easy, right? So Jobs happily painted it, which took all afternoon, knowing that a little cash would come his way. Very useful to cash strapped teenagers! When Dad returned to survey the work, he commented on how good the quality of the painting was on the outside and then went around to the inside to inspect that side. Much to his chagrin, he noticed that the inside was not as well painted. Jobs' Dad asked him what had happened here? The outside of the fence was done with such great panache and care, but the inside was a poor reflection of what was needed. Jobs reply was "who on earth would be seeing the inside of the fence, Dad!?" Jobs' Dad replied that the people who would see that side are "Us, my Son. We will see it everyday, Son. And that's also what counts..."

You see, what we say to ourselves on a daily basis then forms who we are as people. If we do a bad job inside then we are going to eventually present ourselves to the world in this same way. It is these daily rituals that we go through that programme us to speak, act and behave in a certain way. That forms our personality.

If a person is angry at the world, then you can bet your bottom dollar that they're angry inside at themselves. But why would they admit that? That's going to make them angrier.

You've only got to listen to the way someone speaks to get a grip on how they perceive themselves in the world at large. Try it and see what you discover. Listen to what the people you work with say about money, wealth, relationships, hope, themselves, their past, or their future. You will be amazed at what you find. Each nugget of information that they impart tells you a little more about who they really are.

When I work with clients on a personal basis and over a range of issues, they usually become more aware of what they are saying, even though they might never have realised that they thought that way. Through changing the way they think, they can change their entire outlook on life and experience huge shifts towards more personal joy, happiness and reward. If there is one thing about you that you think could be holding you back, what do you think it is? My personal one was procrastination. I've now changed that, and I do procrastination very badly now!

If you could define thinking, what would you define it as? An interesting definition of thinking is that it is a series of questions and answers and an interpretation of that answer which can cause an emotional response, e.g. "What's the weather like outside?" It's raining. "Why does it always rain when I'm off work! I feel down..."

Hence the quality of your life, and the happiness you can ignite could be related to the quality of the question you ask yourself. You might hear it from 'negative' people when all you may ever hear are phrases like "Why me?" or "If there's something bad going to happen then guess what? It's going to happen to me!" And guess what? It does, as they attract the bad luck that they are seemingly prophesising.

When Mr. and Mrs. Smith are going to a party, with Mrs. Smith hating parties, then what type of questions is she asking herself just hours before the party? "Who's going to be there that I don't like? Will I look good in that new dress? Will I have to eat?" (I'm on a diet), "What time does it finish?" Maybe perhaps the worst question possible that one could ask oneself: "Will I feel lonely?" What do you think these questions are doing to Mrs. Smith's preparations for her night out? How will she be feeling before she's even got there? Not good...

Mr. Smith will be asking a totally different set of questions. These may include: "I wonder who's going to be there to have a laugh with?" or "Will there be food as I'm starving?" perhaps "How much booze can I consume?" And so on. Do you think he's going to be in a good mood? As Einstein put it: "We cannot solve our problems with the same thinking we used when we created them."

A woman in America had seen her mother abused by her stepfather and was then abused herself at the age of thirteen, falling pregnant. After the baby was delivered stillborn, the girl was devastated. What could she do? Yes, she wanted to die, but instead she decided to ask herself some powerful questions. She could easily have fallen into prostitution and drugs and become another casualty of circumstances. What she did decide was to ask herself how best she could recover from this ordeal and how best she could pursue in life what mattered to her. She knew that she loved drama, music, plays and writing, so decided to follow her purpose in life. Her dramatic and tortuous upbringing would not stop her from living her life. She went on to become successful in journalism and television.

You may know her better as Oprah Winfrey. Oprah decided to ask herself the most powerful question you can ask in life in her teens: "What do I love in life and how can I serve?" This caused her to focus on the great possibilities of life. The powerful questions she asked gave her powerful answers which drove her to becoming the icon that she is now around the world to both men and women. She was able to control her state and channel her energies into fulfilling her potential through enormously intelligent action and tenacity to create a life for herself. How far are you willing to go create a great life for yourself?

What you are thinking about at any given moment can change your state at that time. Jealousy, love, happiness, envy, anger, frustration, hysteria, sadness, anxiety, depression or joy are just some of the countless emotions that are at the mercy of your mind (your thoughts). You are therefore the summation of every thought and decision you have made until now. If you're happy with your life then carry on with what you're doing. If you need to make a change in an area then change the way you are thinking about that...starting right now.

One quick way of doing that, which has been scientifically verified all over the world, is the power of gratitude. What are you grateful for in your life right now? What's right about your life? Keep asking yourself that question for the next 30 days but with consistency and focus, and I promise you that your life will change for the better. I absolutely practice this as a ritual on a daily basis. It's easy and you can do it starting *now*. It *will* change your life.

Gratitude is like a muscle. If you go to the gym for six months and work diligently, you will more than likely improve your fitness and body strength. The same principle works with gratitude. Applying gratitude will undeniably highlight to you what is great about your life, and ensure you are happier than you've ever been.

Let's finish off with a note about that 'computer guy', Steve Jobs. When his team of circuit board makers had produced the internal circuitry for the first *Apple Mac* back in the 1980s, Jobs, on seeing the finished work, said "I want you to redesign this computer circuitry boys! It's ugly!" The technicians could not understand why and they asked, "Steve, who will be seeing the inside of the computer?!" Jobs replied, "We will. And that's what matters!"

When the design department had re-created the internal look of the computer, which the public would not see until the later transparent case models, Jobs asked his lead designer to sign the circuit board. Asked why this was needed he replied, "Because all artists sign their work".

"Choose a job you love, and you will never have to work a day in your life"

Confucius

David Rahman is a therapist and coach at Start Smiling Again. In his one to one sessions and workshops he helps clients defeat stress, anxiety depression, ME/Chronic Fatigue Syndrome. Techniques used in the combine therapy and coaching include: Cognitive Behavioural Therapy, Neuro Linguistic Programming, Emotional Freedom Technique, Counselling, Time Line Therapy, Hypnotherapy, and Strategic Interventional Coaching.

0800 023 6263
david@startsmilingagain.com
www.startsmilingagain.com

Denis G. Campbell: Finding Your Unique Voice

Throughout and after the 2012 US Presidential election, senior members of the US Republican Party bemoaned their crushing loss by saying they had a "branding problem." Political pundits and experts lined up to quickly to say the Republican brand had been tarnished by the party's emphasis on interfering with women's reproductive rights, class warfare, their alliance with the fringe Tea Party, and efforts at voter turnout suppression.

Twenty years ago, brands were strictly for corporations. It was how you saw the public face and values they stood for. Slickly produced and packaged, brands had logos you only needed one glimpse of to recognise, because they immediately created a series of impressions, built on your experience, with an understanding of that brand.

No one thinks twice when you see golden arches, three stylistic blue IBM letters, or a swoosh on the side of a sneaker. You know instantly what they stand for because they have been imprinted on your memory, and these symbols conjure up both a set of branded impressions and perceived corporate values.

Even within specific business categories, certain brands own specific attributes. The automobile industry, for example, has spent a lot of time and money on this. When you see the *Volvo* logo, you think safety. *Ferrari's* lion is aligned with high performance, expensive, and speed. Even the *Mini Cooper* and *VW Bug* have youthful, chic, must-have images. So the questions are:

- What image do you, or your business, have?
- What image do you *want* to have?
- How can you use it to grow your business?
- Does your brand remain consistent from business to personal, or are they designed to move independently?

When you think, 'genius computer nerd', your mind probably conjures a picture of Bill Gates. When you think 'global philanthropist using his wealth to eradicate malaria and other diseases and convincing other multi-billionaires to do the same', like Warren Buffet, you also think of Bill (and Melinda) Gates and their foundation.

As an entrepreneur, my corporate working brand is different to my author and journalist brand. That is by design. When working with clients I remain off-the-record, deliver more than I promised, and focus on helping them achieve. The approach is direct and specifically cost-benefit focused.

As an author, journalist, and television host though, my image is direct and truthful, focused on getting to the bottom of the story. I lean progressively left and worry about the message to be delivered, and the consistency of it. Your personal / business brands can be different or they can be one and the same. So let's look at ways you can approach building a consistent personal brand.

It's a technologically leveled playing field

Six years ago, *Apple* took smart phones to new levels with the launch of the *iPhone*. Today, reporters in the field for news radio station *WTOP* in Washington DC, record interviews, their voice-over intro and close, cut, edit, and upload field reports direct to air from their *iPhone*.

What used to require a huge microphone and reel-to-reel tape kits that needed to spliced and physically cut, were first replaced by early digital voice recorders. The reporter, however, still had to return to the station to sit in an editing suite to create the radio package. Not anymore, as technology and apps make audio and video editing simple.

If you watched the film *Apollo 13*, you saw Mission Control scientists in the early 1970s calculating re-entry glide slopes for the stricken ship via maths slide rules. Man landed on the moon with NASA having but one computer, the size of football pitch, filled with vacuum tubes in a hardened silo in The Bahamas and another in Houston. Yet today we all carry in our pocket a virtual super computer that also works as a telephone. Even the 135 launches of NASA's Space Shuttle were done using '70's technology. Most of us today could run a flight mission from our home computer.

This matters because there is greater opportunity to use your voice and television in ways previously not considered. The revolutionaries in Cairo's Tahrir Square were armed with cell phone cameras and uploaded images of horrific beatings by police as visual evidence. This eventually brought down a 30+ year dictator in just eighteen days.

When putting our television programme together, I spoke with a man who had invested £30,000 in a broadcast-quality camera, edit suite, and associated kit. This was a mortgage to be paid for monthly from work generated. That kit owned *him* financially. We produce the show weekly with HD webcams, a good microphone, *Skype*, and an editing package worth £99. While his broadcast quality would be marginally better, is it worth the investment?

You can never compete with the video quality of a satellite uplink, but now, even the mainstream networks such as *CNN*, *BBC*, and *ITV* use *Skype* video-telephony for interviews. So you do have the technology. The field is level. What do you do with it?

Brand You starts with you

Who are you? What image do you wish to project? Do your actions match this? Jot this vision of yourself down, place it where you can always see it, and move on from there. Seven years ago, I wrote a simple statement of values and beliefs. No matter where I sit in my office, it stares me in the face to remind me:

> *"Speak truth always and in all ways to power. Be a voice for those without the power or ability to speak for themselves. By lifting others up, you lift yourself up. Show the market that news reporting can have an opinion and disagree or object without becoming personally disagreeable or objectionable."*

What would yours say? What are the guiding philosophies of your business? Start with you and get clear about who you are and what you do.

Rolling on covered wagon wheels

Next, find a wagon wheel photo or diagram. Notice how the exterior of the wheel needs spokes connected to the centre hub? This is designed to allow the wheel to sustain weight. Remove a spoke and the weight is distributed poorly, which could lead to a breakdown. Without the hub, there are no spokes, and the wheel is crushed by the weight of the wagon. It's a fine balance.

You are the hub of the wheel. Whatever it is you sell, do or try to advance... that goes into the centre. Everything else emanates from that hub and the wheel holds it together, because everything you do is inter-related and part of what keeps the wheel going.

When I work on a story or start a business venture, I pull out a wagon wheel and start there. Many people make the branding mistake of thinking the spokes are your values. No, the spokes support your values and they have to be real and generate money or business, otherwise we're off in airy-fairy land and not running a business. If you are not looking to monetise everything you do, you're not running a business: you just have a nice hobby.

So, when people come to me with the next best social media 'thing', I immediately hold it up to the light to discover one thing: is it a thing on its own that could become the hub of another wheel, or is it a tool to support a money-making spoke? If neither, I can live without it.

Understand your wheel... then BREAK IT!

Starting *World View Show*, we took the traditional route: pitch to large television entities in the hopes that they bless and fund the project. Wait until the concept is perfect in a business where 99% of the time commissioning agents say "No!", and, even if successful 90% of the time, you fail to garner an audience. If the venture *is* successful, you see pennies on the pound as the originator because the networks have teams of lawyers opposing your cousin, the solicitor, and you know which way that's going to go.

After four months of pursuing, we realised the old model was badly broken, so we made a new one.

Technology and viewer habits have changed dramatically. We no longer wait until 10 pm for the BBC News, or trudge to the newsagent through the snow. The Christmas buying season of 2011 was the year of the flat screen television. 2012 was the year of the tablet computer.

YouTube videos are consumed at a rate of four billion per *day*. So why not break the model altogether and build your brand on video? We always used to say, "the money is in the mailing list." Today you can add that "the money is in the YouTube clips library." Build a clips library and it grows and grows daily. The bigger the library, the bigger the income and, therefore, the broader the brand.

With your clip library as the starting point you add: membership websites, sell merchandise, plus sponsorship from people trying to reach your niche etc., and pretty soon every spoke of the wheel has a revenue bucket driven from a consistent hub: brand YOU!

Denis G. Campbell is editor of UK Progressive Magazine and host of World View with Denis Campbell. He is the author of Billionaire Boys Election Freak Show about the 2012 US election fiasco, and Egypt Unshackled, the story of 18 days of revolution told via social media, tweets and communiques.

editor@ukprogressive.co.uk
Twitter: @ukprogressive
www.amazon.com/author/deniscampbell

Elizabeth de Benedictis: Bridging the Gaps in Language and Culture

Translation helps to bridge the gap between two languages and two cultures. But what should you take into account when preparing information for a multilingual and multicultural audience? Translation is about more than just swapping words. Translation and interpreting services can help your business or organisation in many ways.

Communicate effectively

Translation can ensure effective communication with people who do not use or have a limited understanding of English (or your main business language). This is particularly important for public sector organisations.

Global economy

We live in a global village and the world really is your oyster, so get out there and make the most of it! Even in countries where computers aren't as easily accessible, mobile browsing via smartphones is rapidly increasing. If you don't have a translated website, you are quite simply missing out.

Increase profit

Billions of pounds of potential profit is lost every year in the UK because many potential customers go elsewhere if a product or service is not presented to them in their native language. It may seem obvious, but to consider buying products and services, customers need to understand them.

Prevent discrimination

Translation ensures everyone can access and understand the information they need. It helps people from different countries and cultures make informed choices based on the same information.

Policy

It might be part of your organisational language or equality policy to provide translations of documents. Increasingly, public bodies are delivering services in multiple languages and require accurate translations across multiple departments.

Stand out from the crowd

You might just want to go the extra mile to show you value your clients. Individual foreign-language, or multilingual, websites, or marketing materials show you understand and value your customers. It will give you an edge over your competitors.

Don't cut corners

Using professional translators and interpreters can help get your point across succinctly and quickly. A native speaker of the target language will have a natural understanding of any linguistic and cultural nuances. Don't be tempted to simply plug your text into a machine; even the most advanced machine translation systems provide inaccurate translations and require a large amount of post-editing (by humans of course). If you have ever put a paragraph into one of these translators, and then pasted back that translation to return it to the original, you'll see what I mean.

Some top tips on dealing with translators and interpreters:

- Provide reference material and background information if available (this helps give the linguist background and context).
- Choose a professional linguist who is a specialist in your sector, e.g., medicine, marketing, etc.
- Always use a native speaker of the language you want to translate into.
- When using an interpreter, speak using plain, simple English wherever possible, and speak in short bursts. This gives the interpreter time to get the target message across.
- Proofread written translations in their final format; i.e., website or print file, to ensure that nothing has been lost or incorrectly formatted.

Writing linguistically and culturally appropriate copy

In a recent survey, 90% of European users said that, when given a choice of languages, they would always visit a website in their own language. However, a slim majority (53%) would accept using an English version of a website if it was not available in their own language, and fewer than one in five users (18%) said they would frequently or always buy products in a foreign language[3]. Therefore, if you want to advertise or market your product or service to a non-English speaking audience, translation is crucial.

Translation is all about accurate copy, ensuring your message is translated succinctly and is consistent with the original message. This could involve translating websites into local languages (e.g., a service provider in Wales having a Welsh and English website), or making information more accessible to speakers of other languages (e.g., a medical surgery offering medical advice leaflets in multiple foreign languages).

3 European Commission, Eurobarometer survey, 2011

It's about more than simply plugging the text into a machine translation tool and hoping for the best – that would result in badly written copy, and nobody responds well to that. After all, would you buy from a company that had spelling mistakes and nonsensical phrases on its website? Translation tools can be useful for finding out the general meaning of a phrase, but even the most advanced systems can't accurately translate grammar, cultural references, humour, and other linguistic nuances.

Translated copy should read as though it was originally written in that language, and readers should be able to understand every nuance and cultural reference in the text. Translation is about more than just words. It's about ensuring that your copy is culturally relevant, correctly formatted and doesn't offend.

Using a translator who has specialist knowledge of the subject matter is crucial. Would you entrust your end of year accounts to someone who wasn't a qualified accountant? It's the same with translation. A specialist legal translator, for example, will usually have trained or worked as a lawyer or solicitor and therefore has specialist knowledge of the legal sector in their country, as well as a deep understanding of the legal system in the source country. You've worked hard to become a specialist in what you do, so why shouldn't your translator be similarly skilled?

When it goes wrong

Idiomatic expressions and slang phrases should be used with care, as many companies have found themselves in difficult situations as a result of using them.

Having a nice cold beer on a summer's day may be the perfect way to unwind for some, but not if you're drinking a Coors beer in Spain. The company's catchphrase "Turn it Loose" became "Suffer from Diarrhoea" through bad translation[4]. American Airlines' Spanish-speaking first class passengers thought they were getting something more exciting than just a comfortable seat when they read the airline's new advert. The airline was trying to promote its "Fly in Leather" slogan to first class passengers. Instead, it wondered whether they'd be interested in "Flying Naked"[5]. Pepsi seemed to lack cultural understanding when they attempted to translate "Come Alive With the Pepsi Generation" into Chinese. The translation read "Pepsi Brings Your Ancestors Back From the Grave"[6]!

Mistranslations show a lack of respect for the target culture and can seriously harm a brand's image, however amusing they end up being for the rest of us.

More than words

Correct use of images is just a crucial as the words you use. Not only should they be culturally appropriate but they should also reflect any wording used. In the U.K., for example, we say "break a leg" to wish someone good luck, whereas in Italy they use an expression that literally translates as "in the mouth of the wolf". So, in an advert based

4 Matt Haig, 2011, Brand Failures: The Truth About the 100 Biggest Branding Mistakes of All Time
5 Matt Haig, 2011, Brand Failures: The Truth About the 100 Biggest Branding Mistakes of All Time
6 Bruce David Keillor, 2007, Marketing in the 21st Century

on the concept of luck, the choice of image would vary greatly depending on the target country.

Colour is also an important element to consider. Red means danger in some cultures and brings luck and good fortune in others. Black is associated with death and mourning in most Western cultures, but is an honoured colour in Chinese culture. Yellow is said to signify sadness in Greek culture and jealousy in French culture.

Getting cultural references right is crucial. Many advertising campaigns in Muslim countries have failed because of a culturally insensitive portrayal of women. Be sensitive when using jokes, idiomatic expressions, and references to politics or society, as these often don't translate well.

When *Nike* launched its "flaming air" logo in 1997, it received a barrage of complaints from the Muslim community, which believed it looked too similar to the Arabic for "Allah". Nike was forced to pull more than 38,000 pairs of trainers from the market as a result[7].

When DIY chain *B&Q* expanded into China, the store initially flopped, because the company failed to understand that DIY is not a popular activity in China, and there is a stigma attached to manual labour: the emerging Chinese middle class prefer to pay others to do the work for them[8]. After more careful consideration, the stores allowed customers to hire someone to do work for them, and became a success.

Think about layout too. Arabic and Punjabi, for example, are written from right-to-left, whereas ideographic languages (such as Japanese, Korean, and Chinese) are more flexible in their writing direction. They are generally written from left-to-right, or vertically from top-to-bottom. We tend to write quite succinctly in English, and foreign language copy is often longer than the original English. Think about how you would require extra space on your website, for example, where character space might be limited.

A translation is not just about language it's so much more.

- Cultural sensitivity
- Understanding why a certain expression may work in one culture but not in another
- Using the correct technical and legal terms
- Being aware of cultural stereotypes
- Thinking about layout
- Ensuring that your copy and any associated images do not offend.

---

7 David Ahlstrom, Garry D. Bruton, 2010, International Management: Strategy and Culture in the Emerging World

8 Jonathan Reuvid, 2011, Business Insights: China: Practical Advice on Operational Strategy and Risk Management

Use a professional who can guide you through any potential issues and ensure you receive a perfectly succinct, accurate, and culturally relevant translation.

Elizabeth de Benedictis is a Partner at Ditto Languages, offering translation, interpreting, localisation, copywriting, proofreading, editing, transcription and desktop publishing. She has lived, studied and worked in the USA, France and Italy. She has specialist experience in technical translation for manufacturing, construction, systems, and health & safety.

02920 508105
elizabeth@ditto-languages.co.uk
www.ditto-languages.co.uk

Emma Jennings: Customer Service

It's not rocket science is it? So why do so many businesses get it *so wrong*?

I have an absolute passion for delivering excellent customer service, not just paying lip service to it, but actually living and breathing it. So much so the mission statement for our business is simply *customer first*.

We provide customers with city centre conference and meeting places in Birmingham and Manchester that are bright, innovative, and great places to be. We believe if you need a new idea, you need to change the view; no good sitting in the same four walls and thinking you are going to find a solution to a challenge, motivate and inspire people, or have that moment of pure excitement as your brain starts ticking with that first inkling of a new concept, product, or service. The rooms we offer have to be great and the spaces in between have to be better, but the glue that holds it all together is the team, and the way they make our customers feel during their experience with us.

We operate in an extremely competitive market and we ask our customers for their feedback after each booking, because we genuinely believe we can learn from the information and get better at what we do. The first question is: why did you choose us? The top reasons are "been before" or "recommendation." My vision is that people will answer this with "why would I go anywhere else?"

Incidentally, we incentivise our customers to provide us with feedback with bacon sandwiches on their next booking, ice-cream on the roof garden, post-event drink in the bar, discounts on future events, etc. They choose, we deliver. We also ask them what their favourite sweet treat is. Whatever they have told us, we mail them that treat with a hand written thank you note for taking the trouble to provide us with feedback. It's a really small thing, but how nice would it be to receive a surprise *Twix, Galaxy*, or *Curly Wurly* to enjoy with a coffee?

The reason we are better than our competitors is because we live and breathe *customer first*. What this basically means is that, whatever you are doing in the business, you must *always* put the customer's needs first.

We firmly believe this is about recruiting the right people start with. A few years ago, I worked for Virgin Atlantic. They commissioned research into what actually made certain people great at delivering customer service, and why others were poor. The basis of this research was to find that ingrained 'thing' in people that genuinely makes them want to help and please others.

Virgin went onto to develop very advanced, expensive psychometric testing that was carried out at secondary interview process, and it was generally the person you had the positive gut instinct about on first impression that turned out to have the right attributes.

I like to call it the 'weevil'. For example, imagine walking up to a reception desk and asking the member of the team, "Do you have a photocopier?" Good customer service will be a smile and the response, "Yes, we do. It's over there and it's 5 pence per copy." A happy customer gets the answer they wanted with a smile. However, I want the person that goes that little bit extra; their response again with a smile would be, "Yes, we do. What do you need doing? I can do that for you and bring it to your meeting room so you don't have to wait around."

These stars of your team, they don't have to think or be trained to deliver great customer service. They just do it because it's their natural state, and they get a genuine buzz from helping people and using that old and overused saying "going the extra mile."

You can, of course, train customer service, but it's not a skill that is delivered well, or believed that if they don't mean it, you will get 'good', not 'excellent'. In our team, it is often talked about when we are recruiting as, "Oh, they are very studio," or equally, "I don't think they'll fit in as they are not very studio!" This is the mysterious "weevil" in action again. Once you have a core team who are all on the same page in delivering brilliant service, they tend to self-recruit. These genuine people-pleasers tend to move in those same circles, and are attracted to working with and recruiting the same traits. If ever we have made a mistake, they don't last very long. They stick out like a sore thumb as not being "studio!"

One of my favourite examples was when one of our receptionists, who had welcomed and shown a group of guests to their meeting room that morning, realised that many of the guests were deaf and communicating via sign language. During her lunch break, she took the time to learn how to sign, so when the guests left she could communicate "thank you and goodbye."

I couldn't have trained this as good customer service. This was her ingrained trait of wanting to be good to people, getting a buzz from those people being genuinely surprised and happy that she had gone out of her way.

Brilliant. I *love* these people in my team! How easy is it to run the business if they make our customers feel so great? So, take an honest look at your own customer service and ask yourself whether it's up to the mark. Customer service really is our most valuable asset.

For Gail

Emma Jennings is the director and co-founder of The Studio venue company, who provide modern, innovative city centre conference and meeting spaces. With over 20 years in the hospitality industry, she passionately believes excellent customer service is the core of any successful business.

0800 079 0909
emma@studiovenues.co.uk
www.studiovenues.co.uk

Eric Taylor: If I Knew Then, What I Know Now

Would I start a business again? Would I be in a different place than I am now? Almost certainly! When I started in business it was as a result of a redundancy and I didn't have much of a nest egg to kick-start my new career. With a young family and a wife at home, planning was not something I had time to do. I just needed to get out there earning somehow. Since then the journey has been long but the time has flown by. Mistakes have been made, and lessons learned.

My decision-making process to become self-employed stemmed from the fact I had been at the stage of my career prior to redundancy that would only produce a suitably paid job in the sales side of our industry. To do that I needed an established contact list of potential clients (which I had), and a new employer prepared to take me on at a reasonable salary – and there was the rub. As an employee the best I could hope for was a basic + commission, with a vehicle and fuel allowance. Back in those days mobile phones were new and not usually part of any package. I did some calculations and it was apparent that to earn the amount of salary we had become entrapped with I needed to start in business with a success rate usually attributed to about 2 years' work. This is often the case for people contemplating self-employment over being an employee.

For me it was squarely a financial decision from the off. I surmised either way was going to be difficult, but that it was easier to achieve a higher percentage commission from smaller sales volume working for myself, than a small commission from larger sales volume for someone else. So having decided self-employment was for me the choice was to decide what I would base my business on.

Always stick with what you know

This depends upon what you know, and I suppose what financial support you have or can acquire to kick-start your enterprise. I was traditionally trained as an engineer, worked in technical publications and publicity as a technical illustrator, then went on to develop wider skills in technical design, artwork and printing. It was obvious to me that that should be my initial approach.

I didn't have the funding to set-up in bespoke premises so I placed myself at the premises of my first main client as a sub-contracted member of their wider team. This is a good way to start in business, whilst at the same time minimising financial investment. The difficulty with this approach is that it can constrain how you can grow your business, as in reality it has the day-to-day appearance of a full-time job and doesn't allow you to easily attract new clients.

By sticking to what you know you are on familiar ground and your output – whatever it is – is the best it can be due to your experience. Your experience gives you a better chance over your competition. A new direction of career doesn't have the benefit of that experience so is harder to do. If you do have the time and financial backing to plan a different career / business then fine, but I believe most people who are successful in business start out by developing existing knowledge and skills. People buy from people for sure, but people buy from people who know and understand what they are doing more readily.

Be visible even when perhaps you're not

If your business is starting from scratch, this is probably one of the most difficult aspects when attracting new work and growing your business.

It is well known that you have to wear many different hats at the start – admin, accounts, receptionist, sales, production, marketing, debt collection, maintenance, delivery – to name just the obvious! The way I managed this initially was to have my phone diverted to my mobile so I could answer a call whenever I wanted. I also broke my week up by having a regular day off mid-week to do other essential activities. Today businesses can benefit immensely by signing up to a Virtual PA or Telephone Answering service. We still use one so we don't miss a call when all the other lines are busy.

A website for most businesses is seen as essential, but beware – a badly designed one can have an adverse effect!

Buying-in services from other providers is seen as hard to justify initially I know, as money is usually very tight. But in truth it is exactly what you should do when it is making your business more efficient or visible.

Expect to become accustomed to long days, evenings and yes, weekends too in order to get your business established. If you want a 9-to-5 job don't start a business. Great as a goal, but it has to be worked for.

Business networking is all the rage and very important if you are personally going to get to know potential clients, customers and / or suppliers. There are a number of different types of networking groups to choose from and all have their value, depending on what type of business you have, where you want it to operate, and who you want to gain access to.

Other ways of being more visible when perhaps you aren't would be the use of targeted PR, advertising or social networking. There are many ways you can connect with these, either through direct business engagement, networking, business alliances, radio competitions, sponsorship and charity support to name but a few. Don't get bound up or tied down by any single area of activity, there is a plethora of ways to spread a message, special offer or your expertise.

Tried and tested

Take the time to meet other professionals in and around your own area of business activity, they are living the same dream as you and therefore make terrific allies – don't assume that because they are competing they can't be of assistance. You can probably learn more from those people / businesses than from any other. Spot when they do something well, or badly, and think how that might help your business.

I spent many years dreading meeting or speaking with my competition for fear I might give something away that would lose me business. I now embrace such like-minded business people. I have and do collaborate with several competitors to our mutual benefit. One even asked me to represent them in front of their client, as my experience on certain aspects of our trade is greater than theirs. That is what networking is all about. But do keep your own council initially. 'Meet, Like, Know, Trust' is a commonly used phrase in networking. Don't miss out the first three stages before employing the last!

There is a myth that social media was going to be the only way forward, but that is coming full circle and many businesses are returning to more tried and tested traditional marketing methods. Businesses have been persuaded that online marketing is the best way to grow sales, but whilst it is useful to a varying degree for most businesses; it should NOT be seen as the ONLY marketing tool to employ. Take for example the fact that many businesses are sending out regular e-newsletters. Speaking for myself, I do subscribe to some of these, but I rarely read them. They appear in my inbox, but I see them as something to be read later - when I am on my computer, I am actually working - so don't have the time to read them when they land. Unfortunately with the arrival of many more emails through my working day that e-newsletter moves down and off the visible part of my screen... never to be looked for again.

Conversely, a printed newsletter, addressed to me personally and arriving with the postman can be left somewhere to be read during a break from my computer. Sure there is a production cost element to a printed newsletter like any physical marketing tool. I think it is far better paying something for something that will be seen and read, rather than paying little or nothing for something that won't be read!

Learn to say "No"

This is probably one of the most difficult but most important things to do when you are running a business. I have seen businesses fail where someone would simply not say "No – I'm sorry I can't do that... in that time frame ... or at that cost... or to that quality". There is no shame in being honest. In fact it is a pre-requisite in business. As difficult as it is to say 'No', better that than to let your client or customer down.

I once asked one of my long-standing clients why he continued to give us so much work, when I knew he could probably get some of it done cheaper elsewhere and his response was - "because with you I only have to make the one phone call. You have never let me down on either quality or service, you have never changed a quoted price on me, or missed a deadline… and in short - you make me look good in front of my superiors. I can't guarantee that with anyone else". Now, I have said 'No' to him on several occasions over the years, but in doing so I always explained why and discussed a suitable alternative solution.

Love your work!

Whatever you do, do it with passion. Hopefully your business will be successful. It will germinate, and grow to become it's own entity. Almost like your baby that needs to be nurtured and supported. It will, if all goes well, mature to look after you later in life – or through whatever plans you may have for it. The effort taken to have a successful business cannot be underestimated. You will spend long hours, days, weeks and months working to make it successful. You can't do that if you don't have the passion for it – the love of what you are doing. The quality of your output on those endeavours will be greater when you love your work, and will show in the finished product or service you deliver.

I have the work, so now I can relax – right?

Actually, NO, you CAN'T. Today any work is hard won, and it is still easier to lose a client than gain one. An old adage is that any business is only as good as the last job delivered and I agree with that. No business ever lost a client through good service, so it is paramount that whatever else happens, you have to provide that. Always base your service on your customers' expectations – then exceed them! If you have two weeks to deliver a job – but can do it in 10 days – do it!

You should always be looking to be getting the next job whilst working on current projects. Continuity is the life-blood of most businesses, it is what enables you to forecast, plan and develop your business and is the foundation that financial institutions use to assess your level of risk, and their level of support.

As your business develops and grows and as you can afford it, it is important that business finance is dealt with in a continuing, professional way. It gives you credibility in front of your backers and will help guide your business through the inevitable peaks and troughs of day-to-day business. Service providers who can help you with this would include bookkeepers and accountants. Financial Directors are excellent and whilst not always affordable on a full-time basis, there are some FD's that offer their services on an *ad hoc* provision basis of one or more days per week/month. Good luck in whatever business you have started because even with the best approach, experience, methodology, control, levels of support etc – you will need a good helping of luck too.

Cancer research is a serious business, and it's great to be a business serious about cancer research.

Eric Taylor is Managing Director at Ricta UK Limited, offering graphic design, pre-press artwork and printing services in all aspects of business-to-business marketing and promotion, with over 30 years' experience in the Industry.

0161 351 0161
eric@rictauk.com
www.RictaUK.com

Fran Tyler: Cancer And The Small Business

My story starts in January 1994, when my daughters were 12 and 15 years of age and my husband, Phil, was an officer serving with the *Royal Air Force* at St Athan, South Wales. I was diagnosed with breast cancer and given a 40% chance of survival.

Ten years later I was discharged as a cancer patient, and became a cancer survivor so I metaphorically "Put it in a Box" on the top shelf where I could see it, but not open daily!

I was always very supportive of cancer research; sponsoring people, and donating my unwanted items to a cancer-related charity shop. I also spoke openly about having had breast cancer so that I could help other people.

In May 2010 I launched my accountancy business, without a client in sight. Friendships soon grew from the *4Networking* groups I attended, and I began to get some work. Out of the blue a previous colleague contacted me and another platform for my business was born.

By early 2011 the business was growing but not soaring. But then I had a few health problems, even if it was nothing that worried me, or my doctor.

I thought a holiday would put me right and we booked a week in Corfu. Then the "fun" began! The little niggling pain in my leg started getting worse. I have to point out that what I would term as a little niggle, or an ache would be excruciatingly painful for many people, that only become apparent after this ordeal.

I became a regular visitor to our family doctor – in fact I think there was a chair with my name on it in the waiting room!

By late July 2011 I could not put weight on my leg and was admitted to hospital in August. Thus began my three weeks in hospital, a diagnosis of bone cancer, and being told it was in my skull, shoulders, spine, ribs, arms, hips, and legs.

While I was in hospital, Phil, now an engineer, undertook the weekly client payrolls, bringing into hospital anything he could not complete. At this point life decided to send me another blow. The bookkeeper I was collaborating with did not work while I was in hospital and so all of the accountancy work had to wait until my discharge.

However, before I could be discharged I had to be assessed by hospital specialists, to ensure that I was able to get up stairs, get in and out of bed, and make short walks. I was determined to go home as soon as possible, but before that an extra banister had to be fitted to our stairs, two temporary toilet conversions, a zimmer frame delivered to our home, and a wheelchair was borrowed from *Bristol Shopmobility*.

I couldn't cut up food and getting out of an armless chair was almost impossible. After three long weeks I was told I could go home. A physiotherapist home visit was arranged weekly for the first few weeks and I still see her to this day.

Now I had to make some decisions. The biggest of which was did I carry on or cease trading? So what do you think I did?

I went to the pub with my husband and discussed it. There was no giving up – I am an Aries after all! Over a lovely steak meal and a couple of drinks we decided to look for someone who had the same working ethos as I did who could back me up should I go into hospital again. In effect, someone to substitute for me who understood the Government Direct Payment Scheme which replaced the old Home Help for mentally and physically disabled people. The hunt was on!

My first situations vacant entry attracted so many applications it was difficult to handle, especially as I was only typing with one hand at this point. The post advertised was for an experienced bookkeeper yet replies came from tyre fitters, shoe shop assistants, stay at home mums who had never worked, and even a fork lift driver – but everyone got a reply.

Eventually applications were sifted down to four candidates. Tarah fitted in well, even though she had not done accountancy for some time. However she was a personal assistant to a disabled person, and therefore an ideal candidate.

There were other challenges to face in this new world of disability. The *MacMillan* nurse assigned to me while in hospital filled out a Disability Living Allowance application and applied for a disabled parking permit on my behalf. I couldn't drive so Phil was my chauffeur, and getting into the car was painful.

Getting up and dressed in the morning was another task to overcome. A temporary attachment was fixed to our bed so I could pull myself out, and I had to have help dressing. The hospital advised purchasing pull-on garments so at least if Phil was at work, I could get dressed slowly in something suitable for the home.

I have a client in Bath with a contract for weekly accountancy at their premises and luckily Phil was able to juggle his work commitments to fit that in. This meant two journeys to Bath every week instead of one, and duplicate journeys were required for every client meeting, putting a massive burden on Phil and doubling the traveling costs to the business.

4Networking kindly allowed Phil to accompany me to meetings as apart from not being able to drive, I was unable to cut my food, lift the orange juice jug or even reach for it, let alone get up from a chair unaided. I think it freaked some people out to see me putting my little drug dispenser on the table, but that was now part of who I was, and in the main no one was bothered.

More costs were added to the business, as there were two breakfasts to pay for instead of one. Something had to give and then we got a letter saying I had been awarded Disability Living Allowance and could use part of this allowance for a mobility car of my choice. I gave grateful thanks and chose a car with high seats and room in the back for a wheelchair, but it would be 23rd December 2011 before I could collect the car.

I was still having physiotherapy at home every two weeks and Jenny told me that she had never seen such a weak arm. I had favoured my left arm for over two years, so this was not really a surprise and the corrective surgery had weakened it further. My leg was still stiff and painful; I could only walk very short distances, and could not propel the wheelchair, or turn the steering wheel of a car, so I had a long way to go in my recovery.

During one of these physiotherapy appointments I explained to Jenny that I felt a sharp, pulling pain in my right leg and by that evening I was in hospital again with the possibility of a Deep Vein Thrombosis (DVT). My worst fear! I was back in hospital where I stayed eight days until DVT was ruled out. Tarah continued working – texting or e-mailing me if she had a query while our Bath client was very sympathetic and waited until I was out of hospital.

Oncology appointments took up a fair bit of time in the early months of 2012. One appointment was needed every four weeks for an infusion of a bone thickening drug, and another every three months to see the specialist. It was lovely to have some "stolen" time out of the day to read a book whilst having the infusion but of course these appointments happened in business hours and had to be factored into business plans.

Tiredness was also something I had factor in. I had undergone two major procedures, one to pin the break in my left leg and after more consultations and x- rays, another to pin the break in my right arm. Cancer had eaten through both my femur and humerus. After any major surgery there is always a period of recuperation, and I often went to meetings, only to return to bed for a few hours sleep. The time had come to move out of our home office as Tarah was working from our dining room, which wasn't ideal.

I still wanted the business to be local as, if I was ill, I could call in for a few hours to make sure all was well and then go home. Stairs were a challenge for me as I was still using a wheelchair and could not walk more than a few yards with a stick and so the premises had to be a ground floor. We moved into our first office over Christmas 2011. The business started to grow quite rapidly and I now had two people who wanted on site accountancy work every week as well as the growing number of clients that were using our payroll and accountancy services.

We moved into a bigger office at the same location over Easter 2012 and things were beginning to get a bit easier for me. I still had a lot of pain in my right arm and typing was a challenge but now I had the mobility car and was driving. The wheelchair had been returned and I was using a normal walking stick as an aid.

Then another blow! I became ill and telephoned the oncology centre. More tests and scans followed and it was found that neither the infusion nor the oncology drug were working and had to be changed. At least it gave me back that stolen morning where I read a book, but it also meant that I was referred to a spine specialist. Three months, four specialist appointments, thirteen x-rays and two types of scans later I was delighted to hear a Registrar suggesting that they leave well alone – if I could bear the pain – and thankfully his boss agreed with him! No spinal operation for me!

Today is the 20th January 2013, seventeen months since I was diagnosed with bone cancer. So where am I now, and am I still running a business? Of course I am!

I have had to adapt my original business model, but who doesn't? I try my best to live and work within my capabilities and not "make excuses" for living with cancer, merely adapting and accepting it. If it is a bad day – I tell people, I might miss a morning networking meeting or sit down rather than work the room.

I stay in bed if I don't have to meet with someone. I take a painkiller if it hurts too much. I pass work on to another member of staff if I can't manage it.

I firmly believe that things happen for a reason – business started to soar with clients being referred almost every week, and so Steph, a Certified Chartered Accountant joined us in October 2012.

I am so very lucky! Business is not always about money – there are other aspects as well. Both members of staff accepted their posts knowing my medical history. They are supportive and have the same empathy with clients that I based my business on. They treat clients with respect and enjoy giving them all the help they can. I can only say a very big thank you to both Tarah and Steph, as they support me so well.

Finally, I have to say a huge thank you to my fantastic husband, Phil, who has supported me in everything I have ever done, and never once doubted my ability to carry on with the business.

And me? I have smiled and laughed throughout the worst of the last seventeen months and continue to enjoy working in the business. *Life is for living.* My experiences, both good and bad, have made me what I am and I continue to enjoy every single minute. Bring it on! First Call Financials can deal with all the challenges life brings to it!

Fran Tyler is the Owner of First Call Financials, an accountancy company offering "Hand Held" accountancy solutions to clients including general book-keeping through to specially tailored management and year end accounts, on or off site. The Payroll Bureau specialises in providing Payroll solutions to disabled people. Fran has worked in accountancy for over 40 years both in practice and for international clients.

03335 779810
enquiries@firstcallfinancials.co.uk
www.firstcallfinancials.co.uk

George Savva: Why is Smoking So Hard To Kick?

Smoking is a complex behaviour so, here's a crazy question for you to consider!

Do you know that smoking actually has little to do with cigarettes? Many think that smoking is a bad habit, others think of it as an addiction. It is, of course, both of these things – but first, it is a complex behavioural pattern.

Removing the cigarette still leaves one with 80% of the problem unsolved. Stopping – and staying stopped – is a difficult thing to do because of this 'unsolved' problem. Oftentimes, people who quit, find themselves 'taking up' other substitutes like eating or drinking.

How many smokers do you know who promise that they will stop smoking, only to start again shortly afterwards? Or, if you are a smoker, how many attempts have you made, patches have you used, or gums have you chewed, all in the hope of kicking the habit once and for all? The numbers of people who successfully stop smoking using will power alone is very small because smoking is very firmly rooted in the brain.

Part of the 'survival wiring' in our brain is our ability to 'learn quickly'. At the dawn of time (in human terms), when we first appeared on the planet, part of our survival strategy was the ability to learn what was harmful to our existence and what was helpful. The neural pathways in our brains aided our survival by forming 'quick links' which become easier and more effortlessly accessible the more we use them.

As an example, consider a time when you were new to any particular place or venue – a university lecture hall, for example. At a primeval level, this new environment represented a 'potential death' condition simply because it is an unknown quantity. But you chose a seat and you sat down. What happened at your next visit there? The chances are greater than you'd have chosen the exact same place to go and be seated! Why did that happen? What was it that made it so much easier to choose that same place at your next visit?

Is it possible that to your brain, that particular situation didn't kill you last time, so it must be safe? What is important to consider, is the sheer speed with which that decision process was made. It was almost impossible to interrupt.

So, here is the trouble with these pathways; those unhelpful behaviours like smoking, also become linked, making it very difficult to interrupt the resultant responses to any number of given stimuli.

People who do not smoke, for example, can discern that the discomfort caused by thirst is alleviated by drinking water. Non-smokers respond to the thirst stimulus by drinking water, or *Lucozade*, or a cup of tea, or any other recognised thirst quencher. For a smoker, that discomfort is decoded by a smoker's brain to mean it's time for a cigarette.

In order to stop smoking successfully, it's important to figure out what the triggers to a smoker are, and to replace the responses to the various stimuli with the appropriate responses. The important thing to remember is that the journey of stopping smoking is exactly that – a journey.

Too many of us, (who are smokers) focus on the 'event' of stopping smoking, and forget that the process of *keeping on smoking* has been part of our behavioural make-up for many years. We don't stop to consider that we actually have relationships with cigarettes and all the paraphernalia attached to smoking.

On the subject of relationships... consider the advent of the 'social' which now goes with smoking. The fact that smoking has been banned in the work-place, and indeed places of social gatherings, has given rise to what is now known as "the 'smoke-break social". These smoke-break socials, actually create strong and binding relationships between the people who belong to those groups. There is a strong sense of identity between these members – and so, the logical argument that goes with all the reasons why one should stop, are supplanted by this desire to belong to a group.

This gives rise to an altogether new difficulty and that is that the greatest experts on smoking and stopping smoking are non-smokers. They inflict unsolicited advice on hapless smokers such as: Why do you smoke? Why are you carrying on like that? Just throw them away! Non-smokers feel free to do this with little idea of what they are talking about. This condition often makes smokers find solace within their groups, but more disturbing is that it makes them dig in their heels and to say "You can't order me about! You can't tell me what to do!"

I remember an incident in 2005. I was working with a lady in Tredegar. We were in the third week of the intervention and I was explaining the week's assignments. About fifteen minutes into that meeting, she stopped me dead in my tracks, stared at me with a defiant glare and demanded "What the hell do you know anyway? You have no idea what I am going through!" That marked a turning point in our relationship, because the fact was that I had been exactly where she was some twenty years earlier. So, I knew exactly what she was going through; and this was very important to her because she realised that I could identify perfectly with her experiences.

Please don't misunderstand the previous thought though – I am in no way vilifying non-smokers because most are very well meaning when they dispense their advice. The trouble is it is advice based in logic and not in insight. Smokers know at every level that they should stop. This is, of course, logical.

Medical practitioners will be the first to tell you just how much pressure the body is put under every time a smoker lights a cigarette. Almost every major organ in the human body is directly affected when a smoker lights up a cigarette. In fact, every cigarette lit causes the following direct pressure on the human body.

- Central nervous system sounds a 'state of alarm'
- Adrenalin rush; affecting all organs
- Heart beat accelerates, heart strain + lack of oxygen = heart disease
- Blood vessels constrict, blood pressure rises
- Coagulant increases – risk of clotting increases
- Lungs over-inflate, lose elasticity, potentially causing emphysema
- Digestive process stops, blood diverted to arm and leg muscles
- Circulation to hands and feet cut off – gangrene & amputation can follow in time
- Eyes damaged by lack of oxygen – cataracts can form
- Brain cells destroyed by the lack of oxygen in blood
- Liver is stressed and functions impaired
- Overworked insulin emission causes / aggravates diabetes.

The human body is a beautiful and artistic work of engineering. All the above have reasons for happening which I really can't go into in this piece, but if you'd like to know, speak to a medical practitioner who'll probably be happy to explain why all of the above are executed each time a smoker consumes a cigarette.

But, probably, one of the major problems that smokers have to face is that most of them started smoking when they were under 20 years of age; a time when they were emotionally immature, vulnerable and impressionable. It is during this period that young people become hormones on legs, which adds to the many different feelings raging within them. This could be why so many of the neural pathways that are formed and linked to cigarettes remain unchallenged, and for that reason, become 'true' for them.

So, the truth is that nicotine is powerfully addictive and research has shown that a teen can become addicted from smoking *just one cigarette.* Initially this addiction will make new smokers smoke over and over; soon enough, however, what they begin to discover is that whenever they feel bad, a cigarette will somehow give them a lift, so that they feel better. And, sooner than soon the cigarette has become an integral part of their emotional support system and will become even more entrenched in their emotional life. In fact, in an article published in *www.michaelshouse.com* (the Drug and Alcohol Treatment Centres), cigarettes are rated more addictive than cocaine and heroine. This should give you some idea of what smokers have to deal with!

Now, when a smoker stops smoking, he or she can recover from the addiction reasonably quickly. Many of the discomforts they experience may have to do with a chemical imbalance in the brain which also passes. Exercising helps restore the chemical balance. The 'misery' they endure is mostly due to the loss of their emotional support and to the fact that they have to 'change identity' overnight. I am very fortunate that I get to work with smokers directly, and when we start to unpick the entire mass that binds smokers to their smoking, it is astonishing just how major an *issue* the 'emotional support' bit really is.

Finally, stopping smoking is a very simple thing to do, but please do not confuse simple and easy. Things which are simple are not necessarily easy.

Achieving a state of 'non-smoker' is magnificent because the advantages that go with it begin to arrive, slowly at first, but with astonishing speed after a few days. If you smoke, and you're undecided as to whether you'd like to stop or not, just look up some of the benefits that will come your way. And then, pledge to give yourself some of those gifts.

In the end, smoking is a personal choice, and there will always be that die-hard who will not stop under any circumstances. Well, that is their right.

For those who wish to stop – this enemy is eminently defeatable.

For my Father

George Savva is the Managing Director of It Takes 7 Seconds Training, helping people to improve the quality of their lives through recognising and using the enormous latent power that each has within. George has helped 1,000's of people quit smoking (and stay quit) since 1988.

07906 556307
info@ittakes7seconds.co.uk

Lady Helen Child Villiers: Running Your Social Media

I keep hearing from people that social media isn't working for them, that they're not getting enough business from it. So here are some of my top tips for making it work.

Listen

It's not all about you! On your personal profile on *Facebook* you are free to make it all about you. Rant, rave, spill your guts and garner as much sympathy as you want. *But, don't do this on your business page!* Listen to what you customers want. That's what social media is all about, listening. Use it to gauge reactions, to ask opinions, and tell people you follow you're sorry if they're having a bad day.

Use a photo of yourself

Nothing puts a follower off like an egg on *Twitter*, or a question mark on *Facebook*. Even a logo isn't a great option. If you are an SME you need to identify with your followers. Your photo should be representative and appropriate. We all want the best possible photo, but you need to make sure it looks like you.

None of this looking flirtatiously into the camera from below either! Trying to look sexy whilst representing your business is not only a bit gross, but it also sends totally the wrong message. In this case, sex doesn't sell, and your prospective clients will subconsciously be turned off. Especially if when they meet you, you don't look anything like the photo!

Don't snipe

We all have fallings out with people at times, it's part of life. But criticising them and their business publicly might make them look bad for a while, but in the end it just makes you look bitter and twisted. If you have a problem with someone, go and confront the situation in private. If you have made a small situation worse you may end up having to publicly apologise, and in a worse case scenario, you could be done for libel or slander!

Say "Thank you"

If someone retweets or follows you, be polite and say "thank you!" It's an opportunity to build a relationship, and people like to be thanked!

To sell, don't sell

If you think you're going to make money the second you sign up to *Twitter* or *Facebook*, you're wrong. Just as in real life, using social media takes time to build relationships with people. I sell an awful lot through both those platforms when I try, but I've taken the time to build relationships and customer loyalty, and even then I don't always get sales.

But, I do have a presence, and what I do best out of now is referrals. I've had so many referrals in the last couple of months it's been fantastic, but that has come after three years of tweeting. It takes time! I'm still shocked when people think about it!

Be happy!

Remain upbeat and positive. Even if you're saying a negative, try and find a positive. Everyone has bad days, but try not to moan about them too much, for example saying: "Rubbish day, really fed up with it all, don't know how much longer I can take this." It's a huge turn off compared to: "Rubbish day, but glad to be home, now, where's the wine?" Can you feel the difference when you read them both? Moaning about having to stay up late to work, or telling your clients things have gone wrong, is not going to make them want to buy from you! I do use *Twitter* to vent sometimes, but I never rant about my work, it's professional suicide.

Don't lie

Liars always get caught, and they can never repair the damage they've done to their reputation. Don't do it. #thatisall

Don't spam

Nothing is more irritating than your feed getting filled up with auto tweets. One every three to four hours is enough if you really have to do it, but seriously, you need to make sure they have a personal touch. Don't just use social media to sell! Remember, it's about personality too!

Don't auto direct messages

Just don't. Or use *Twit Validate*, unless you want to turn people off straight away!

Don't swear

In real life I swear like a sailor (probably because I was engaged to one once!) but on *Twitter*, you'll only very, very rarely see me swear. If I do, it will usually be 'bloody' and at a push 'shit'. The 'f' word is only ever implied (it's 'effing'), never the word itself. Seeing those words written down make them seem a lot more harsh because they leave a longer imprint visually. It cheapens your brand, and is against all the rules!

So there you go, some of my top tips! I hope they help you feel a bit more in control of your social media.

Lady Helen Child Villiers is Owner of Adore Social Media, empowering businesses to feel comfortable using social media to promote their products, services or events. She trains companies of all sizes and all over the country. After successfully building cupcake and fudge making companies through social media, as well as advising other businesses on how to get the most from their social media activity, it seemed a natural step to start Adore Social Media.

helen@adoresocialmedia.co.uk
Twitter: @adoresocialm
Facebook: www.facebook.com/adoresocialmedia

Helen Davies: Cold Calling for the Fearless

Cold calling is simply the first stage in the selling process. Most products and services are there to provide a solution, the key with cold calling is to ascertain what your prospects problem is, and how you can fix it. The fear of *picking up* the phone is worse than *being on* the phone and making calls. Always remember you have a fantastic product or service and you are bringing it to a potential customer's attention. Let's pick apart some familiar excuses not to cold call.

"I don't want to appear pushy or desperate"

You have a product or a service that your potential clients may need. Calling them is a key way of drawing their attention to what you are selling. Think of it as building a relationship with a prospective client.

"Cold calling won't get me the sale"

Cold calling will open the door to a conversation, that could lead to an appointment, which in turn could lead to a new customer. By engaging and qualifying the prospect you have the opportunity of new business.

Cold calling doesn't have to be used in isolation; it can be used together with other marketing methods, such as direct mail. This then becomes a 'warm call' as you have already made contact with the prospect.

There is a difference between being persistent and being pushy. People buy with their emotions... then they use logic to justify the purchase. People rarely buy what a product *is.* They will buy how it makes them *feel.* As Helena Rubenstein put it; *"In the factories we make 'make up' but in the factories we sell hope"*. You are solving a problem that they have; focus on the relationship you are building, rather that the sale. Think about how you are going to solve your prospects' problems, why they would need your product and what the key benefits are.

Components of a well planned call

- **Planning and preparation**: Set out your objectives for the call. Are you looking for an appointment, or are you looking to close the sale over the phone? Understand the Features, Advantages and Benefits your product can offer.

  Target specific industry sectors that are relevant for your business and find out who the decision maker is. Outline a call frame; work with the key information you would like to get across.

- **The introduction**: Be clear and concise about who you are, and the reason for your call. Something like "Hello, my name is Sam and I'm calling from... we help customers with... last year we saved our customers X% and we would like to do the same for you." Essentially you are highlighting the value that your clients receive by doing business with you.

- **Qualifying questions**: Empathy, and the ability to listen, are crucial here. Encouraging the prospect to talk by asking open questions (*who, what, how, where, when*) will provide you with a wealth of information. It's a powerful way to build rapport and gather key information that you can use later in the call or the sales cycle.
- **Build interest**: Connect the benefits and value you can offer with the problems the prospect is experiencing, and demonstrate how your product can alleviate their issues.
- **Overcome objections**: A good way of finding out the reason for an objection is to reflect it back to the prospect, "What makes you say that?" Asking a series of "why" questions will open up the underlying issue as to why the sale is not moving forward. Usually it's due to the prospect not understanding fully how the product can help them.
- **Close:** Close for an appointment or a sale. Try to leave every call with a call to action, even if you just ask for a referral from the prospect. If they are really not interested do they know someone who might be? Or perhaps schedule a call back in a couple of months.

Next steps

Keep full notes on the call and complete all relevant paperwork. Confirm appointments in writing and keep a diary of any follow-up calls that are due.

How to get past the gatekeeper

Be open and friendly. Gatekeepers are your allies; develop strategies for getting them on your side. You can find out a great deal about the decision maker, for example the best time to call, when they are out of meetings, etc. "I wonder if you can help me" will frequently get you all the information you need.

Know the name of the person you are calling *before* you pick up the phone. Do your research on the internet and build a customer profile. LinkedIn is a valuable source of information. If you are unable to find out the person's name then ask the gatekeeper for their help, which they will be glad to provide.

Let them know who you are and your company name before they ask for it. If they ask you for the reason for the call, be honest as they will check with the decision maker before putting you through.

Questioning techniques

It might be tempting to launch all of the benefits of your product or service at the prospect straight away. However, telling isn't selling, and you have just thirty seconds to make an impact on your prospect before their mind starts to wander, and you lose their interest. Get them to do as much of the talking as possible. The best way to do this is by asking questions. You need to know what their 'problem' is before you can solve it with your product. It allows them to become more engaged with the call instead of being talked at, and it will maximise the chances of a successful outcome. Remember that throughout the call the prospect will be asking themselves "What's in it for me?"

The first, very simple and most effective question is, "Is it convenient to talk?"

If they say "No" then ask for a convenient time and date to call them back. Make sure that you do ring them back when you say you will.

The types of questions you might ask are:

- What challenges are you facing?
- Have you had any difficulty with...?
- How much of a headache would it be if...?
- What are the costs to your company associated with...?
- Is it difficult to manage this level of uncertainty in…?

These types of questions are called *concern questions* and they are designed to get the prospect thinking about how *your* product can solve *their* problems.

Objections revisited

If your prospect has raised an objection, it's a good sign. They are giving you an opportunity to answer their concerns and explore the reasoning behind it. Here are the three most common objections.

- **"Send me some information"**: Ask the prospect further qualifying open ended questions such as, "How are you currently carrying out..?" Relate it back to your product. Show the prospect how your product would benefit them and whether they would consider using your product as a solution to their problems.
- **"We have an existing supplier":** Ask them why they are with their supplier. What makes them special? Asking more qualifying questions will enable you to find out how you can offer a better service.
- **"We don't have the budget":** Explain how you are confident that your product can provide them with the solution to their problems, and that by meeting with you they will be able to see it for themselves. They can address any budgetary constraints at a later stage.

Closing the sale

There are several techniques you can use to close successfully on the phone.

- **A direct close**: This is where you ask for the appointment or the order up front, following your pre-qualifying questions and when you are sure that your prospect is ready.
- **The value close**: Where the prospect believes that s/he is getting a better deal or saving money when you say "I can add another for you for just 10% more".

- **The scarcity close**: Typically something like, "We only have two more of these items in stock and you will need to order today as they fly off the shelves."
- **The trial offer**: This is particularly useful with software sales as once the prospect has started using the software they are unlikely to want to stop using it if it's made their life easier and saved them time, effort or money.

Cold calling is an inexpensive way of getting your product out to a wider audience. It will grow your sales pipeline with qualified leads, and develop your business by at least two new customers a month... based on regular, daily activity. There are millions of customers out there that you can make contact with. All you need is persistence and belief in your product.

For my mum and Anne. Who are still bravely fighting and inspire me everyday.

Helen Davies is the owner of Hurricane Telemarketing, offering specialist lead generation, appointment setting and sales solutions. Helen's great passion is helping businesses transform, flourish and grow.

01633 530054
helen@hurricanetelemarketing.co.uk
www.hurricanetelemarketing.co.uk

Jacqui Malpass: CRM Explained

When was the last time you were pleasantly surprised by how well the person on the other end of the phone knew you? They were probably using a CRM system. Choosing a Customer Relationship Management (CRM) solution for your business can be a time-consuming process. It is also fraught with conflicting thoughts about whether it really will make a difference, and how it will influence your bottom line. Making the wrong decision can lead to an inefficient system that doesn't meet your company's needs and, worse still, doesn't get used.

I pulled these steps together based on my work as a marketing manager and consultant. I developed my own CRM system back in my IT days, and also selected and implemented many others over the years. So, I know the pain not only of looking for one but also of persuading others to implement it, and then getting them onside.

I believe that no matter what size of business you are, a CRM system is vital for your growth. Of course CRM is not just about technology. It is a strategy to learn more about customer needs and behaviours in order to develop stronger relationships with them. CRM is the way companies manage their relationships with clients. By implementing systems and processes, such as a CRM system, you will have information to hand that will enable you to make better decisions.

You will never alter the fact that people buy from people and fantastic customer service is the key to great relationships. However, a CRM system is the technology that works as an enabler in that quest.

The system can be a filing box, Excel, Access or one of many CRM systems specially designed for the job. What is important is that you follow a process for choosing the best system for your business.

What can you use a CRM system for?

- Profiling customers and prospects
- Tracking all contacts with a customer or prospect
- Managing all communications, including emails, letters and proposals
- Managing sales campaigns and tracking results
- Tracking sales targets and commissions
- Managing and scheduling follow-up sales calls
- Managing problems and complaints
- Improving customer service.

Benefits of a CRM system

- Increasing sales by understanding trends and needs better
- Identifying needs more effectively
- Maximising cross-selling opportunities
- Better targeting of marketing communications
- Enhancing customer satisfaction and retention
- Increasing value from existing customers
- Reducing costs associated with supporting and servicing customers
- Increasing your overall efficiency
- Reducing total cost of sales.

Think big, start small

It may sound overwhelming to implement a CRM system. My advice is to think big, start small. When you have the confidence, then build quickly. You can start with the goal of creating intelligence around your top 20-30 customers, including data on sales pipelines, marketing, and products.

CRM systems are for everyone, even solopreneurs. Work out a process that works for you and your business. To do that you'll need to define your CRM requirements and objectives:

- What do you want the system to achieve and deliver for your business?
- What are your company's business objectives?
- Who will be using it?
- What kind of functionality do you need?

Start by obtaining a list of needs and wants from everyone within your organisation; this includes sales, marketing, executive team, admin and customer service. Consider who else may need to have access to customer information. This implementation could fail if you do not get the buy in of all stakeholders. Remember that a 'customer' in this sense can be anyone that your organisation contacts – so include suppliers, partners and other organisations.

Your requirements list

- Supplier profiles
- Functional requirements
- Processes and work flow (now would be a great time to review them)
- Technical requirements (e.g. in-house or cloud-based)
- Integration requirements (hardware and other software)
- Your budget
- Implementation issues
- Training and support
- Productivity and customer service goals.

Once you know what you want (and only then), should you start to look for a potential solution. Don't start with a piece of software and try to bend it to your will.

Research potential suppliers

Armed with your list of needs and wants, search the internet looking at potential suppliers, reviews, and ask others who they chose and why (although 'bad' reviews should be treated with caution, they may not have done their homework or properly implemented it). What you are looking for might include:

- A track record or familiarity with your industry, or a similar one.
- Look at case studies and the solutions they came up with.
- Talk to real users of the system for their view about the implementation process, what users think, reliability, training and support.
- Check the financial health and longevity of the supplier.
- Narrow down to a short list of 5 possible solutions, and get remote demonstrations of each one.
- Then, narrow down your list to a final 3 to contact in person.

After contact, consider which of them:

- Demonstrated that they understood your business and technical requirements?
- Gave you the sense of going the extra mile to earn your business? This doesn't guarantee great customer service, but it is an indication of what you might expect.
- Offered you a list of users to talk to?

Although you may have set a budget, it is the system and supplier that provides the *best value* that will save you money in the long term. Beware of people giving their goods away for nothing, there is no such thing as a free lunch, and these systems will probably cost you more in the long-term. Also be wary of any company going through an acquisition, as your software may get dumped and you will have to go through a costly migration process soon.

When you get to your final three, share the results with your CRM selection team and start the in-house demonstrations and evaluations. All feedback should be welcomed.

Demonstration and feedback time

It's time for your supplier to show that they understand your business and show off their system, people, processes and customer service in the best possible way. Review and compare how each of the systems work. Try to map out your processes and don't just think because their system can't work to your process it's not worth considering. Your processes may just be rubbish (and in my experience they often are). Ask your potential supplier to show you how various processes could work, and look at how creative they are at solving your problems. Sometimes these demonstrations can really get us questioning our business processes.

Once the demonstrations are over, ask your team to evaluate and report back with their findings. Address any of their issues with them, and the supplier. Once you have everything addressed it's time to get a consensus. No matter what the size of organisation, it needs to meet everyone's needs. If you are a small business that outsources activities don't forget those workers as well.

Budget and value for money

Cost is not just the price of the system; you need to be looking at the ongoing support and customer service. You may pay a bit more for your system, but you will also get peace of mind.

If you are buying a system off the internet the price is usually fixed and it is harder to negotiate. However, if you don't pick up the phone and call you will never know. A great way to get money off is to offer to be a reference site or to use their affiliate links and share it with your fellow businesses. Read the small print, and confirm what the get out clauses are. Check that if you are not happy you can get your data out of the system so that you can re-use it elsewhere. Before you part with your money sleep on it and buy the system that meets and exceeds your needs and offers the best overall value.

Implementation time

The number of system users and the nature of the system you are putting in will determine how you implement your CRM. My suggestion would be to find yourself a champion and start small. Once others see someone enjoying the benefits of a new system they will want to be part of it. If you are doing it all yourself, the same rules apply, start small and get each part to work before you go onto the next. Invest in training, whether that is classroom based or online, nothing beats learning how before you jump in and try.

Which software?

Wow, how long is a piece of string!? Over the years I have used many and have always followed my own advice and really thought about how I will use it now and for the future, what my objectives are, how easy it is to implement and use, what integrates with it, support and value for money.

Your business will doubtless have different needs to mine, but as a guide, here are some of the criteria I was looking for:

- Cost effective
- Easy to learn
- Easy to use and a simple interface
- Customisable
- Fully hosted cloud solution
- Integrates with *Google Apps*
- Easy to import and export data
- Tools to keep the database tidy
- Autoresponder integration
- Task manager to diarise and prompt actions
- Social media integration on multiple platforms
- Opportunity tracking.

What next?

- **Define 'customer' and 'lead'**: Every customer relationship begins as a lead. Leads must be nurtured under the right conditions to grow. This means creating processes so that you stay on top of your leads. Before starting any lead generation activities, it's essential to know what you're looking for. What's the profile of your ideal customer? Look at your current customers and consider what makes them great customers and ask what else would you want? From there, you can answer the question, what makes a good lead for our organisation?
- **Create a process**: The goal of marketing is to generate leads that lead to new customers. However, without an effective lead-management process, leads may not be tracked effectively making it hard to know if your marketing efforts are working.
- **Nurture your leads**: Successful lead generation goes far beyond simply acquiring leads. It's about building relationships, then tracking and nurturing them. An effective nurturing process seeks to truly understand the customer and their needs, challenges, goals, and when and how they want to receive communication from you. Respect those concerns and wishes and you go a long way toward building the relationship.
- **Track and tweak**: Just because you have software and processes it doesn't always follow that these will be successful. My belief is that there is no such thing as failure, only feedback. When you find that something isn't working, find out why, tweak and retry.
- **Use the reporting systems**: All CRM comes with a way to report back to you, make these meaningful, and make time to analyse the data. This is where you will learn what has been successful and gives you amazing insights into your business. Sometimes business comes from the places and people we least expect.
- **Use it every day**: This goes without saying, use it or you will lose it. I open my CRM first thing every day to see what I need to be doing and when I have an interaction, I record it.

Jacqui Malpass is an author, coach and consultant offering book coaching and mentoring, marketing, and personal branding, consultancy and training. She has over 25 years in marketing at senior management level and consulting with SME's. She specialises in systems and processes for lead generation and getting the most from your CRM system.

07862 260095
jacqui@jacquimalpass.com
www.jacquimalpass.com

Jason Vaughan: Building Your Reputation

I started training in Tae Kwon Do when I was 8 years old but due to issue with transport (and girls!), I stopped at around 13 as a black tag. This is one grade below black belt. I joined the army at 16 and really wanted to get back into training. However, due to the commitments of the unit I was with at the time no clubs were interested in taking me on, as I could not train or attend for several months at a time.

I eventually got back into regular training in 1996, aged 25, but had to start from white belt all over again. So, although I had five years previous training and grades I had to start from scratch. This was all due to the length of time that had elapsed, and the politics of the sport, but that's another story.

At the time I stopped training regularly I'd achieved a 3rd dan black belt. If you break it down it takes around 3½ years to get 1st dan, then 1½ years to go from 1st to 2nd, 2 years from 2nd to 3rd. That's around 7 years training. I trained in the AIMAA (*Action International Martial Arts Association*) which was under a 9th dan Korean Grand Master, Hee il Cho, who I took all my dan grades under. I trained at all the clubs I could in my local area and used to train 5 or 6 nights a week. The sport has taken me all over the world.

In 2001 I started my own club in Ledbury with just four people. They were all friends who wanted to see what I kept going on about. Only one of them lasted more than a week but I knew they probably wouldn't stay the distance. However, I had budgeted for six months where it would not matter if I got any students or not. After that if I had none I was going to be in trouble. I printed my own flyers on my PC, and put together my own A4 posters. It was all done on a shoestring budget really.

There was one other club in the area but the instructor was not teaching it in a traditional way. Parents liked the military discipline aspect for their children as it taught them respect and discipline as well as real self-defence. The root of Tae Kwon Do is a military combat technique. As such it goes beyond being just a series of kicks and punches, it's also a disciplined way of thinking and acting.

The club picked up students fairly quickly once I got some local kids interested and they were participating regularly. Word spread as their parents would tell other parents and so on. It took off a lot quicker than I had expected it to. Being in a small town like Ledbury I had thought I would be lucky to break even, but the numbers continued to grow, and I was attracting people from quite a distance. Once that happened I even started getting students from the rival local school come over and join at our club.

I soon built a reputation as being able to practise what I preach and keep even the worst 'problem' kids in line. I've always believed that the presence of a strong role model, particularly for young boys, is important in terms of their emotional and inter-personal development. The so-called problem kids generally seemed to lack such a role model in their lives. They may have had an aggressive role model, but not one that coupled discipline and strength with respect and dignity, something which Tae Kwon Do promotes. I had found something that was lacking in some kids' lives in one way or another. And parents liked the effect it had on all aspects of their children's lives from manners, to school work, through to health, fitness and general confidence. Tae Kwon Do doesn't just teach martial arts moves, but a real discipline of the mind and body as well.

One crucially important thing I learnt from developing the club was the importance of a good reputation. One quality referral is worth a fortune in advertising. This has so many parallels in the way we shop in general – whether we base our opinions on a product or service on our own experience, or on the recommendations of others, we respond to reputation instinctively.

What does your business say about your personal reputation, and vice versa?

I knew what people were saying about my club because I asked them. I sought feedback and opinions. How about your business – do you know what people are thinking about you, and even more importantly saying about you?

These days there are so many ways that a bad reputation can be spread quickly – *Twitter* and *Facebook* come to mind readily, as well as all the specific online forums that meet the needs of special interest groups. If you're moving in these circles regularly you'll know only too well how quickly the rumour mill works, and how people make, and pass on, good and bad comments about the people they deal with. As a photographer now I operate in such online communities, and I see people getting slated and complimented every day.

The club, and my style of delivery, became a magnet for success for the club. We would regularly compete at national competitions and come back with large hauls of awards – far more than other clubs based on just size alone. Although we'd grown, we were by no means the biggest, best funded or best equipped in the country. I honestly believe that it was the ethos of the club that drove this competitive success. We were always confident in the arena, but never cocky. I never allowed my students to humiliate their opponent – win by all means, but not at any cost.

No matter how close someone is, or you think they are to you, don't trust them with anything to do with your business. I look back and really wish that I had just made sure I had done all the teaching myself, as I'm sure that if I had it would have still been going now. Due to work commitments I would get senior students, or my partner at the time, to take a class for me. However, I was putting them in a situation that they were not capable of dealing with in the same way that I would. They didn't have the skills, or the understanding of the principles I was teaching to do a job that was consistent with my goals.

If you have something that works make sure that anyone else you are going to trust to deliver that product or service really can do it with the same consistency, and does it the way you want if you want to maintain the reputation you have worked hard to create. When people go their own way and without your knowledge, it is a recipe for disaster. This was part the reason my club started to fail, as I misguidedly trusted others to teach when I could not, and people started skipping on training because the same demands were not being placed on them.

It was *my* goal to start and run the club, *my* vision. As soon as I involved others I ran the risk of diluting that vision, and were I to do it all over again I would do things differently. I'd certainly demand the same levels of commitment to the direction of the club, and find genuinely like-minded individuals that shared the same ethos. Because, when it all comes down to it the reputation of my club was too important to mess up.

To my late father Charles Vaughan

Jason Vaughan was in the army for 10 years, trained in martial arts since the age of 12, left forces as personal trainer gym instructor, sports therapist and martial arts coach. He was three times AIMAA Open British Heavyweight Champion.

Jeff Boycott: Achieve Perfection

Proofreading is the final step to your finished business document. It is a detailed analysis of correctness, and must be applied to every document before it is published. When you write an email in business, or upload a blog to your website, or even print your new business cards ready for a networking event, you are in fact publishing.

Whether you use a pen, keyboard, or smart phone in business, proofreading your work should be considered *the* most important step. Unfortunately, it is a step that is commonly underestimated. All too often we see clumsy errors on business documents: a poor choice of grammar, typos, or long and complex sentences that lack correct punctuation, which affects communication and therefore risks the credibility of the document, and, essentially, *your* credibility.

For some, proofreading could be running a spell checker. This is, of course, an easy way of locating spelling mistakes or minor grammatical errors, but it is not the extent of proofreading.

Before this, you must determine whether or not your finished document serves its purpose. For example, the purpose of a cover letter for a job application is to convince the hiring manager that you are the perfect person for the job. A marketing document should raise awareness of a product, and encourage the target market to buy it. An invoice should clearly and accurately indicate the products, quantities, and prices agreed between the seller and the buyer etc. Proofreading is essential; it is the difference between settling for mediocrity and achieving *perfection*.

Let's look at seven valuable proofreading techniques that can be applied to *any* business document.

Does your document serve its purpose?

It is important to understand that, before even considering spelling and grammatical errors, your document serves its purpose. It may read perfectly well from your point of view; however, you must consider the person who will ultimately be reading your document. Ask yourself whether or not, in their position, the document does exactly what it should be doing. If not, then you must proofread and thoroughly analyse the ways in which you can improve your work.

The following examples will briefly outline some of the common errors made in business-related documents, and some considerations that can be applied to perfect them.

Emailing a cover letter and CV for a job application

Your CV sells you. All the years of study and education, and your struggle to break into your field of expertise, has to be crammed into a few pages. It could be the best CV ever written; however, the hiring manager must first get past the cover letter to reach it.

The proofreading stage of a cover letter for a job application is of the utmost importance. You must ensure that the document does exactly what it should do, which is to get you the interview and progress you to the next application stage. Your goal is to capture the attention of the hiring manager and encourage them that you are the best person for the job.

Listing your experience and achievements does not quite cut it. The cover letter must demonstrate more than the CV Without exceeding one A4 page, try to engage the hiring manager with a conversational tone instead of just listing facts. Be concise, but at the same time, clear and specific. Use power verbs, e.g., *accomplished, recommended, obtained* etc., and adjectives, e.g., *competent, proficient, organised* etc.

The single most important part of the cover letter is the very first line. This is the line that determines whether or not the hiring manager will read on, and should be examined methodically. Sell yourself. Once you are happy with your cover letter, read it not as yourself, but as the person hiring. It may look perfect to you, but will it look perfect to them? Put yourself in their position: "What do I want to read?" and "Do I want to learn more about this applicant?" If the answer to the last question is "No", then the cover letter needs to be revised.

Using email-marketing systems

Marketing is the process of communicating your products and services to your customers, a strategy which plays a vital role in every business. Popular marketing techniques for small businesses may include websites, social media, websites, cold calling, workshops, networking, elaborate case studies, and referral networks etc. Whether your marketing costs exorbitant sums of money or is cost-free, it should simply do one thing: create and build awareness of your products and services, and, ultimately, generate business.

Email-marketing systems are a great way to market your business products and services to hundreds, if not thousands, of inboxes at one click of a mouse. They allow you to build an email campaign using your very own custom-made templates (including logos, website links, and pictures etc.).

Once delivered to your target list, you can monitor the activity of your campaign; i.e., how many were:

- opened
- clicked
- unopened
- bounced
- unsubscribed from.

If, for example, only 12% of your emails were actually opened, it means that the email might not have served its purpose and therefore needs reviewing. How many of us receive an email and instinctively hit the *delete* key? Similarly, if we open the email and the first line reads, "Hi everyone..." it is likely that the email will be immediately transferred to the trash folder.

No business can expect 100% of their target list to indulge in their products and services. However, there are ways that you can use email-marketing to improve your results. It all comes down to proofreading.

Initially, you must establish a relevant target list. It would be pointless to send an email campaign marketing your fantastic French translation services to a plumber. Keep your marketing material relevant and exclusive to your target audience.

Secondly, address your email to each person by his or her first name; this is a simple tool that comes with most email-marketing systems, making the recipient feel more valued.

Finally, you must analyse the email subject line. This could be considered *the* most important factor when proofreading your email-marketing campaign. Spend time thinking what would make *you* want to open the email and learn more. Keep it short, catchy, and, most importantly, free of spam content.

Reread your campaign thoroughly, correcting any spelling mistakes. Does it serve its purpose? If the answer is yes, then it is ready to go. Understand that good email marketing does not take effect overnight. You must adopt a marketing style and stick with it, ironing out and improving any concerns along the way.

Proofreading your invoice

Your invoice should clearly and accurately indicate the products, quantities, and prices agreed between you and your customer. It is a simple process, but should be approached with great care when proofreading.

The invoice bridges the gap between being paid, preferably on time, and not at all. It goes without saying that all numbers must be correct. Staring at a page full of numbers can be confusing, which is why each figure and value must be scrutinised thoroughly.

When using a template confirm that:

- each box is correctly aligned with those surrounding it
- you indicate the terms of payment; for example, "payment due 30 days after invoice date"
- your contact details are correct
- customer details are correct
- bank details are correct.

It may even be a good idea to save a copy of your invoice in pdf format before you send it to your customer. This way, its content cannot be altered, and could reduce the risk of conflict should something go wrong during the payment process.

Many of the latter come down to common sense, however, if not proofread accurately, an incorrect invoice can cause unnecessary problems, and even affect your credibility as a business.

Give the same attention when creating your business cards prior to printing. Ensure that your mobile number reads "07979..." and not, "o7979..." It is not perfect and therefore does not evoke perfection. The last thing any business wants is 1,000 beautifully clean, erroneous business cards. So, be sure to spend time analysing, in great detail, the purpose of the business document that you are producing. When, and only when, the document does precisely what it is supposed to do, is it then ready to go.

Now you can achieve perfection

Now that your finished document serves its purpose, it is time to achieve perfection. Proofreading for spelling, grammar, punctuation, terminology, and formatting should be considered with great care and must not be rushed. It is *the* step that will ensure that your document is perfected before submission. Let's look at some of the less obvious issues that could potentially risk the credibility of your document.

Spelling, grammar, and terminology

When using *Microsoft Word*, for example, it is just a case of activating the spell check function, if you just want to find misspelled words. But it won't necessarily pick up on misused ones.

Of course, it is important to note that the language selected is relevant to the target audience; e.g., US English uses a 'z' where English UK uses an 's', (organisation versus organisation). When writing in a foreign language, the same must be applied. The writer must ensure that an audience in France will be reading the document in French (France), and not French (Canada).

Terminology must be subject-related. Use an online dictionary to determine the best choice of words and compound words so that they fit the right context. For example, *council* and *counsel*: A *council* is an administrative group or assembly, whereas a *counsel* means giving formal advice (to someone). Phonetically, the two words sound exactly the same; however, when written wrongly, this single word could corrupt the sense of the entire sentence, or even the entire sentence.

Other common confusions in terminology include *prescribe* and *proscribe*, *effect* and *affect*, *fiscal* and *financial etc.* Take great care when proofreading your choice of terminology, and confirm that it is relevant to both your document and your target audience.

Formatting and editing

The *Track Changes* function in *Microsoft Word* is a very useful tool which notes any changes you make when proofreading your finished document. Any changes appear in the margin. They can be compared to the original document and then individually or collectively confirmed to accept the final changes before submission.

Be consistent with formatting. If you leave a space between paragraphs, maintain that space throughout. The same should be applied to alignment, indentation, and time references; e.g., *2 o'clock*: the correct way to write the time, in formal business writing, is to insert full stops and leave a space before the abbreviation, i.e., *2 p.m.* It is a minor factor to consider, but a necessary one. Small changes can mean everything in the finished document. It's normally a job that gets overlooked, but, in actual fact, it is one of the most important jobs.

Proofread your finished document meticulously for any errors in terminology and punctuation etc. Minimise the risk of loss of credibility should these errors affect an otherwise good business document.

Clear of any distractions, read the document out load to yourself

It is always a good idea to carefully read your document through several times, but even better if you read it out loud. Lock yourself in a quiet room with no distractions, calm yourself, and begin to read out loud. This way, you are more likely to identify errors in punctuation. Make the change, reread it, and, only when you are satisfied, continue reading. Family members may worry that you're talking to yourself, but at least you will have a perfect document.

Read the document backwards

It sounds crazy, but reading the document backwards is a great technique used when proofreading. Without even noticing it, you automatically say each word slowly and carefully in your head. You may notice mistakes that you would have skipped if you read it normally.

Print out a copy of the document

If word-processed, it may be a good idea to print out the document to read, instead of reading it on screen, which can be difficult for some people.

Punctuation is critical!

Good punctuation is, of course, fundamental to the quality of your finished document. Poor punctuation risks the credibility of the document. Pay close attention to the use of commas, full stops, capital letters, and apostrophes. *Your* and *you're* (*you are*) are too often confused. It is such a simple error to make, and equally simple to miss when proofreading, so keep a close eye on this.

Be consistent with numbers

If you refer to times of the day, be consistent in the way you present them; i.e., *a.m.* or *am* and *p.m.* or *pm*. Choose one and follow this pattern throughout. The same applies to the presentation of dates and figures.

Use the Track Changes function when using word processors

Track Changes is a useful tool. Any change you make when proofreading your document will be indicated in a coloured box in the right-hand margin. Once you have made all of the changes and you are happy with them, you can review and confirm your changes either individually, or collectively.

Get someone else to read it

The document may make perfect sense to you, but may not to a family or friend. Get someone else to read through your document. You'll be surprised at the number of mistakes you missed.

Jeff Boycott is the owner of Jeff Boycott Translation. He is professional French translator specialising in business and marketing, and a highly proficient English proofreader and editor. Jeff is also the co-owner of The Arena, an effective home fitness programme that requires no equipment or gym membership, but works for everyone. Jeff has 6 years experience in the fitness industry, specialising in elite fitness and extreme weight loss.

07979 181538
jeff@jeffboycotttranslation.com
Twitter: @jeffboycott22

John McAleer: Fire Safety - Assume Nothing

In my opinion, the three most important words in the English language are tried, tested, and trusted. This comes from many years on the road carrying out Fire Risk Assessments of commercial and industrial buildings, including numerous office premises, pubs, restaurants, hotels, residential care homes, buildings in multiple occupation over many floors, and houses of multiple occupation.

As a member of the public, who may possibly enter one of these establishments, you would like to think that every effort has been taken to ensure your safety, and you would hope that the person or persons responsible for fire safety have taken this task seriously. Unfortunately, even with the changes in fire safety legislation, which have been implemented in recent years, this is simply not the case.

Many successful prosecutions have been brought by local fire authorities and regularly courts issue large (fines plus costs). In 2011, two cases led to custodial sentences. However, many property owners and occupiers still fail to comply. Please bear in mind we are talking about the safety *of people's lives* here – a building can burn down and most of the things inside can be replaced...lives cannot.

I have always taken a very simplistic view on safety systems – if you need to use it for its intended purpose there is already a problem. A fire extinguisher, a fire alarm, or a fire-resisting door, there's no difference.

Fire extinguishers on commercial premises are seen by the maintenance engineer only once per year. So, let's say the maintenance inspection is carried out in January every year. If a fire extinguisher is tampered with, damaged, or moved away from it's intended location in February, in May when someone needs to use it, there is already a problem. There will be much more of a problem if no checks are carried out to ensure the equipment is available for use and free from tampering or damage. If, in this example, the occupant of the building carried out a monthly check on their fire extinguishing equipment, then this problem can be more quickly rectified, therefore making the fire extinguisher ready and available for use.

It is very scary when I think of the number of times I have entered a building, whether on a professional visit or not, to find fire extinguishing equipment missing, damaged, tampered with, or completely inappropriate in its specification. Clearly, these things are rarely being checked, as well as occupants assuming that "it won't happen to me." Everyone appears to assume that they will have the right thing in the right place, tamper free and ready to go if needed. Wake up! Assume nothing.

Fire alarms work on the same principle. If you need to use it, there is already a problem. Sadly, testing of fire alarms is rarely carried out correctly. Simply pressing the *sound alarm* button on a control panel is not sufficient. Yes, it will make a noise, but this is not the way fire alarms should be tested. There are different methods of testing fire alarms, depending on the model. Some have a key to insert into a break glass call point to activate the alarm; others have a reset key; but regardless of the method, testing must take place. Too many people assume that just because it is installed it will therefore work.

The worst example of this I have come across was a solicitor's office where I was carrying out a Fire Risk Assessment. It transpired that their fire alarm system had no power going to it. It wasn't faulty, it was switched off, and it would appear that it had been off for approximately 4 years. No testing was ever carried out, and nobody even *knew*. It was switched back on that day, but it still remains untested, and without the required maintenance being carried out.

Testing of fire alarm systems should be carried out on a weekly basis. Have maintenance carried out as required. It may be that your building does not have a fire alarm system, whereas perhaps it should. Whatever method you have to raise the alarm in case of fire, check it can be heard throughout the building, especially in areas where there may be additional noise.

Test it. Check it. Assume nothing.

Training

How difficult can it be? Everyone knows how to use a fire extinguisher, don't they? *Surely* everyone knows how to get out of a building safely? Everyone *must* know where the assembly point is... it's at the... hold on... have we got an assembly point?

Training in fire safety is vital, and not so difficult. Every person employed at a premises should receive induction training as soon as they join. They need to know:

- how to use the fire extinguishing equipment
- when to use it,
- more importantly, when not to use it
- they should hear the sound of the fire alarm system...now there is an opportunity to test it
- where their assembly point is
- how to raise the alarm
- the action to take on discovering a fire
- what to do when they hear the alarm

Training should be repeated on a regular basis. People in a panic situation may not react the way you would expect them to. It should not be glossed over, or hurried. Make sure everyone knows what to do. Assume nothing.

Fire exit signs can often be confusing. I have seen fire exit signs placed incorrectly. For someone who is not familiar with the building, they could find themselves in a dangerous situation. Check your signs. Assume nothing.

These points may seem obvious, but they form the backbone of a good basic fire safety policy. In summary, the items mentioned above are all too often taken for granted, so test and record all testing in a fire safety logbook. Assume nothing.

Fire safety in the home

Here's a quick checklist of things to consider in the home.

- **Ensure you have sufficient smoke detection throughout your house:** Many people have a smoke detector, but here is a piece of information most people don't know: there is more than one type of smoke, so more than one type of smoke detector. The vast majority of smoke detectors are ionisation smoke detectors; these are the ones that go off when you are cooking. You probably can't see any smoke but the detector is so sensitive that it activates at the smallest amount, because ionisation smoke is made up of very small particles. Smoke that is generated by a fire involving an electrical appliance is made up of larger particles, and this is called optical smoke. Ionisation smoke detectors will not react to optical smoke, and vice versa.
- **Smoke detectors should be installed in pairs**, particularly in areas where people sleep. Remember that smoke alarms alert you to a problem. If you are awake you will see and smell smoke, but if you are asleep you must be woken to survive.
- **Battery-operated smoke detectors should be checked weekly**. Batteries should be changed once a year, not left until it starts beeping in the middle of the night and then probably not replaced at all. Pick a memorable day, like a birthday or anniversary. My personal preference is battery operated smoke detection, which is what I have in my home.
- **Mains operated detection equipment will also have a battery back up.** You may have to refer to manufacturer's instructions of the frequency of replacing batteries in those units. Some modern smoke detectors claim to have a battery with a recommended ten-year life span.

Fires that householders (whether owners or tenants) are likely to be involved in will most likely be the result of an electrical problem (either with the mains or an appliance), carelessness, or arson. To avert the first two possibilities you can take some simple precautions.

- Every privately owned house should undergo an Electrical Installation Condition Report (EICR) at least every ten years.
- In rented properties, an EICR should be carried out every five years, or at the change of tenancy, whichever comes sooner.
- Electrical appliances should always be used with care, particularly when the appliance generates heat.
- Ventilation slots should never be blocked, as this will allow an appliance to overheat.

- Carelessness often involves smoking materials (legal or otherwise), the consumption of alcohol and drugs, and often cooking. So, avoid cooking if you have consumed alcohol.
- Always make sure your escape route is clear at all times. I know of lots of people who store items on their stairway. Always know where your keys are, so you can get out quickly. Keep doors closed, particularly at night.

Did I mention?

Assume nothing.

Know!

John McAleer is a Director at Red Point Ltd, a fire protection company offering supply and maintenance of fire extinguishing equipment, fire alarms, emergency lighting, fire safety training and Fire Risk Assessments. John has many years of experience in dealing with failings, which lead to problems relating to life safety in fire situations.

0800 849 6432
info@redpointlimited.com
www.redpointlimited.com

Jo Jocelyn Pearce: Take a Break

Life is busy, and people are always rushing around in their own little world. They go about their work and enjoy their time, doing all sorts of things in a busy week. If you can have an Indian Head Massage, it will help you to relax. It helps you to unwind and it takes the stresses of the week away.

Indian Head Massage first came to the UK from India back in the 1600's. Over in India, everyone in the family will daily sit down as a family, and all have a go at each others head in a long line.

For those of you unfamiliar with what this is, I'll briefly take you through the process.

Indian Head Massage can be done sitting in a chair or lying down on a couch, depending on which way you prefer. It's generally performed through clothing, unlike many other forms of massage, so it doesn't need to feel exposing for the recipient.

Starting off at the back with some essential oil, commonly lavender, although other oils can provide a different experience. The back of the neck is massaged in a few different techniques, working on any knotted muscles or aches and pains. Moving slowly up the neck and then on the head. Starting at the scalp in a nice rubbing movement. The hair is then massaged gently, lifting the scalp. Then it is raked and lifted, and tapped like raindrops, with flicking and plucking movements as well.

These very gentle movements help the blood to circulate and improve the condition of the hair. The objective is to take away any tension, pain, and stress.

Moving on to the face, lots of pressure points are gently touched to help give more energy, and to de-stress. The face is left feeling more toned and relaxed.

This massage helps the whole body; arms are also moved in a light stretch and circular movements. It can help you to sleep, will give you more energy, and help with relaxation in general.

Almost anybody can try one, although it's not suitable for people with some medical conditions, and advice from a doctor may be required before some therapists will do one. Even a mini massage can have a positive effect. It can help with shoulder tension from sitting at the computer for many hours.

A full hour will give you a lovely treatment and set you up for the week ahead.

Sometimes, you may feel a little different the next day, a bit groggy, which means that a blockage has been cleared and is normal, a bit like a detox. Just rest, slow down, eat light food, and drink plenty of water or herbal teas.

You don't have to be in pain or stiff to benefit from a massage like this. It brings a great calmness. It takes away aches and pains. If you need a break from the stresses and strains of being in business, an Indian Head Massage is certainly an excellent way to treat yourself.

To Muriel Brand a lovely lady who went too soon suffering from Breast Cancer, died in 1986. Thank you for being there for all your lovely family, who struggled hard without you. Love from them all xxxxx

Jo Pearce is a Reiki master and Psychic Clairvoyant Medium, at AngelsHelpandGuide.co.uk, offering Indian Head Massage, back, neck shoulder massage, Reiki treatments, and Animal Healing. Jo has over ten years of experience in Indian Head Massage, and also teaches Reiki.

01275 474105
jopearce@hotmail.co.uk
www.angelshelpandguide.co.uk

Karen Hensman: Intellectual Property in a Nutshell

The term *Intellectual Property (IP)*, refers to a work or an invention that is the expression of an idea. It usually takes four forms:

- Patents
- Trade marks
- Copyright
- Registered and unregistered design rights.

Any creative work can contain one or all of the four types of IP. They protect different things but can also work together in harmony.

Patents

These protect inventions. For example, if you design a new car windscreen wiper, this would be protectable as a patent.

In the UK patents usually last for 20 years, giving the inventor protection whereby no other parties can use, produce, or sell the invention without their permission. At the end of this period the patent becomes public, and anyone can produce the invention.

Patents can be expensive, but hugely valuable if you have an invention. However, not everything is protectable. A patent can only be granted if the product is new (i.e., not already in existence in the world) and inventive.

Certain things are excluded from patentability and these include software (this is protected as a literary work under copyright), a discovery, a scientific theory, a mathematical method, a method for playing a game, the presentation of information, or a method for doing business. These sound very restrictive, but, in practice, they are not that bad. For example, you may not be able to protect the method of playing a game, but you should be able to protect the apparatus for playing it.

If you want to know whether your invention is patentable, seek the advice of a qualified and regulated Patent Attorney. A word of advice though. If you do have something that you think may be patentable, DO NOT TELL ANYONE! The moment you tell someone, it then becomes information in the public domain, and you have destroyed the novelty of your product, making it un-patentable.

If you wish to talk to a potential business partner, or need help getting the product to market, make sure you give any information under the protection of a Non-Disclosure Agreement (NDA), or Confidentiality Agreement. You can find good, free to use NDAs on the Internet. Just make sure that you are as explicit as possible when explaining what it is that you are revealing and for how long it will be effective.

Trade marks

These protect anything that acts as a badge of trade origin. A trade mark is usually a brand name or logo, although it can be musical (jingles), shapes (three dimensional product packaging), or a company livery (petrol station forecourts).

Trade marks can be unregistered (usually denoted by a ™), or registered (denoted by the ® symbol).

An unregistered trade mark is simply something that the owner feels is his or her trade mark. The indication of ™ places no extra protection on the mark. I often recommend people not to use ™ as it simply highlights that you haven't protected your trade mark properly by registering it. If you do not register your trade mark, you will need to rely on the common law tort of *Passing Off* if a third party copies your mark. In order to do this, you would need to demonstrate, with evidence, that:

- you have a reputation in the mark,
- the other party are misrepresenting themselves as you, and
- they have caused you quantifiable damage.

This can be tough to prove. If you register your trade mark you can rely on trade mark law which is much easier to prove in law.

A registered trade mark lasts for 10 years, but can be renewed indefinitely upon payment of renewal fees. The oldest trade mark in the UK is the *Bass Brewery* triangle, which was registered in 1875. By registering your trade mark, you are granted a monopoly right, which will let you stop anyone using anything identical or similar to your mark for identical or similar goods and services to those which you offer.

When you register a trade mark, you register it in the class(es) of goods or services for which your activity lies. There are 45 classes: 1 - 34 are for goods, and 35 - 45 are for services. A full list of the classes can be found on the *UK Intellectual Property Office* website, *www.ipo.gov.uk*. The price of your trade mark registration will depend on how many classes you wish to protect it in.

Not everything is registerable as a trade mark. If your trade mark describes your products or services, then you will not be granted protection. For example, you cannot register *soap* for toiletries, as people would need to use the word in order to describe your product. However, if you created a visually distinctive logo, which contained the word soap, or something which alluded to soap, you would be granted protection, but it would only really protect the stylised look of the logo.

You also cannot register anything that is against public morality, anything that may be a geographical indication of where the product was made, the *Olympic* symbol, or anything that bears a Royal crown or an Armorial crest.

Here are a few examples of what would, and would not, be registerable:

- **Yes:** *Suds* for toiletries, *Speedy Builder* for building services, or *Hardcastle's Yorkshire Bitter* for alcoholic beverages.
- **No:** *Soap* for toiletries, *Bristol Used Cars* for car sales, or *Arctic Leather* for clothing.

Copyright

This protects anything that is creative. For example, music, literary work (books or blogs), drawings, paintings, photographs, sculpture etc. Copyright is automatic; as soon as you create a creative work it is automatically there. There is no facility to register copyright officially. There are companies offering registration, but they are simply allowing you to lodge a copy with them and this acts as a record of when you created the work. This can be useful, because almost all copyright cases are won or lost based on who can prove they created the work, and when they created it.

A good alternative to paying an external company is to send yourself a copy of the work in the post. Don't open it, as it will be independently dated by the post mark, and, if you need to rely on it at a later date, you can open the envelope in front of a notary or other legal body who can testify as to the contents of the envelope. This is often much cheaper than paying a company to 'register' the work for you, and carries as much legal weight.

Copyright duration varies depending on the type of work and how it has been used.

- Literary, artistic, or musical work: 70 years + the life of the author / composer / artist.
- Typographical arrangement: 25 years from the end of the calendar year the work was created.
- TV Broadcast: 50 years from the end of the year the work was created and first broadcast.

Registered and unregistered design rights

Design rights protect anything that has a visual appeal. This can be purely aesthetic (think of shoes and handbag designs), or more industrial (think of the shape of an *Aston Martin* car). Many things to which design right would apply are also covered by copyright. Unregistered designs are protected automatically, in the same way that copyright is. They last either 10 years after the first marketing of articles that use the design, or 15 years after creation of the design, whichever is earlier. For the last 5 years of that period, the design is subject to a licence of right. This means that anyone is entitled to a licence to make and sell products copying the design. Registered designs in the UK last for 5 years, but they can be renewed for up to 25 years upon payment of renewal fees.

Registration of IP

All IP is territorial. If you protect your work here in the UK, and wish to expand your business to the US, for example, you will also need to protect it there. In the UK, in order to be registerable, a design must be new, and have individual character. Not everything is registerable. Anything for which the design is dictated solely by the products function would not be protectable.

Monetising your IP

If you have IP that you cannot market yourself, consider licensing it to a third party. For example, if you have an invention, but do not have the facility to produce the product yourself, you can grant a licence to a third party. You might take a percentage of the profit they make from your product, or sell them a royalty free licence for a set sum of money.

Another way would be to use your brand to endorse other people's products or services. For example, many sportswear companies, such as *Nike*, use the image rights and trade marks of professional sports people to endorse their products. *Nike* pay for this privilege. Is there a company that would pay to be associated with your product or service?

Thirdly, you can franchise your business brand. If you have a localised brand that is well recognised in your area, think about franchising your business and making fees this way.

Finally, if you are not using your IP, you could just sell it. IP is just like any other property, as it can be sold like any other physical asset.

This is merely an outline of the principles of IP. For guidance specific to your requirements, always seek professional advice.

Karen Hensman is the Owner and Trade Mark Attorney at Innovate IP Ltd, offering registration, enforcement and advice regarding all aspects of intellectual property including patents, trade marks, copyright and designs. Karen has over 10 years' experience working in IP both as an in-house attorney and in private practice.

01454 203694
info@innovateip.co.uk
www.innovateip.co.uk

Kirstine Hughes: Where Do I Start?

2009 was going to be a great year! My husband and I were in our tenth wedding anniversary year, we had plans, but as we all know plans do not always go the way we want. In April I trapped a nerve in my neck; I was in bed for three weeks and could not move. So, me and my laptop become very close. It was during this time I received a call from my father. The cancer he had in his bowel has moved to his liver. It had been operated on and they had, at the time, thought they had got it all. Well this call was to say it was back in his liver. I knew an operation was not viable this time as they had taken so much from him at the last operation.

The reason I am telling you this, as this is the start of *Angel* at work. Husband and I really wanted to renew our vows, on our tenth wedding anniversary so while all this is going on and with my Dad, I became a planner for our blessing which was booked for the 24th October 2009.

We lost Dad in June of 2009, due to an infection in a stent that was fitted to the vein from his liver. Looking back, that was the day I became a grown up. So what was this grown up going to do? In the last four years I have grown, as a person, and finally into an adult.

First I started *Angel Bridal*, a wedding planning advice company and I have helped with around twelve weddings since, all of which were different but great. All had issues on the day, but the bride was completely unaware of any problems. I love doing this helping out, it's in my nature to help people.

I have since fallen from one job to another. I have to be a little careful with my work as my husband has Multiple Sclerosis and needs help sometimes, so I need to make sure I am at home to help when needed. We also have two children, aged 14 and 8, so home life can be pretty hectic.

I needed to do something for myself, and in 2010 my hubby brought me a lovely food mixer. It looks stunning in my kitchen and he said the words that started everything, "As I got you this, you need to bake me a cake!" Sounds so easy, but I was decidedly *not* a cook. I was so worried about it but I found how to do it in a cook book. It was not pretty, but I was told it tasted good (well, Husband survived!). From there it sort of just took off.

Last year I started to sell cakes, as friends told me they would buy them if I did. So I went about it the right way. I went on a few courses for icing and Health and Hygiene, then registered my kitchen with the council; I achieved 5 stars out of 5 when they rated it. I'm constantly learning new things about my new business at evening classes. I was very impressed with myself, very proud indeed, as I am sure my father would have been too.

I love baking, and although I don't eat any of it, I really love seeing how people react to my work and how it tastes. I like trying new things, so I often leave my husband to watch sport and I go off and make some tasty new things for him to try. *YouTube* has been amazing, and I have made some really good friends in the online cakey world. While there are lots of very nice and wonderful people, others leave a lot to be desired. Fortunately the nice people seem to be in the majority.

I have baked all sorts of things. Cupcakes, in all sorts of designs - love hearts, roses, baby shower /new baby cakes; I am told not only do they look good, they taste good too. I have done a few tiered cakes and am hoping this year to do at least one wedding cake. This will of course give me sleepless nights but I am sure will be worth it in the end. The ones that are great are the oversized cupcakes. They look amazing and you can decorate them as you want in whatever colours you like - the impact is great.

Why the name? Well I have Angels looking after me so it's because of my Mum and Dad that I have been able to do this, with the confidence to put myself out there.

Over the next year I would like to grow as a person and a business, I need to have more confidence in myself, and my work, and this is coming over time. My self-belief is increasing as I get honest feedback about what I do. If you're just starting out in business you can often feel self-doubt, but if you want to continue you'll need to be resilient.

It's hard sometimes not being able to get the things you feel you need, you may not need them at all. The early days of any business will require sacrifices to be made. You need to accept that you're going to have tough choices ahead, but have the courage to face them anyway. Being in business for yourself isn't easy. But then the alternative, being employed, isn't easy either.

For me, life is much easier working from home. I can work flexible hours around the needs of my family. It is brilliant to be at home... being a mum, a wife, and a business owner, and I love it.

To my father who passed away in 2009 due to cancer...the guiding light in my life. I miss him every day. You are still my inspiration. Also to Steve Hughes (a.k.a. Mr Angel Bakes) my best friend, my husband, and my rock.

Kirstine Hughes is the Owner of Angel Bakes, supplying all sorts of cakes from cupcakes to wedding cakes and everything in between. She's been trading since 2011.

07920 263554
angelbakes2012@gmail.com
Facebook: www.facebook.com/angelbakes2012

Lee Rickler: How to Get Your Startup Up

December is that time of the year when you're so frikking bored of eating turkey and playing snakes and ladders for the millionth time that all you want to do is get back to the office.

But wait, hold on a minute, remember – when you're sitting at your desk working on that report your boss needs delivered before 5pm, normally you can't wait for the clock to fast forward to 5.05pm. Then you can start getting ready to go underground on that hour long journey with a sweaty armpit stuck in your face. Just to veg out on the sofa shouting at the z-listers on britain's-got-celeb-dancing-in-the-jungle-factor.

Oh, how you wish you were the boss, running your own company, working the exact 18 hours each day that you choose, on the projects that you want for way less than minimum wage.

Well, guess what, you can, starting right now, with these seven tips to getting your startup off the ground.

The difference between a hobby and a profession is getting paid. Half the battle is having a passion for what you're doing, so choose something that you actually enjoy. You can't sell something without fire in your eyes. There will be no trust, no belief and people will see right through the fakeness and they will go somewhere else.

For the first few weeks/months you'll have no/low income so you better love your new excuse for getting up in the morning or you'll be back researching "how the fiscal cliff will affect European inner city 'i-generation'" with your tail between your legs before you can say "I really can't be arsed going to the gym tonight".

Bootstrap the mother

Seriously, trust me on this one – sniffing around for investors, drawing up 45 page business plans, or sitting in your local bank waiting for your 'business manager' (whose entire experience of running a business consisted of a paper round when he was 12 and helping out at weekends in his Dad's shop to pull himself away from updating his LinkedIn profile just to tell you that your loan application has been refused) really is a total waste of your time.

All you really need to start up a business is a phone, a laptop and a website. Use *Skype* for the company landline or when you're really busy, use a telephone answering service to take your important calls. Get a shared hosting account, and install *WordPress* in 1 click to get yourself online. And look at co-working spaces like *Google Campus* and definitely get into using *Google Apps*.

You're not the CEO, you're just someone with a laptop and a WordPress theme

A really simple way to win over people, and therefore clients, is to just be yourself. Would *you* want to work with someone with delusions of grandeur – "I'm the Chief Social Media Guru and International Head of Making Stuff Up" – or would you prefer someone that doesn't just need a hug? So concentrate on making your products the star, yourself the twinkle and give people benefits not bull.

Any cowboy can set up a company but it takes balls to run a business

You're good at drawing / coding / sales / electronics...? Great, that's the key product right there BUT you are a Corporation of One and need to learn new skills – and fast – accounts, HR, online legalities, negotiating, networking, sales – the list goes on … and on … and on.

If at first you don't succeed, outsource. Don't restrict yourself to everyone having to drag their arse across the city just to clock in at 9am everyday. Look at building a distributed firm where your co-workers are able to work from the location of their choosing, at a time to suit them. You'll save yourself a fortune in holiday pay, empty desks and stationery.

Build up a network of reliable people who you can outsource to, especially all the stuff that you are useless at.

Let's say that you're charging yourself out at £50 an hour and it takes you 8 hours a month to sort out your accounts. Surely it'll be cheaper, and less stressful, to pay an accountant to do it, which will leave you to concentrate on doing what you're best at.

Leave him, he's not worth it

Come here a second, I need to let you into a little secret. No… closer, closer… right… your idea… the one you've been slaving over for the last 20 minutes – it's been done. It's not original, you're not the first. No, seriously, the location-based, socially-aware shopping experience app that you think is the most radical thing since threatening to leave *Instagram... done.*

In business as in life, you're not unique. In business as in life, there are those that do stuff before and even better than you – there are plenty more that are way, way worse, but the ones you need to have in the back of your mind are those doing their stuff bigger and better than you. So, what do you do, get all baby-crying jealous of them? No way, you build a better product, you develop a more disruptive method, you puff up your chest and grow bigger balls. This is business, not the playground.

Focus, adapt, rinse and repeat

The day you start your business, write a note to yourself. Write, in 140 characters or less, your main pitch for your new business – what is the main product and/or service that you're unleashing onto the world? Put that note in an envelope and on the front write the date as it will be in 3 months' time.

To survive as a business you need to be able to adapt. Look at the recently defunct *Comet* – they failed because their system was stuck in the dark ages of retail shopping. The beauty of your Corporation of One is that you can be nimble, Jack. You can change quickly to embrace a new found technology or skill, you can accommodate your clients' wishes quicker, and you should be able to dig yourself out of a hole easier.

But take care to always focus on the core products and services that you are getting known for. You'll find yourself being driven into a niche area but should always look to be offering more.

After 3 months, open that envelope you stashed away and see how much your core ideas have changed. Have you grown, what have you learned and is the passion and focus still there?

Choose life

There are 24 hours in a day. You can only give a maximum of 100%. You are only human.

No matter how many times you say "Yes", your clients will always want more.

No matter how many new projects you take on, there will always be more.

No matter how many all-nighters you rack up hunched over your machine, stuffing your face with pizza and beer, you need to stop, and stop that right now. That is not what you signed up for. That is not what you dreamed of. That is no way to run a business, family or life.

Your family, your friends, your clients will all be more thankful if you put yourself first, them second and your work third. Never be afraid to delegate, out-source or even just say "No".

Enjoy!

Lee Rickler is the Director for Point and Stare who primarily work with companies using WordPress as a CMS. Lee has over 15 years online experience, with around 10 years spent running his own company.

0207 1936 109
info@pointandstare.com
Twitter: @PointandStare

Lesley Allart: Exhibitions

So, you've made the decision that exhibiting at an exhibition, trade show, or fair is important for your business and is worth a chunk of your marketing budget. The first question is determining which event to attend, and what questions to ask to make sure you're getting value for money.

We are all bombarded with event offers with hugely varying price tags, and all claiming to be able to do wonders for our business. It's not unusual for the phone to ring with a 'too good to miss' last minute opportunity to take one of the 'few remaining stands'. How do you sift the wheat from the chaff, the events which will give you a return on investment from the ones which are a waste of time, poorly organised, poorly attended, or which don't attract your target audience?

Why exhibit?

As with any marketing decision, be sure why you are considering attendance at a show in the first place. What do you want to get out of it? Perhaps it is:

- For brand awareness
- To be seen in the right places
- To establish yourself as a market leader by taking advantage of speaking opportunities
- To generate leads
- To sell products or services on the day.

All of these are valid reasons, and I'm sure you can come up with more; however, until you are clear on your reasons for attending, you can't decide which event is right for you.

Questions to ask

In your interactions with the people selling space, particularly for the bigger exhibitions, remember that these guys are trained to close you and they are only really interested in the bottom line. It's your responsibility to make sure you ask the right questions! So, what should you ask?

- Ignore estimated attendance figures; ask for actual figures from the previous event. That's attendance figures, not the number registered, as these often vary significantly. If the previous attendance figures vary wildly from the expected attendance for this one, alarm bells should ring; if they match, happy days.
- Check how many have pre-registered for this event, and how this compares with the previous event.

- Take a look at the event advertising materials and critically evaluate whether you would invest the time and costs to go.
- Is it being well advertised and promoted?
- Is there added value in attendance for delegates, for example, seminars, workshops, networking opportunities, etc?
- Who attended the last event? You may not get names, but you should get a sample of job titles and market sectors. Are these the people you want to target? If not, the event is unlikely to be for you.
- How many exhibitors have rebooked? Ask if you can call any for a reference. If the answer is 'no', us a search engine and hunt down their information, then pick up the phone.

What's included?

Armed with this information, let's assume you've decided this event *is* for you, and you've decided to go ahead and book space. You'll need to understand what is included in the price.

Space only means just that: simply the space on the floor, so you'll be completely responsible for providing everything to go on it.

A better option for many small businesses on a limited budget is a 'shell scheme'; this often includes closed sides to the stand, carpeting, a name banner, and perhaps some lighting. Sometimes a table and chairs are included, other times not, so check.

If you need to hire stand furniture it can be a very expensive exercise, especially as larger shows often insist on use of the approved supplier and you aren't allowed to bring your own.

Is electricity is included in the stand cost? Sometimes this can be a hefty extra and most people will want to run a screen or laptop at least.

Think about where it is best to be located on the exhibition floor. Avoid dead ends or around the edges, as traffic in both places is often slow. Instead, choose a centrally located spot. If the show has seminar or networking areas, close by is good, as traffic will be higher. However, organisers are usually clued up, and these areas tend to be laid out for larger, more expensive stands.

Go with a shallow, wide stand. It's your shop window so width counts, not depth (which can be expensive and difficult to fill properly). Also, try to negotiate a stand with more than one open side—stands on corners with two corridors provide two opportunities to engage with visitors.

Before you agree to buy, haggle on the deal you're getting. Ask for a shell scheme for the 'space only' price, or a larger stand for the price of a smaller one. If there are speaking opportunities at seminars, see if you can get one included in the price, or an additional sponsorship of a break-out area. Don't take anything at face value because there is always room for negotiation, and if you don't ask, you don't get.

Preparing for the event

You've chosen your stand location, know what you're getting, and have got a good deal...the hard work has just begun! Most people launch in to an exhibition thinking about how they are going to make the stand look, and then forget about the event until two days prior before they start planning. This will not lead to maximising the budget you've spent! Once you've decided to attend and have booked your stand, the planning starts immediately.

First thing for the plan is your follow up strategy!

Surely you worry about that after the event? Not if you want to maximise your investment and make sure that you act on leads generated before they go cold. Remember, attending this exhibition isn't an ego exercise, it needs to generate a return, whatever your reason for attending. So, working out what leads you want to capture and how you are going to follow these leads up should be the first thing you plan, not the last. This is relevant, even if you are selling something directly from the stand. How are people going to find you for repeat sales or all the other services or products you offer?

One of the things I have done with great effect is to have a follow up email saved as a draft on a mobile device. A simple thank you, with links to your website, products, case studies, information sheets, etc., and a call to action will suffice in most cases. During a quiet moment on the day, I'll move aside, go through the business cards or email addresses collected, and send a personally 'topped and tailed' email out to those who have visited. With so many people now carrying smartphones that receive mobile email, the power of receiving a "Thank you" before even leaving the show is highly effective.

Attending a show or exhibition is a huge investment of time, funds, and energy, and if the follow up isn't done correctly then you are flushing those resources down the drain.

How you are going to advertise your presence and maximise your opportunities for engagement? This might involve looking for PR opportunities, if only by writing news articles and blogs for your website and lodging these with free on line PR hubs, such as *http://onlineprnews.com*. Ask the organisers what PR they are organising and try to get a mention – but don't pay for it!

Promote your presence through your own social media channels. Avoid blatant 'buy my stuff' campaigns, and instead talk about your preparations, your excitement at attending, etc. Be conversational and engaging. This makes great material for a blog series.

Use social media to connect to others attending the event. If there is a *Twitter* 'hashtag' for the event, use it in your own tweets and check out who else is using it—then connect with them! Check LinkedIn and see if there is a group for the event, or if it is being talked about in other relevant groups. Use social media to break the ice and start the engagement early. Keep monitoring these channels during the event and continue to make connections with visitors on the day.

Check out the other exhibitors at the event, and prioritise the ones you want to meet. Use social media to connect with them and start networking early, or email or pick up the phone to set up a time to buy them a coffee and have a chat. Be open to overtures from other exhibitors too—there may be synergy in the most unexpected places...

Don't forget to invite key people who may be interested in the event to attend. You have a number of free passes, or you can get them priority booking at seminar sessions. Promote to your existing and former customers and your prospect list that you are going to be at this exhibition, and that you'd love to see them there.

On the day

Think about your strategy for the day itself: What is your method of engaging with customers and contacts? How will you attract people to the stand and communicate your message? A lot of this is very specific to your business and business sector, but a draw to your stand is essential.

How are you going to handle capturing contact details and feedback? For business-to-business events, most people will have a business card. Collect these and annotate the card with a few key words to remind yourself of the conversation.

If you wish to collect details from people who don't want to engage in a conversation, think about a giveaway in return for business cards. Sticking your business card in a box to win a bottle of champagne is always a good one, but the giveaway could also be one of your products or services.

Don't think you need to have lots of printed material for people to take away. A good follow up email with pdf. files attached and web links is more effective, and cheaper!

When laying out the stand, consider the angles from which people will approach and make it as eye catching and engaging as possible. Don't push everything to the front and block people from stepping in. Sometimes it's better to move most of the information to the back of the stand to draw them in. Whatever you do, don't be tempted to set up a desk and stand or sit behind it. You are placing a barrier between you and your visitors and this makes you appear unapproachable.

If you have more than one person working the stand, agree beforehand how you're going to share the workload, and set behaviour expectations. Agree what is to be worn. You might consider branded clothing, but at least similar smart business attire. Don't eat or drink on the stand, as it looks unprofessional. Do remain engaged and outward facing, even if the stand is quiet. Sitting down, chatting, and staring at a mobile phone doesn't invite engagement.

Post-event

Allocate time immediately on return from the show to follow up, know who will follow up which leads and how, and make sure this happens. Keep track and, if someone other than you is doing the follow-up, get regular reports on progress.

If you know you'll be struggling for time to do this, make sure you engage additional resources to help; a freelance virtual assistant or telesales person could be worth their weight in gold. Be honest with yourself and book their time for the week after the event well in advance. Leaving the follow up for a month, promising yourself you'll find time and then not doing so, and then trying to bring in a freelancer will dramatically reduce your chance of getting results.

The devil's in the detail

A previous boss of mine was a former Army Major, and he used to work to the 'six P's': 'Prior Planning Prevents P*ss Poor Performance.' This maxim is so important in maximising your substantial financial and time investment in attending this type of marketing event. The rewards can be considerable for a well-organised event, and a complete waste otherwise. The outcome is up to you.

For my Dad, who lost his short battle with Leukaemia in 1997 aged 65, but whose love and character continues to inspire.

Lesley Allart is the Owner and Marketing Angel at The Marketing Angel, offering down to earth and cost effective marketing, social media, sales and business consultancy for small business. Lesley has a wide range of experience gained through her time working for and now running a small business, as well as excellent communication skills honed by several years of Secondary Teaching, and the analytical brain of a Scientist. All these combine to bring a unique and skilful take on Marketing and Business Challenges.

07896 654596
lesley@themarketingangel.com
www.themarketingangel.com

Liam Hamilton: Top Tips for Online Setup

There are a number of things concerning website hosting which you really should consider. This is likely to put you one step ahead of your competition, and at the very least make sure you don't lose visitors. Best of all, some of these tips are very easy to apply.

Domain names

Domain names are important, and most of what we do online has something to do with a domain name. They are much easier to remember than IP addresses (the generally unmemorable set of numbers that are behind every site), which is why we use them. They are also a very easy place for businesses to make mistakes.

Common spelling mistakes

When most businesses purchase domain names they often think about buying a domain name that matches their business name. That's great, but what if you have a commonly misspelt word in the name? You should look at buying the misspelling too, and simply redirect it to your main domain. It might cost you £10 per year, it but that's worth it.

Numbers confuse

My company (*1 Click Website*) had an issue with the number *1* in our domain. If you see it on a piece of paper, fine, you know to use the digit in the domain. But if you hear it instead most people will write the word *one* down when it comes to typing in the domain name. To resolve this, we purchased oneclickwebsite.co.uk as well, which redirects to our main site.

Alternative extensions

As surprising as it might seem, even if people see yourdomain.co.uk they might still put yourdomain.com (or vice-versa). Yes, it certainly is worth buying both. People often expect to see a *.co.uk* for UK websites; however, the *.com* domain frequently has the greatest level of brand awareness (if a domain *extension* could ever have a brand!).

Redirect email too

I know most of us cringe at seeing a full e-mail inbox, however, we want to get business leads to come through. If you have purchased additional domains to re-direct website traffic, do the same for your e-mails. Someone thinking they have your email address correct and receiving an "email does not exist" reply from a server is going to make you look bad, assuming, of course, they don't notice their mistake. Simpler to anticipate their error and prevent it.

Use your domain for email

Businesses should be using their domain name for all sent and received e-mail. Using free services, designed for consumers; e.g., *Gmail, Hotmail, Yahoo, BTInternet*, etc., doesn't look professional when you're representing a business. The format of email addresses also comes in here. You should use one of the following formats for business e-mail addresses:

Initial.LastName@companydomain.com. e.g.: J.Bloggs@companydomain.com

FirstName.LastName@companydomain.com. e.g.: John.Bloggs@companydomain.com

Remember, it is easy to change an email address. You can just forward an old one to a new one and archive all the previously sent email.

When it comes to advertising your email address, mistakes are often made, the biggest one being the way email addresses are often displayed publicly on websites. It doesn't look good and encourages spamming. Yes, we all want to be contacted, so use an enquiry form (it also gives you a good chance to catch a phone number too).

Next, of course, are the people who think they can place a so-called 'anti-spam' email on their website. They look something like this:

name[dot]name[at]domain[dot]com

This format can still be harvested for spam with bracketed words being switched to symbols, and it looks even worse than just putting an email address on a website.

The law does, however, require that you put an email address somewhere on your website. You are best off placing it in a downloadable pdf file with any other contact details that you are legally required to provide.

Hosting

Website hosting is what all businesses require in order to make sure they actually exist online. This service takes your website and makes it available whenever someone wants to view it. It is a very cutthroat industry, which has many ways to cut corners, costs, and service levels, without making clients aware. So, here are some warning signs to look out for.

'Unlimited' hosting packages

A number of hosting companies claim that they provide unlimited web space and bandwidth. Don't believe them. You *will* be limited, either by the capacity of the server, or their terms of service. It also proves that they oversell their servers. It's not possible to sell finite physical server space an infinite number of times.

Overselling

Just like hotels and airline operators, most website hosting companies oversell. It is one of the many things that you get when you buy cheap. However, they get away with it, as everyone who they have oversold a particular server to can still go on it, as long as they don't all try to use their full space quota at the same time.

A few hosting companies do not oversell and advertise as much. The advantage of a hosting provider that doesn't oversell is a faster service. It is often noticeable when you compare providers directly. Even with some of the larger companies, however, it can go undetected until you make such a comparison.

Annual contracts

A number of website hosting companies force you into annual contracts with higher fees after the first few months. Again, it isn't the only industry that does this sort of thing, but a few companies do get away with it. Others will offer you flexible terms, giving you the choice of monthly, quarterly, semi-annually, or annual contracts. By allowing you to choose, they are putting the power back in your hands. Normally, I recommend shorter payment terms, as this allows you to move if you are unhappy.

Website builders

Some website hosting providers offer some sort of system to build your website with. This is, in theory, a great idea, as it provides the chance to build your own website quickly, and normally for free. Actually it is a bad idea. Using a website builder means the website can't be moved easily, if at all. Therefore, should the support be terrible with that provider, and you wish to move, you're stuck. If you are thinking of considering this, you are far better off using a company that will build you a website for around £500-600, or by installing WordPress, using an installation script that the hosting company will often provide for free.

There are ways of ensuring you get the best from your website. You just need to understand the pitfalls *before* you commit to spending a lot of money on something that is likely to be as important as this for your business.

Liam Hamilton is Commercial Director at 1 Click Services Limited, offering website hosting and development services primarily to businesses. Liam has experience inside the website hosting industry and experience on laying out websites for end users. He's author of several web- and technology-related books including The Consumer Tech Annual *series.*

Twitter: @ukwebsitehost
l.hamilton@1clickwebsite.com
www.1clickwebsite.com

Leanne Hugglestone: It Couldn't Happen to Me

To you this is just a story in a book, but I live with this every day of my life. You'll put this book aside and carry on with your life. Today, and tomorrow, I will face the reality of yet another day with all the challenges breast cancer brings.

That's the thing, even when it happens to loved ones, and we feel the pain for them, it's still happening to someone else. Sufferers and survivors alike must all have felt that "It couldn't happen to me". And then it did. And it comes as a shock.

When the reality of having cancer sets in, it changes your entire life, and your outlook. Things come in to focus, and other things become less important. As a thirty-something single woman I never imagined I'd have to face up to my own mortality. I was a party girl. I didn't see myself as being a victim.

I still am a party girl, and I'm certainly not a victim.

Many things have changed with having cancer, for one I am now blogging regularly and trying to help other people in a similar situation to cope, just as so many others have helped me. I could genuinely fill the space allowed in this book with grateful thanks to so many people who continue to be there for me. It feels like mentioning some, but not others, is disrespectful, but that's not intentional. I was asked how cancer affected my work and social life, so that's where I'm going to focus on.

You see, this disease has pulled together the family behind me in a way I couldn't have imagined possible. But, just as importantly I've remained a part of work life too, thanks to colleagues who have continued to send me texts and emails, phone calls, and regular personal contact. I still know what's going on at work, and when I return I shouldn't need long to get fully back up to speed, I already know most of the latest gossip! And that's really important to me because my *career* is important to me, and it's good to know that I'll fit right in when I get back to work.

I'm going to unashamedly name-check people at work, because they are a part of my story – they are one of my pillars of strength.

So, here goes with thanks to Luisa for the gifts for hospital, the notebook I use to write my lists and the trips out. To sisters Lisa and Beth for keeping me updated on the goss and visiting me as much as they can! Jon, for being a fab buddy, to Chris for always texting me and keeping me updated about work (as well as sending me lovely gifts).

To the whole of my department and the S&S committee for my (now very well used!) *Kindle*. To the whole of Companies House in Cardiff, who have supported me when I've fundraised. To those of you who all ask after me to my Mum (who also works there), and to the directors for giving me the opportunity to raise awareness and get my message across to the workforce. A shout-out to Griff for the comms, and a special thank you to Diane Reed for all the lovely gifts.

You Are All Brilliant!

Doesn't that restore your faith in human nature just a bit? It would have been so easy for me to have drifted out of people's consciousness. "Who's that girl that used to work here? Isn't she on the sick or something?"

No chance of that! And it matters. A lot.

Thanks to *Twitter* I have also been lucky enough to be involved with *The Big C: Choir of Hope* through *Tenovus* (the cancer charity) - and through Sarah Jayne spotting my tweets about my blog and my fundraising. *Tenovus* has been a crucial part of that - thank you Rosie! As have the production team, Gabe, Kristian and Will, for being so sensitive and understanding through filming such a tough ordeal. To Ian at *Exclusive*, for ensuring we are all looked after, and to Cat the choir master for her never ending enthusiasm and contagious excitement!

I also want to thank all the other members of the choir, each with their own cancer story. Whether they are terminal or not, male or female, old or young - their stories are inspirational, and together we discuss treatments, how to cope with side effects, get to know each other and our families, and encourage each other through the 12 weeks of filming.

We all belong to a club we never wanted to join - we are all Cancer Buddies. But through cancer we have found each other, and been given such wonderful opportunities, doubtless with many more to come!

You see, without every single one of you I wouldn't be where I am today. From your support, advice, texts, tweets, status updates, visits, help and general keeping in touch - I would not be this good at this point. You all have made a huge difference in your own way and I want to thank you for being such amazing individuals.

Thank You.

You may think it's very self-indulgent to be saying so many thank-you's, but it's important. I count myself as hugely fortunate that, in addition to my family, and friends, these two areas of my life have opened up.

My ability to work has been devastated by having cancer, but the people are still there. My ability to engage in a social life was curtailed, but the choir has come into my life. Without these lifelines to a normal life I might have gone under. And I realise that many people might not be as lucky as I have been; they might be facing this - cancer, treatment, the thought of dying - all without family, or friends, or colleagues, or a social network.

If I could do just one thing, it would be to ask you to remember people when they are ill. Drop them a line, there are enough ways of doing it these days. Pop round for a cuppa, if only for ten minutes. Don't let them hide away from the world, scared and alone. Don't just remember them in your head, but show them that you care.

Because it matters.

A lot.

To my parents, sister & twin brothers. You have been strong for me, when being a bystander is often harder than going through treatment. Love you all. X

Leanne Hugglestone is currently undergoing treatment for breast cancer. She's a determined thirty-something who wants to reach other young women in the same situation. She blogs regularly, between treatments, and is passionate about offering whatever support, advice, information and tips she can.

Twitter: @Huggzy
http://huggzyvsbreastcancer.wordpress.com

Lucy Scott: Getting Organised

At this point some of you will be thinking "Why should I get organised, I'm perfectly fine as I am?" That may be so. There is every possibility that you are bumbling along with your own very unique system thinking you know precisely which pile that quote request was put in, or exactly which folder that presentation is in that you did last year, right up until you actually want to find it... then it takes you ten minutes! Or maybe only two minutes on a good day.

But consider if twice a day you need to find a document or an item and it takes you two minutes to locate, (which from my experience is conservative). Just two minutes a day will equate to approximately *two days* a year looking for missing files. I would bet that many people spend much longer than that.

The benefits of being organised

Obviously a major benefit to being organised is saving time. Be honest, how much time do you spend a day looking for things that you 'know exactly where you put' last time it was read, saved or used? How much is that actually costing you? Most of us will know someone who has missed their tax return deadline. "That's £100 please", says Mr HMRC. Rarely is it because there is some incredibly technical difficulty, such as no postal service since May or no internet access anywhere since October, that prevents you filing the return. It is just being disorganised.

Another benefit to being organised is that it improves focus thus making you more productive. The effect clutter has on people's well-being and psychological health is well documented. The physical environment impacts on self-esteem and a person's ability to think clearly. It stands to reason that a person surrounded by future projects, past projects, and all of the things needing an immediate response, are going to be easily distracted, probably many times in a day.

With a clear deck and improved focus you are far more likely to achieve what you want. There is a reason for the saying "Can't see the wood for the trees". Additional time you've created and orderly surroundings equal fewer distractions and more productivity, as you can work in a more methodical way.

I can already hear all the creative amongst you screaming "but that's not going to work for me". I'm not talking about removing all stimulus or inspiration. I'm referring to distractions. If you are working on a particular project you may well need pictures, words or books around that inspire you, but you are unlikely to require your accounts paperwork, latest insurance quote or child's school report on your workspace too. These are just distractions!

Consider too the image you are portraying to potential clients who may see your work area. Are you promoting yourself as an expert in your field with your finger on the pulse of business or a slightly chaotic eccentric who will find that file any minute?

I had the misfortune to employ a solicitor many years ago and on entering her office I found her desk piled with files, as was every corner and edge of the floor. She scrambled around looking for a blank piece of paper to write her notes on my case, having to move several confidential case files to do so. Needless to say, as an organised person I was not inspired by her professionalism. I had no confidence in her keeping my notes safely, that she would actually ever find my case ever again or be organised enough to get things done in an orderly manner. I decided on *not* pursuing her services so not only did this lose her the custom, I have never felt able to refer her and she never billed me for the advice provided. Quite a costly result of not being organised and I was just one client.

In summary, by not being organised you risk losing time, focus, creativity and money.

Knowing, and doing

Knowing the need to be organised and the varied benefits of being so are one thing, but actually getting it done is another. The major objections that I hear are that 'I don't have time' or 'I can never find anything when I have a tidy up.' My response to these are, short-term pain for long-term gain: label, label, label and get systems and processes that work for you; think them through before you start and stick with them. Be consistent. In case you didn't notice that last phrase I'll repeat *BE CONSISTENT!*

So where do you start? First of all think about how your business actually works. Every business is different but whether you are a person painting teapots at home or you're selling security to multi-million pound organisations you know what you use on a daily, weekly and monthly basis and more importantly what you don't use.

Firstly, ensure you have a dedicated space from which to work. Many new businesses start from 'the kitchen table' which can be very effective to start with, but you need to dedicate that area just to your business. Obviously the table probably needs to be used at other times of day but maybe there is somewhere else you can use instead. A corner of a dining room, a spare bedroom, a summerhouse or shed. I've seen a very effective office set up under the stairs alcove with everything in one place. I've seen a very ineffective 'office' set up on the kitchen work surfaces with nowhere to put anything.

Maybe you are lucky enough to have a dedicated office and if that is the case don't let it become a dumping ground or a place where others use the space or just 'hang out'. Avoid using your bedroom if at all possible because mentally you need that separation from work and relaxation, no matter how much you love your business. Keep work for work, relaxation for relaxation, it'll make life easier as your business grows.

What can you do today?

Starting from a physical aspect, getting organised is a fairly simple concept, *work from the inside out* and *be consistent.*

- Anything you use on a daily basis keep close to hand, on your desk or in a drawer, somewhere you can just reach for.
- Anything that is used weekly keep within 'grabbing' distance, somewhere you can wheel your chair to or just need to get up and reach.
- Items used on a monthly basis can be put further away, maybe a higher shelf.
- Things that are used annually further away again, hence working from the inside out.
- If you have something on your desk that you haven't used for a week, it doesn't need to be there.
- If you have finished with paperwork but need to keep it, such as accounts, archive it well away, maybe a different room, an attic, garage, store room or off-site storage.
- Get creative with your space as there is no need to keep all your office paperwork within your work area if it is technically finished with.
- Ensure that you set up systems that are expandable, simple, easy to understand and consistent.
- Think about each area that creates paperwork or even electronic documents and how these can be systematically kept.
- It doesn't matter whether you want to keep things in date order, alphabetical order or by project, as long as you stick with the method you choose.
- At some point you will want to archive documents, so think through what is most suitable for your business.
- Remember the simplest systems are often the best and much as we like to think we are indispensable it is always better if the system can be interpreted by other employees, even if that is only an aspiration at this stage.

Labeling

Ensure you label accurately and relevantly, and be consistent! Labeling is as important for electronic information as it is for physical documents, if not more so. What makes sense to you as a working title now may make no sense to you or anyone else when you are trying to retrieve it in two years' time. Use folders and subfolders and if possible use the same method as you use for physical documents, i.e. if you decide to keep information by project then save electronic documents by project. Did I mention being consistent?

Now is the time to implement the 5D's. Part of your new organised environment will of course include a bin close at hand as, believe it or not, that is not what the carpet is there for! So the simple way to cope with everything that comes over your threshold is:

Discard it

Bin (paper recycle hopefully) or shred it. Make a quick decision, does it benefit you?

Deal with it

If it's quick and effective to deal with immediately then do so. At least determine the action that is required.

Diarise it

If something requires action give it a time slot to do it. Use a bring forward file, electronically flag it to follow-up but do not use this as a way of avoiding the other 4D's, don't just use it to postpone or procrastinate.

Direct it

Is this something that someone else should be dealing with, is it more relevant for a colleague to deal with or of more interest to a peer?

Deposit it

File it away in its relevant location – remember, be consistent!!

Now you have an efficiently laid out office with everything labeled and things to hand that are required. There are no piles of paperwork sliding off the end of your desk when you accidently elbow it whilst looking for something else. You know exactly where to find that quote that now needs revising. You have labeled everything and *you are being consistent.* Well Done!

To my mum, who has fought cancer once and beat it, and is kicking its butt again.

Lucy Scott is Owner of Admin And Errands, a Personal Assistant service for people with busy home and work life. From spreadsheets to filing, de-cluttering to research, she does the important items on your to do list, making it a done list.

07970 984601
www.adminanderrands.co.uk
Twitter: @LucyScott_

Martina Mercer-Phillips: Copywriting To Increase Sales

I don't normally start articles writing about myself, but I realised that many of you who have picked up this book may not have heard of little old me. I'm a copywriter, journalist, and blogger. Some like to call me successful; I think I fall into the workaholic category. As my mother said, when I received my last writing award, "even if you were stacking shelves in *Tesco* working the hours you do, you'd win the best shelf stacking award without a doubt". I do like to believe that my talent also plays a part but I leave that feedback up to my paying clients.

I do believe that anyone who can spell can add compelling copy to their website. All it takes is a little insight, some tricks of the trade, and bingo, your visitors are hooked from the word go.

Keep it simple

This is why many start-up businesses hire someone else to do the copy, as they believe good copy involves a plethora of adjectives and lots of four syllable words. In fact, visitors will be put off if your copy takes effort to read. Conversational is the key. If you wouldn't use the words when having a chat to the supermarket checkout lady, you shouldn't use them on your website.

At best, the overuse of the online thesaurus will make you look pompous and pretentious; at worst, you'll actually lose custom as you make people feel a little bit stupid when they need a dictionary to translate your website!

Remember the twenty second rule

Is there something you're thinking of buying at the minute, or services you are considering using? Pretend you need a domestic cleaner, have a *Google* and have a look at the websites that catch your eye. No doubt, *Google* will have thrown up hundreds of results, so how do you make sure you pick the one that's right for you? You scan! We are all a nation of scanners and this is how we do it. We land on a website and if the copy doesn't pull us in within twenty seconds, we leave. There's just so much choice these days and the consumer has all the control, so we must bear this in mind when creating compelling copy.

Forget left to right

On top of the scanning, visitors will read a webpage differently to how they'd read a magazine or book. The general consensus is this. On landing they'll view the top right hand corner first (insert contact details here); then they'll look at the top left; they'll assess some of the middle before having a glance at the bottom left (look at websites, this is usually where the phone number or social media links are). The bottom right-hand corner is quite useless. Unless you put an animated gif of a juggling cat there, it's unlikely to get any attention, so use this as storage or leave it blank; there's nothing wrong with white space on a webpage.

Forget beginning to end

Now you know where to put the copy you need to know what to put. Visitors will only read the first and last lines of a paragraph and then only the first and last few words of a sentence. This is scanning at its best. I believe the pyramid technique works well here, start with what's important. Highlight your unique selling point straight away, then if you've drawn them in, they're hooked and you can expand a little on the detail to compound the notion that you are the best and they won't find better elsewhere. Good copy will entice from beginning to end and it will encourage a user to learn more, which lowers bounce rates, to click to contact or to buy it now.

Cut out the clutter

A cluttered website will be an assault to the senses and will put people off in an instant. Try not to worry about white space, and use 50% less copy than you believe you should. Less is more in copywriting, and every word counts, which is usually why copywriters charge by the word. Streamline the appearance by making it digestible in bite size chunks. Use meaningful titles, make use of bullet points, and only sell one point per paragraph (as only four words will be read anyway, you don't really have chance to promote anything else).

Use a little psychology

One trick all copywriters use (and if they don't they're not a copywriter) is to harness the power of writing in the second person. Talk to your audience, appeal to your target market, and let visitors believe you've written the copy and developed your business especially for them. Let them know how your services will help them and how choosing you will be the right step to take. So use phrases such as, "we offer you an unrivalled service that promises to make you smile, enhance your life, and leave you thankful that you found us as soon as you did".

Add a personal touch

As a journalist for *The Integrated Retailer*, one thing I often report on is retailer marketing, such as *Omni* channel solutions and so on. I've talked to bigwigs such as the CEO of *Marks and Sparks* and picked the brains of the best PR gurus in the country. All of this has confirmed what I already believed; we want the old days back!

We all love the convenience of shopping online, but we do miss the good old days where we'd go to the shop with cash in our hands and have a little natter as we waited for our change. Remember buying penny sweets and as the doorbell tinkled a friendly woman would come out and greet you? That's how welcoming your copy should be. People need to feel appreciated before they'll part with their hard earned cash.

The truth is, although we all reminisce about these days, we really haven't the time for chin wags and browsing, so, to cater for your consumers, you need to give them what they want quickly, and your copy will help with this.

These tips are just for applying to your homepage as the rules change the deeper you delve into a website. For instance, if a visitor has taken the time to click on your *About Us* page, then they are already interested, and you can use copy to utilise that. Your frequently asked questions should answer every eventuality, even if not frequently asked, as visitors will want to be reassured that you've considered their needs when they flick through your FAQs.

To get started, just try one of these tips. You'll be surprised how much your new copy will lower your bounce rates; your next step is to add SEO!

Martina Mercer-Philips is a journalist, blogger and copywriter whose clients include British Gas, Calpol, Austin Reed, Linens Direct, Funky Giraffe and LavenderWorld. She also produces web copy, press releases and SEO-friendly blogs. Martina is head journalist for the Integrated Retailer.

admin@martinamercer.com
www.martinamercer.com

Maz Hawes: 'Right-Brainers' in Business

It's well known that our brains are divided into two hemispheres, left and right. Although it's a huge generalisation to say each is responsible for a different type of thinking, it is probably true to say that creative people use their right brains more than their left. This is not a scholarly article on brain physiology and function, but a personal attempt to explain why some of us in creative industries find it so darn hard to run a business.

Many definitions exist to describe the curious traits of those whose right brain is dominant. So we are all on the same page here, let me describe myself so we can get a feel for the challenges of being a right-brainer.

I'm a head-in-the-clouds over-thinker, emotional and slightly introverted, a fluff-brain idealist-creative with tendencies to fear and self-doubt, self-judgment, comparison, procrastination, distraction, denial, and a feeling that I don't quite fit. In common with my right-brain peers, I tend to focus on *how* something is said rather than just the *what*. Thoughts happen randomly and haphazardly; there is rarely anything sequential about my thought process.

I have a love-hate relationship with money; "It taints the purity of my artistic vision, darling." I won't read instructions, and my boredom threshold is low. I'm intuitive rather than analytical. Whilst I love process and structure, I just can't do it. My bookcases are ordered by colour not alphabet; there are at least half a dozen books at my bedside, corners folded, scribbles in the margin and underlined, all being read and annotated concurrently. And I have a strong belief that vulnerability is a means to growth, so I really don't mind sharing that all with you!

It's not a black and white thing; my left-brain is clearly there and working perfectly adequately, but its muscle is weakened and intimidated by its bossy opposite. Occasionally she will rise up and slap the right hemisphere into place but I have to watch that 'Right' doesn't run shivering into a hole. 'Right' may be mostly dominant, but she is a gentle and sensitive giant, a bit of a wimp and easily intimidated.

It's my perception that there are a lot more left brains running businesses than right; the way we do business, culturally, is based on left brain principles; most business education is designed for left brainers. I am visually oriented; business books are not. Developing skills of financial analysis, business planning, even writing a to-do list, if I'm not careful, challenges me to move out of my comfort zone and into fear. Over the years I've been running my business, I've learnt much about what works for me, and conversely, what is likely to propel me into a state of paralysing 'stuckness.'

Here are my top tips in a predictably unpredictable order for getting ahead in business as a right-brainer.

Understand that we may not all fit into the traditional working week

Our bodies and minds eschew the 9 to 5. We are either 'off' or 'on'; and when we're on, it's a wave we have to ride, even if it means an 18-hour day. We are all cyclical beings; our physiological processes and cognitive functioning vary with the time of day, month, and year. I've learnt when my most alert, productive, creative, and distractible times are; there's little to be gained in trying to run at 100% all the time. Even if your business needs you to be present 9-5, you can identify when you are best equipped to do different tasks within those hours.

Keep doing personal projects

This is especially important if you've developed your business out of a hobby, as I did with my photography. Keep that right brain stimulated and entertained and don't let your passion wither on the vine. Your passion for what you do is your USP (unique selling point), a precious and finite resource, and personal projects will keep it nurtured.

Collaboration is crucial.

It's all too easy for us to feel isolated in our creative niche. Get out, network, find your tribe. Find a guide and a mentor. Give back to your community. Be open to connection.

Don't plan **too** *much*

A too-precise, ultra-focused set of goals and targets may leave little room for unexpected opportunity. Leave yourself an open mind in order to welcome the serendipity that is the life-blood of the creative life. Once you open yourself to the possibility of synchronicity and serendipity, they will pop up everywhere. Careful, though, that it's not an excuse for distraction! Ensure these happy chances really do fit in with your goals and values.

Do whatever it takes to keep you grounded, happy and whole

It might be yoga or mountain biking or digging the allotment; exercise nurtures your body and spirit. Good sleep, nutrition, and computer downtime are all vital. Know what feeds your spirit and what depletes it. Protect your energy reserves and remember that the potential for building wealth is within you, not external to you, and your energy needs constant nurturing.

*Accept that some sh*t is necessary*

Accounts have to be prepared and paperwork does have to be filed. Know where your own strengths lie, and get help for the other stuff. It will free up your time and your mind to do the things that will drive your business forward. A caveat however; it is essential to at least understand these aspects of business, even if you do choose to delegate them.

Remember to maintain balance

Passion can easily lead to obsession, and obsession to burnout. When you're 'in flow' on the creative stuff, it's easy to neglect the business end of things, which may result in you being taken advantage of... or going broke...

Don't take it all so personally

Rejection is a fact of life. Don't confuse your own personal value with the value of your work in a competitive marketplace in a depressed economy. Learn to protect yourself from heart break, but not by shying away from risk. Lean into the fear and do it anyway.

Get good systems in place. A nagging thought that you've forgotten something, or are avoiding it, can corrode your creativity and stop you from doing your best work. Use a productivity system to capture details, ideas and to-do's so that you are free to move on knowing that nothing is going to slip through the cracks.

Face up to procrastination

The nemesis of the creative brain. Action leads to the risk of failure, criticism or ridicule, hence inaction is always easier. There are many methods to overcome procrastination; break big tasks down into 'next steps'; make yourself accountable by saying what you're going to do and when; chunk your time into bite size pieces (e.g. the Pomodoro technique); don't delay tasks because you haven't got the systems in place; understand when perfectionism is blocking you (95% is usually good enough.)

Embrace your eccentricities

You don't have to be like everyone else. It's easy to waste a lot of energy in trying to conform. Leverage your differences as part of your unique brand.

Develop your left-brain muscle too

Carl Jung advised us to strengthen our non-dominant brain in order to strengthen our skills overall. I know that when I've got the organisational side covered, it frees my creativity. It's like athletes cross-training; it makes them stronger, faster, more focused overall.

Use your creativity to envision your dreams

Use pictures, colour, glue, paint; whatever it takes to make a vision board illustrating your goals. Pin this above your desk, and when you wobble, return to this vision, and get yourself back on track. Instead of sitting in front of your computer, use colour, shape, paper, post-its, pencil and pens to plan your work. Right brainers need little excuse to buy stationery supplies! Get up and move. Draw mind maps instead of lists to help you think of creative solutions to your business problems.

Change your attitude to fear and failure

The most successful right brain entrepreneurs, designers and creatives have truly embraced 'failure' as 'learning'. When we believe failure is an opportunity for growth, we can (almost) take the fear out of our creative lives.

Stop comparing

I'm exposed every single day to the exceptional talents and creativity of photographers and artists around the world, and if I let it, it would freeze me into total inaction. It's a fine line; inspiration is vital, but comparison is a creativity killer.

Consider multi-tasking as an overrated skill

Choose to focus instead! It's shifting gear between two different tasks that's hard: the segue between the left and the right brain. Try and be fully present, in the moment with each task in turn.

Get over the money thing

Because it's a passion, because it comes easily, the tendency is to undervalue what you do as a hard fought skill, to think there's nothing special about you, and to not charge enough for it. Money is not dirty, it's a necessity! So charge for your services and products appropriately.

Even if you aren't one, some of your customers will certainly be right brainers

Consider how you market your product or services to them. Tell a story, use imagery, and tell them what a difference this will make to their life. Don't just give them facts and figures. Your aim is to secure their loyalty to your brand and to influence how your product is received; not simply to increase bottom line revenue.

Take a break

Go for a walk, visit the coffee shop, do some retail therapy; remember as a creative entrepreneur this counts as work too. Just make sure you carry a notebook with you to jot down the inevitable random thoughts that will pop up when you're not consciously thinking!

Be open to new experiences

Welcome the chance to meet new people, visit new places or work in different environments. Even though you may have a tendency to introversion or a feeling that you have to be tied to your desk/studio, overcome this and enjoy the results.

In summary, be grateful for the amazing and privileged position we are in. Getting paid for something we love to do – does it get any better than that? Learning to run my business around a passion is so much easier than being in possession of a proficient business brain but struggling to engage in any creativity.

Ultimately, I do believe it's possible to be an artist and an entrepreneur, to have artistic integrity, and to create wealth.

Maz Hawes runs Light and Day Photography, offering natural and vibrant family and business portraiture. A self-confessed Right Brainer, Maz has spent 3 years learning how to channel her creative passions into a sustainable business.

07966 376490
maz@lightanddayphoto.com
www.lightanddayphoto.com

Dr Michelle Clarke
You Are Your Brand

7 steps to bringing more of yourself to your business

"Just be yourself, kid – people will like you and that makes everything else easier", that was always my Dad's advice to me. As a seven-year old finding my way in school, as a teenager working out who I was, whenever I had relationship challenges, and particularly when I went into the world of work, he was always there with the same advice.

I have to confess that most of the time I didn't believe him. Even when I experienced what happened when I tried to be someone else's version of me, I didn't really think that the answer was to listen to my Dad!

As it turns out, and since starting my own business two and a half years ago, I've been able to explore this more fully and guess what, he was right. I believe it's true now more so than ever. If you run your own business, whether as a solopreneur, or with a team of people, *you* are your brand and if you have several versions of 'you', not only does that become exhausting to keep up, but the messages you give out to your market place can become very mixed.

How you show up at a networking meeting counts, what you say, how you treat people, and what you wear. It all forms part of who you are, your brand and how you are perceived by your peers, clients and prospects. We know that people buy from people. We understand that on an intellectual level, and yet many of us can still fall into the trap of showing up in our 'work' persona and leaving the 'real' us at home.

Connections are made when we feel we have something in common with another human being. Whilst that can be purely related to life at work, it's far more likely to be a shared hobby, having kids of a similar age, the same home town, or school, a similar holiday experience, the love of a certain music or perhaps the same devotion to a particular sports team.

Think of someone you connected with easily at a networking event and have since gone on to do business with. Was it just their business credentials that made you say "yes", or could it possibly be something far more simple, something far more human... that you just liked them?

What if we just gave ourselves permission to believe that to be true? When we understand how we connect with others, it's far easier to understand how others connect with us.

The following seven steps will guide you through a process of deeper understanding of yourself, helping you to bring more of yourself to your business, and encouraging you to have more fun along the way!

Step 1 – get clear on who you are

That might sound a little crazy, but do you know what your values are? What's important to you in your life?

How do you translate that into your business? What is your message? What's your brand associated with?

How do you see yourself? How do others see you? What's the gap between the two?

Ask yourself these questions and ask them of friends, peers and colleagues. Take some time out to reflect on your brand, your mission and your vision for your business. Are *you* in it? If not, what tweaks need to be made? Don't be scared of adjusting things; your brand can, and will, evolve as you do.

Step 2 – turn up the you dial a couple of notches

How much more of 'you' could you bring to your business? How could you connect more personally with your prospects and clients? How could they get to know, like, and trust you even more than they do already, so that doing business with you becomes an even easier "yes" for them?

Step 3 – be consistent offline and online

What do your social media postings say about you and your business? When people meet you offline, do they feel they already know you from your online presence? Make sure the message is consistent across all the platforms you use. Consistency creates momentum and momentum increases the presence and effectiveness that you have in your market place.

Step 4 – raise your visibility online

Let yourself be seen. Use photographs and videos to increase engagement and build relationships online. Photos are great instant visuals to share and video gives your prospects an experience of who you are before they actually meet you. By creating a connection and building trust, videos enable relationships to build way before you're ever in a room together.

Step 5 – share what you know

You are the expert in *you*. No one else can be you in your business, so understand what it is that you bring to the party and share your expertise.

Talk at events, networking groups, create videos and share online; on your website and throughout social media.

Step 6 – keep it simple

This isn't supposed to be rocket science. Being yourself is the easiest thing in the world, it's the one thing we know how to do more than anything else, and yet we make it complicated. We like to create personas to hide behind, to perhaps not shine as brightly as we know we're capable of, to follow 'shiny pennies' and get easily distracted from what it is we really want to do.

Cut yourself some slack. Ask yourself the question: "How could I simplify this? How could this be easier?"

Step 7 – have fun

Give yourself permission to let business be fun. Remember what inspired you to start your business in the first place, and revisit that passion if you feel that it's not what it once was.

Doing business with someone who obviously loves what they do is a joy. Be that person and clients will be drawn to you. Ask the questions, enjoy the process, and remember... sometimes, just sometimes, your Dad could have been right.

To Unc, love you millions, miss you more.

Dr Michelle Clarke is the Director of Damsels in Success, Cardiff and creator of The Art of Authentic Success. She works with female entrepreneurs to help them embrace all that they are, to develop and grow their businesses which truly reflect their authentic selves and have more fun and success with ease in the process! Michelle has mentored hundreds of women, both in the UK and abroad.

michelle@damselsinsuccess.co.uk
www.damselsinsuccess.co.uk/cardiff
www.artofauthenticity.com/21days

Michelle Dalley: Branding

Let's start with a question and at the same time dispel a myth. What is branding? Most people think that a brand is a logo. The visual that you get on a business card and website, maybe on some flyers or a brochure. Get a nice logo and that's the branding sorted? Surely that's enough? That definitely is not enough – so what is branding then? Here's a definition of brand design to consider:

> *"Brand design is the process of creating a distinct identity and personality in order to communicate and promote an organisation, person, product or service. Brand design is therefore a much deeper and broader process than visual identity design, although graphics are often a crucial way of succinctly symbolising and evoking a brand and its associations."*[9]

Or, "A brand is what your product or service stands for in people's minds".

The great news is that you don't need to be a multi-million pound business to have a brand; you probably have one already, you may not have realised. A good place to start is to talk with your staff and customers to see what they think of your business. Find out why they buy from you, what they like, where you sit in relation to your competitors and how you could improve. Explore the market that you operate in to see how you compare, and then how you could stand out more, and be different. Take a look at the following questions consider how they might affect the development of your brand.

Proposition

What exactly are you offering to your clients? Be clear, be specific, make it easy for your clients to understand and engage with you. Do not speak in jargon, but do take time to find the right terminology. Consider using visuals to help demonstrate what you do and how you do it. Infographics are perfect for this method of communication.

Personality

What is your style? Are you direct, personable, faceless, quirky, funny? This will generally be directed by the type of client you are looking to engage. A great example of this is *Innocent*, the multi million pound drinks supplier. Their approach from the very start has always been quirky, for example when they started they advertised for staff on their bottle labels. This was fun, free and more likely to attract people that already liked and understood their product. They also created the banana phone, which still exists now, so that customers can call up for a chat! I would recommend that you find what style is right for you. Out of all of them 'quirky' is probably the most difficult to deliver visually. However it does look like a lot of fun!

9 The Design Council, www.designcouncil.co.uk

Voice

This will be used across your website, letters, emails, marketing materials but also in the way your company answers the telephone, the way you speak to your suppliers, customers and competitors. Make it consistent from the start. Make it reflect the personality of your business. Are you very formal, conversational, chatty, funny etc.? All of these are acceptable – as long as they are relevant and consistent.

Key differentiators

Why are you different to your competitors? Offering "great customer service" is expected by everyone. So, is it your range of products and services, your experience, or your approach that will attract clients? How can you stand out from the crowd? What makes you different – why should someone buy from you?

Market space

Where do you sit in the market? Who are your competitors? What is the size of the market and the opportunity that you could achieve? What is the future of your market, could you get ahead of your competitors by focusing on current issues such as environmental credentials or communication methods.

Target market

Identify your target market, understand their needs, then communicate in a fashion that will appeal to them. Believing that you can deal with 'everyone' is much more difficult to market than working with a niche sector. Consider what type of clients you prefer to work with; you do not need to work with everyone so make choices that suit your business style. How will you communicate with these clients? Where do they live and hang out – *Facebook, Twitter, LinkedIn*, direct mail, word of mouth, email, exhibitions etc.

Your visual branding

Once you have your brand credentials identified you are now ready to build a visual brand identity that encompasses all of these components. This is your logo, and it should then feed into all of your marketing materials in a consistent and professional way. A great design company will be able to create a visual that will deliver your message in a memorable, unique way. This is the part where lots of people get excited as they consider company names, straplines, colours, fonts, style. Once created this must be used consistently across all of your marketing communications such as email signatures, websites, brochures, flyers, business cards, *LinkedIn* profiles, *Twitter, Facebook, Pinterest, Google+*, forums etc.

Your brand as an asset

A brand is an incredibly important part of your company's financial and intellectual assets. Whether a company is brand new, or established with a good reputation, or has a reputation that is less than brilliant, branding can help the market position and build credibility, or rescue a difficult situation.

Having a clear brand also centres the company's belief system and ensures that all levels of staff understand what is expected of them in the way that they communicate and strive to develop opportunities for the future. Of course this only works if employees understand their part in the company jigsaw, so take the time to make sure they engage with it.

Recommended reading

If you would like to read about branding there are many, many to choose from. Here are two that I would highly recommend:

- *A Book About Innocent: Our Story and Some Things We've Learned* by *Innocent*
- *Steve Jobs: The Exclusive Biography* by Walter Isaacson.

Remember that it is never too late to re-work your brand; in fact it is something that should be reviewed on a regular basis, every six to twelve months. This review may not deliver huge, ground-breaking changes, but there could be new opportunities for your business that can be realised through tweaking your brand and the way you communicate to the outside world.

Good luck, and enjoy the process.

For Gail. With love. Always x

Michelle Dalley is a Director at Creating Media, a full service design house working with clients to provide memorable and impactful branding, logo design, marketing, websites and printed marketing materials. Michelle is passionate about design and maximising results orientated opportunities for all businesses. She also loves her family, food and business.

0845 686 0050
michelle@creatingmedia.co.uk
www.creatingmedia.co.uk

Mike Morrison: Marketing On A Budget

If you're running a small business, particularly if you're a one-man band, your single most important job is that of a marketer. It doesn't matter what your business sells, or what services you provide; you can not make a living *doing* what you do, you can only make a living *marketing* what you do. To some that may be disheartening, because typically people think of marketing as an expense; something that conjures up an image of sprawling marketing departments, 90 page strategy documents and massive budgets.

While that may be true for the large multinationals that is not the world we live in as small business owners, and all the better for it! For what we lack in deep pockets, we more than make up for in our ability to adapt swiftly in an ever changing market. As well as our ability to stretch a penny when we need to.

This is something that has become even more relevant, with development of the Internet and the ways we can now leverage it as never before. Social media has turned what was previously a one-way conversation into a multi-person dialogue, and big businesses are still struggling to adapt – while smaller ones are thriving. That's just one way in which being a small business is more advantageous when it comes to marketing, than being a large one.

Still many of us are approaching this with little to no budget, so with that in mind here are my top five tips for marketing your business on a shoestring.

Create content

Content is quite possibly the most valuable tool there is when it comes to marketing your business online, and the best bit about it is that it doesn't cost a thing to produce. Whether its blog articles, videos or podcasts, using the power of the web to make your voice heard about a particular subject is a fantastic way to establish yourself as the go-to-guy (or gal!) within your field, and develop your site as a trusted authority. It's a great, non-committal way of getting people to give you the chance to demonstrate your expertise to them - people will be far more likely to read your blog article than to read your sales page!

Networking

There's a reason that "it's not what you know, it's who you know" is such a common turn of phrase – because it's true! Networking is an absolutely crucial marketing activity that you should make sure you're engaging in. Few things are quite as effective as simply getting in front of people and talking about your businesses. That doesn't always mean organised networking events either – your friends, family, ex-colleagues, and so on, all form part of your personal network and could hold great value to your business, so make sure they actually know what it is you do!

Networking is essentially all about securing your place on the mental 'Rolodex' of the people you meet – and then by nurturing that relationship moving yourself to the top of their list so that when an opportunity presents itself that person doesn't have to think too hard before recommending you.

Review your spending

This one may be a little controversial, particularly to those people who believe that you have to speculate to accumulate, but I firmly believe that if you have £500 in your bank account, and you want to have £1000 in there, then the best thing to do is avoid spending that initial £500.

That's not to say that you should never spend money, but you should definitely be scrutinising every purchase – do you *really* need this? What benefit does it provide? Could I get the same benefit for less outlay?

I often find that small business owners go to great lengths to justify purchasing something they really want, but in truth don't actually need. I've certainly done that before; telling myself it was absolutely essential to spend £1000 on camera equipment despite my business having nothing to do with photography!

Also with small business there can be an element of trying to "keep up with the Joneses", or perhaps a feeling that if someone is pressuring you to buy something then not buying it would suggest you can't afford it and therefore are not successful. If your purchasing is being influenced by someone else, then take the time to truly question *their* motives, and ask yourself who really benefits. Is your printer really the best person to take advice from about whether you need more leaflets or not?

Make sure you take care of existing customers

So much marketing activity focuses on attracting new customers – you may see such concepts as the 'sales funnel' or 'pipeline' mentioned quite a lot. More often than not once those prospects become clients they're forgotten about. Business owners spend so much time focusing on getting people in through the front door that they overlook the ones who are slipping out of the back!

On average, it costs four times more to procure a new customer than it does to retain an existing one. This stands to reason when you think about it logically. Most of what you're doing when bringing in new customers consists of overcoming their objections, convincing them of your quality and winning their trust; so of course it's going to be far easier to market to those people again given that you've already cleared all of the hurdles.

Sometimes it's simply a case of feeling you have nothing more to offer them, in that your product or service is a one-time purchase. In which case you need to change that – expand your offering, develop follow on products and upsells which will appeal to those people who already have a proven desire to buy from you, and with whom you've already established a commercial relationship.

Fine tune your offering

Sometimes, no matter how great your marketing is or how many things you're getting right, people will still not buy from you. Often this is because what you're selling is simply not right for that audience, and no matter how hard you try you will forever be hammering a square peg into a round hole. Unless you change something, and that change needs to either be trying a different hole, or trying a different peg.

Assuming that in your valiant peg-hammering efforts you've built up some goodwill and developed relationships, it makes no sense to abandon those in search of a new audience – instead consider refining your product or service. So if people won't buy what you're selling, sell them something they will. This doesn't always have to be a complete reinvention, sometimes it's just a case of making some small changes, and sometimes it means taking your main offering elsewhere while focusing a new, secondary product at your already established audience. It's simply a case of putting a bit of extra thought into your product, and your market, and just ensuring they actually align.

Mike Morrison is the Author of Bootstrap Marketing: 101 top tips for marketing your business on a budget. *He also runs MIMO Media, offering web design, online strategy, email marketing, search and local services.*

Twitter: @MikeMIMO
www.bootstrapmarketing.co.uk
www.mimomedia.co.uk

Nicky Marshall: How to Focus On You In Business

I remember as a child hearing people saying to my Dad, "You are so lucky running your own business! You can dictate your hours, take as many holidays as you like, and earn pots of money!" This was all I needed to hear. After a few false starts, working in a bank and training in accountancy, I got to live the dream. A few life changing events meant I discovered Holistic Therapy, so, not only could I run my own business, I could do it in a chilled out and relaxed fashion.

- Step one was to make sure I had stationery; you can never have too much of this.
- Step two was a catchy name and fancy logo; image is everything.
- Step three was a shocker, realising that without any customers paying me all I had was a hobby.

I am sure there are many business owners that had a false start like me. What followed next were hours and hours of long days, doing the wrong things, worry, and doubt. There was also a lot of time spent wondering if accountancy had been the better option. Luckily for me, I have found some great mentors, contacts, and role models along the way, but read on for a host of hints and tips to ensure an easier ride. The best way to live the dream and have it all is to focus on *you* in your business. At the centre of any business, large or small, there is a person, a human being like you and me, who needs some basic ingredients to run their business.

Food

How many times have you ran out of the house after grabbing a coffee, skipped lunch as a project has taken your attention, or got home starving and eaten all the wrong things? Good, basic nutrition will allow your body to run at a steady speed, and ensure you have the brainpower and concentration to get everything done. Cut down on those sugars that play havoc with your body, and instead, choose some slow release carbohydrates. Replacing that bar of chocolate with some nuts or seeds, adding some fresh fruit, and choosing brown rice instead of white can really make a difference.

Feeling sluggish? I have been advising people for years to 'eat the rainbow'. The idea is to choose a variety of colourful foods; e.g., peppers, fruits, and vegetables to give a balanced diet and increased energy. It was only recently that I found a scientific study of the same name suggesting the same thing.

Water

Our body consists of at least 70% water, and there are studies to suggest that a lack of water contributes to a range of ailments, from high blood pressure to sleeplessness, and, once again, a lack of concentration. Air conditioning, central heating, convenience foods, and caffeine all dehydrate us. Ensure there is a glass of water to hand for most of the day, and watch your energy and enthusiasm increase. Cold water can be a shock to the system, so room temperature is best.

Oxygen

In times of stress, our breathing gets shallow, starving us of oxygen, and increasing our stress levels. Get into the habit of breathing properly; even ten deep, full breaths every time you go to the loo or pop the kettle on will reap rewards.

Relaxation and sleep

All work and no play really does make Jack a dull boy. Continual working means our fight or flight reflex gets stuck in the *on* position, which:

- reduces appetite
- reduces digestive function
- causes eye strains
- interrupts our sleep
- and, if sustained, can cause other health problems.

Our body needs quality REM sleep to process the day and get rid of stresses, so light or interrupted sleep means our stress levels build. Partake in something relaxing just before sleep, and, if possible, get out for some physical exercise each day. If your sleep patterns are out of sync, there are lots of meditation and relaxation CDs that can help. The perfect solution would be to start some form of meditation practice. It's said that 20 minutes of meditation equates to six hours sleep.

Just imagine

Our brains can't tell the difference between imagination and actually doing something. This is why championship skiers can be seen at the top of the mountain wavering with their eyes closed as they visualise every turn and jump. Recent studies of stroke patients showed people got better 30% quicker when given an hour of visualisation practice on top of their rehabilitation plan.

Imagining you are doing something that gets the neurons firing in the brain, and new neural pathways come into existence. If you have a business plan, spend time visualising how it will work. Look into the future and see yourself successful and smiling. It turns out there was a lot of truth in that old saying "Fake it until you make it". If you want to be a charismatic speaker, a successful entrepreneur, or a record-breaking athlete, the sky is the limit with some focus along the way.

Happiness

Positive thoughts jump the synaptic gaps in our brain allowing for a train of thoughts. Negative thoughts can't jump, leaving us stuck and de-motivated. Kick those jumping positive thoughts into gear by discovering what makes you happy. It's quite ironic that, when we are relaxed and happy, we usually manage to nurture ourselves, yet, in times of stress, all of the above go out of the window!

Stop!

Rather than working harder, take some time off. Go for a walk, take a day out with family, or arrange a catch up with friends. Take yourself away from the problem and do something completely different for a while. Einstein said that the solution for a problem cannot be found in the place where it originated, so get some distance between you and your challenge, and an answer will appear.

Observe

Was there something that started this downturn in events? Are you tired? Are people around you zapping your energy and being negative? Is there a pattern here; have you been at this juncture before? We are often tempted to take immediate action, and knee-jerk reactions can be a mistake. A little observation of ourselves, and of our surroundings, can bring up other alternatives and solutions that elude us if we jump right in.

Choose

Do *something*. To do nothing is to make a choice, so decide on an action plan and make it count. Share your ideas with some positive friends or a mentor that can encourage you. Initially, don't tell too many people, as this can dilute your ideas and energy. Stay focused and see your choices through, give them time to take root, and remember to nurture yourself along the way. They say it takes 21 days to make a habit, so, by following the above steps for 3 weeks, we can usually stay in this swing for life.

So what do you do when life has got busy, you have got into bad habits, and can't decide what to do next? It's at times like these that we usually start the longer hours and panicked decisions that add to our distress. The solution is as easy as 1, 2, 3.

Sometimes, the best choice takes us a little out of our comfort zone, and that's fine. Every one of us has a gut instinct, so take a moment and feel if you are doing the right thing. Remember, this is the right choice for you, as we are all different.

So often it really is the little things that make all the difference. Try the above and soon you will be bouncing out of bed every day full of zest for life!

Nicky Marshall is the Director of Holistic Insights. She is a writer, psychic medium, Reiki Master and holistic practitioner. Nicky spent 20 years working in industry, starting in finance and progressing to accountancy. When she faced health and life issues she began working as a business owner and entrepreneur with a simple mission: to inspire people to love their life.

07760 483851
Twitter: @nickyllmarshall
www.holisticinsights.co.uk

Nicola Cross: Cashflow

Cashflow funding of a business is key for its survival. A number of businesses fail within their first two years of trading, not because they didn't have a good product or service, or because they didn't have a market. They simply ran out of cash.

Think of your business as something that needs feeding from time to time. To keep it running, and to allow the Owners or Directors to achieve their operational and strategic goals there needs to be cash in the business.

It is something that the Directors of any company whether it be a sole trader, partnership or limited company need to keep focused on at all times. The plan is to always be in a position to not only have enough cash in the business to meet its overheads, but to make enough surplus that the shareholders or investors in the business get a return on their money. There are important decisions to be made to keep any business liquid.

Your initial capital invested

If you are a start-up business it is likely that you as the shareholder will be the first person to put money into the business. Some businesses start up with a couple of hundred pounds, and others need thousands. Every business is unique.

If you are lucky you might not need any equipment to get started, or maybe can get away with a minimal amount. Maybe you can live off your savings for six months so don't need to cost the company anything. Or perhaps you may be putting all the hours you can in at a minimal cost to the business to get it off the ground. You might even be fortunate enough to have a ready-made contact list of potential contracts where income comes in straight away.

The reality is that not every business will be this lucky to start like this. It's far more likely that you will have to invest capital to get equipment, marketing and to support yourself in the early stages.

The best way of determining how much capital you need to get started is to put together a cashflow plan. Put into it everything you need to run for the first six months, being strict with yourself. You can't run a Bentley on a budget for a Mini.

Assume that no income comes in initially. If it does then that's a welcome bonus. Then, a couple of months into the plan, start to show sales income coming in as you would expect marketing activities to begin to take effect. Stay conservative with your sales figures as it is always to best to be slightly under than way over in estimating your overall income, and avoid spending or committing to spend, what you don't have. Always run a plan for twelve months, but take a look at your first six months, this will show as a deficit to begin with as this figure will represent your opening capital.

Plan Ahead

Once you are past your first six months you are hopefully getting into your stride, and looking further ahead. Even if your business is more established and has been trading for many years, if you are not planning ahead you are working blind. If you are working blind you are not preparing yourself for your journey ahead.

Use your cashflow plan as a working tool, it can be updated daily, weekly or monthly. The frequency of your updates may be influenced by the size of business you operate and the tightness of the bank position.

Roll the plan forward a month each time, so that you are always looking one year ahead from the date of the plan. Put in actual figures and compare with your previous estimates every time. This will help you get better at predicting more accurately.

This working tool can now be used to grow and develop your business.

You might want to refurbish your commercial building, buy some equipment, or maybe take on new staff. This cashflow can be used to help you make all of those key decisions, by putting in the cost of these items. It will help you assess at what point you can go ahead with those decisions. You can see in advance that if you make a certain amount of sales that you can then afford whatever it was that you needed to get the business to the next level.

Sample cashflow statement

On the following page is a sample cashflow plan. Yours can be as simple or as complicated as you like. The point of the exercise is that you are putting one together, and that you have it available to use in your decision making process. Our example shows capital being invested at the early stages and general overheads the business might expect to pay for. Note in February and August the potential cash deficit.

There are a couple of things that might be reviewed once the cashflow has been completed. For example, can the capital equipment needed in March and July be deferred? The second capital payment made in March, might need to come into the bank in February. Or, perhaps the Directors' salary might need to be reduced. Alternatively the sales income could increase. By knowing these issues ahead of time you will plan a lot better.

There is also a technique of building up cash to bear in mind. If you see that six months ahead there is going to be deficit, this could be because work is seasonal or contracts are not planned that far ahead of time. Give yourself time to build up the cash reserves to cover the cashflow deficit. Start keeping a tight control of cash outflows and increase cash inflows. The chances of a sudden influx of cash just when you need it may be wishful thinking.

	Jan	Feb	Mar	Apr	May	Jun	July	Aug	Sept	Oct	Nov	Dec	Total
Cash Target				**1000**	**2000**	**2500**	**2500**	**2500**	**4500**	**4500**	**4500**	**4500**	**28500**
Capital	10000		5000										**15000**
Income			335	1680	885	1035	610	360	500	500	500	500	**6905**
Total Sales	**10000**	**0**	**5335**	**2680**	**2885**	**3535**	**3110**	**2860**	**5000**	**5000**	**5000**	**5000**	**50405**
Expenses													
Advertising	200	200	200	200	200	200	200	200	200	200	200	200	**2400**
Capital expend			450				450						**900**
HMRC			200			200			200			200	**800**
Insurance	100	100	100	100	100	100	100	100	100	100	100	100	**1200**
Loan payments	150	150	150	150	150	150	150	150	150	150	150	150	**1800**
Other	50	50	50	50	50	50	50	50	50	50	50	50	**600**
Office Expenses	200	200	200	200	200	200	200	200	200	200	200	200	**2400**
Rent	600	600	600	600	600	600	600	600	600	600	600	600	**7200**
Travel	250	250	250	250	250	250	250	250	250	250	250	250	**3000**
Wages	0	0	0	500	500	960	960	2460	2460	2460	2460	2460	**15220**
Expenditure	**1550**	**1550**	**2200**	**2050**	**2050**	**2710**	**2960**	**4010**	**4210**	**4010**	**4010**	**4210**	**35520**
Cashflow	**0**	**8450**	**-1550**	**3135**	**630**	**835**	**825**	**150**	**-1150**	**790**	**990**	**990**	
Bank Balance	**8450**	**-1550**	**3135**	**630**	**835**	**825**	**150**	**-1150**	**790**	**990**	**990**	**790**	

Your sales income

Prepare a detailed cashflow of your normal business trading from information of past sales if you have been trading for a few years. Use that history to project forward. For a new business set an achievable income goal. Always look ahead a minimum of a year and three years if possible.

Your business may be subject to peaks and troughs due to downtime or seasonality; build these into your forecast. You might even be able to anticipate an extraordinary boost in demand and sales around major events (for example, the *Olympics* or a Royal Wedding).

Don't forget VAT if that applies to your business. Ideally show it separately and offset the VAT on your purchases. Your sudden inflow of cash may end up belonging to the *HMRC*.

Keep a close eye on margins. If you are not making a profit you will eventually run out of cash.

Your costs

Overheads can be fixed or variable. Items like rent, rates, or insurance tend to be fixed, in other words they will occur whether you are selling or not. Variable costs tend to be for materials, wages, heat and energy costs, they will probably go up the more you operate.

Keep your costs in your sights at all times, being conservative and careful with your money. You are more likely to use it a lot more wisely. Always negotiate with suppliers and attempt to use your trade with them over time to negotiate a better arrangement. That is not to say that you shouldn't take risks, as we all know you have to make certain judgements and take certain risks in order to grow and expand any business. But do not spend without making more informed decisions. Be disciplined with yourself. If it was your personal money would you still make the same decisions?

Access to finance

There are many sources of extra finance for running your business. Some can be inexpensive whilst others will cost quite a bit. Here are some examples.

- Gain credit from your suppliers, but always get your supplier's permission or this could have an adverse affect on your credit score
- Loan from family or friends
- Bank overdraft
- Credit cards
- Finance leases from banks and other lenders
- A mortgage
- A re-mortgage
- Equity investment.

Your credit score can even affect you being able to take on a large contract. You will still need the credit from your supplier to make that important sale. By gaining credit it will increase your credit score and make you more attractive to lenders.

Cash truly is king so don't let it out of your sight. Whether you are busy or not, you need to devote some regular time to this very important part of your business.

To my mother who won her battle with breast cancer 10 years ago, and is still fighting strong and enjoying every day with her family. Love you mum. Xx

Nicola Cross runs Cross Accounting & Payroll Service Ltd, offering accountancy services to businesses in South Wales, and specialising in assisting start-ups, sole traders, and smaller Limited Companies. They look at tax planning and the take an active interest in their clients' success by offering regular financial reviews. Nicola has over 20 years' technical experience in a variety of industries.

02920 653995
Twitter: @Nicola_Cross
www.crossaccountingservice.co.uk

Nicola Drummond: DIY SEO – Five Top Tips

Search engine optimisation, or SEO, can be both overwhelming and confusing. Bringing traffic to your website and promoting your products and services online is essential, but most small businesses do not have a huge budget to spend. Competing with established businesses and well-known brands can seem almost impossible.

However, many of the techniques involved in promoting your website to search engines are neither technical nor complicated. If you are prepared to spend a little time and effort following these 5 tips, you should soon see your website appearing higher in the search engine results - resulting in increased visitors to your site and, hopefully, more business.

Choose realistic keywords

If your businesses is new, or you have just launched a website, then it is likely to carry little authority with search engines. You will be up against rival businesses with well-established websites, some of whom may have been working on their SEO for several years. Competition for keywords - the words and phrases typed into search engines - can be very high.

For example, a traditional sweet shop in the Yorkshire Dales might choose to target the keyword 'sweet shop'. However, this search delivers 165 million results from *Google*: there is a lot of competition and it would take a long time for the new website to make an impression. More realistic keywords would be 'old-fashioned British sweet shop' (2.3 million results), or 'Yorkshire sweet shop' (1.25 million results).

Think about the terms that your potential customers would type into a search engine to find your business, and start to compile a list of keywords that you would like to target. If your business serves a defined geographical area, ensure that your list of keywords includes the towns in which the business operates. Search engines endeavour to deliver the most relevant results, and will therefore prioritise websites of businesses that are local to the searcher.

By using *Google's Adwords* tool, you can research keywords to find out which are the most competitive, and which are easier to rank for, whilst still driving relevant traffic to your website. This free and easy-to-use tool will also suggest keywords similar to the ones you type in, which should help you to build a thorough list of target keywords.

Ensure your website is built for real-life visitors, not search engines

It is important to ensure that your website or blog is easy for search engines to find by submitting a sitemap, using clear code and incorporating keywords within the website content. An SEO expert could offer a one-off health check of your website to make sure its code is search engine friendly. However, you must aim your website content at real-life visitors above all else.

Make sure that the purpose of your website is clear: do you aim to get your visitors to call you, or fill in an online contact form? Are these details easy to find? Your text should be clear and easy to read, and your site layout should be easy to navigate. This will help both humans and search engine robots to work out the purpose of your site.

If the text content is overly stuffed with keywords, the search engines are likely to blacklist your website as being 'spammy'.

Equally, if a lot of visitors leave your website after a few seconds (known as the *bounce rate*), this will lower your search ranking, as the search engines believe your website is irrelevant to what visitors are searching for.

Include your keywords within the website text in a natural way, so that it does not look awkward to human readers.

Using *Google Analytics* to examine how your website visitors have found you, as well as the website bounce rate, is a good place to start when investigating any potential problems with SEO and the user experience.

Build up useful, good quality content

Search engines love websites that look like a good source of reliable information. Do you have information and resources that are not currently displayed on your website? Use your own knowledge to build up articles or blog posts with informative and interesting content.

For example, if you have a website for a sweet shop, visitors might like to find out about ingredients in the sweets, and whether any are suitable for diabetics. They may be interested in how traditional sweets are made. Perhaps you could supply recipes that use sweets as an ingredient, or supply ideas for an old-fashioned children's party where your company's sweets could be given out as prizes...the list is endless.

A blog is an easy way to supply up-to-date information to your visitors, and is helpful from a customer service and a search engine perspective. You could use photographs, or even a video, to convey messages to your website visitors. Potential customers will spend longer on your site, and other sites may link to your useful content or blog posts.

Consult your keyword list when writing new content for your website. Include keywords within the text, headings, and image descriptions. Use your keywords as links, to help both search engines and humans to navigate the site and identify important areas. In the past, you would often see the words *click here* used as a link.

However, what is far more useful to visitors, and helpful to your SEO, is to add the link to relevant text such as, "Why not try some of our traditional sweet recipes"

Again, don't overdo it. A typical human visitor to your website should not be aware of your SEO efforts; if they are, and your keywords are screaming out from every page, you will need to reassess.

Build some good links to your website

Ensuring that your website has a good amount of high quality inbound links will help it to rank highly in the search engine results. Link building is time consuming and often a tricky process, but there are basic strategies that everyone can use, regardless of the industry you are in. Creating a blog, linking from one web page to another within your site, and submitting your website address to relevant and authoritative business directories, are just a few ideas to get you started. The emphasis should be on building up high-quality links to your website.

There are sites referred to as *link farms*, which exist solely to spam search engines with web addresses. Avoid submitting your website link to these unscrupulous sites, as they are often blacklisted from the search engines, which could, in turn, flag your website up as being untrustworthy.

Google, in particular, loves to provide searchers with results that are local to them. It is estimated that between 30-50% of searches are for local businesses (depending on the type of business being searched for).

If you provide products or services to a particular geographic area, you could investigate whether there are local non-competing businesses that you could share links with. Asking your suppliers and partners to place a link on their website can also be a great way to increase your links, particularly if these other businesses are well-established and relevant to your niche.

Interact and be sociable

Virtual networking using social media is a great way to make business relationships and build up awareness about your company. *Google* loves social media, and you will usually find that, if you search for your company name in any social media profiles you have; e.g., *Twitter, Facebook, or LinkedIn*, it will appear near the top of the search results.

Use social media to keep customers up-to-date with your latest company news and provide links that your fans and followers may find interesting. Let followers know when you have updated your blog, or created a special offer; always include links back to your website. Remember to interact with other businesses too; social media should be sociable and not just a one-way news feed. If another business posts a blog link or photograph that you think will interest your followers, why not re-tweet it (on *Twitter*), or share it (on *Facebook* or *LinkedIn*)? It is likely that other businesses will repay the favour when you post something interesting or useful.

When will I see the results?

Unfortunately, your SEO efforts will not show straight away. Whether your website is new, or you have made changes to its content, it will take a while for the search engines to find and index the site. Visit search engine websites and look for an option to submit your website link; this will often speed up the process of finding and indexing the web pages.

Monitor your website's progress regularly by using *Google Analytics* or similar tools.

Most importantly, SEO is an ongoing process, so make sure you keep your website content fresh and interesting. Review your list of keywords regularly, and continue to follow these 5 top SEO tips. Good luck!

Nicola Drummond is Director of Calino Creative Agency, which offers web design and online marketing services. She has helped a range of businesses from startups through to large corporations to improve their online visibility and customer reach.

07710 562141
nicola@calino.co.uk
www.calino.co.uk

Peter Hopkins: 'Hunter' or 'Farmer'?

Business networking events are populated by two distinctly different types of professionals. In universal networking jargon, they are characterised as being either *Hunters* or *Farmers*.

Hunters are the New Business Executives, who attend networking events in their droves. Their focus is almost entirely sales-orientated. In their role, they must continually prospect – and as consequence will encounter high levels of rejection. For this reason they must be resilient, never take the rejections personally, and simply be prepared to move on to the next prospect. They will visit as many business-networking groups and events as possible, as regularly as it proves worthwhile. By nature, *Hunters* will be impatient – and not overly interested in forming a relationship with a customer. Nor will they usually join any regular networking groups as a fee-paying member, because they need new prospects on a daily basis.

Farmers are the Key Account Managers in their business, responsible for nurturing and maintaining a selection of existing company relationships. To do so, it is critically essential that they connect with their contacts. Thus, the relationship becomes theirs and not the businesses. Key Account Managers will usually be fee-paying members of at least one regularly held, networking meeting or organisation. They attend as much on behalf of their Key Accounts, as they do for themselves. They gain and share knowledge of, and with, their contacts and fellow networking-members. They will easily refer individuals who they have got to know, like and trust over time. They will liaise with other networking members outside of the regular meetings, and in time may even socialise with them – to varying degrees. They are fundamentally salespeople, but with a longer-term goal of building and maintaining relationships. They are unquestionably more patient than *Hunters*.

Hunters and *Farmers* are both salespeople, but they are characteristically different. Essentially, each on their own would find it difficult to survive without the other. A good product or service sold by a *Hunter*, is still a good product or service. The *Farmer* will recognise the benefit of that product or service – not necessarily for their own use, but to one or more of the Key Accounts they are responsible for. When this situation occurs, both parties stand to benefit. One directly and the other indirectly. Key Account Managers do not make good New Business Executives, and vice versa.

Professional relationships can be as complex as a personal relationship. Indeed, they can become even more so, as some business relationships later develop into permanent (or at least semi-permanent) personal relationships – whilst the same cannot be said as often, the other way around! A critical factor in this process is time.

First impressions *do* count: The *Hunter* will dress to impress, as they will want to visibly convey how successful they are. Their delivery will be a highly charged and enthusiastic presentation. The *Farmer* may also be suited and booted, but they will have a more relaxed approach to networking. They are in it for the long-run. For them, there is no race to the finish line. Both are aware – from different angles of the same reason – that at a first meeting, everybody is on their best behaviour.

Hunters sell on product or price. When the competition is offering a similar product, cheaper – and there's always someone that will be – the *Hunter* will be quick to point out the advantages of their product or service over the competition, but they won't waste much time on trying to compete on price alone. They simply move on to the next prospect.

Make a list of the number of people you know (by first and last name,) who have been in the *same* job, with the *same* company, for more than ten years. Do you buy or sell, to or from them, on price alone? The answer is most probably not. If not, what other factors do you think influence you both to continue doing business together? Odds-on, it's relationship-based.

By and large, and when opportunity allows, people buy from people. It's as natural a phenomenon as night following day. It does not necessarily follow that we have to have a deep and meaningful personal liking of those we regularly conduct business with – but we will naturally default (given the choice) to conduct business with people we relate to best at least at some level.

Of course a commercial decision can be influenced at any number of factors and not usually on one level alone. But if the product, the service, and the costs are as near as identical, from two (or more) salespeople with different firms, who is the buyer going to place their business with? People – and the relationship that exists between them – can make a considerable difference.

Joining a business networking organisation is seldom a quick-fix to radically improving sales figures. The *Meet, Know, Like, Trust* philosophy underlying most structured networking organisations, will mean that new members have to take the time to earn the respect of their fellow-members. This cannot always be achieved easily – if at all – at one weekly breakfast meeting over the course of a few weeks or even months.

The purpose of the networking event is to introduce the businesses to each other. The members then have to work together, to get to know each other better on a professional and semi-personal basis. One-to-one meetings should take place throughout the working week. Spending time with the other members affords an insight into each others business operations and equally importantly, helps their relationships to gel and develop. Almost certainly, other members' businesses will also be discussed in your meeting, providing an overview and impression of their value to the group. Common ground and acquaintances are explored, whilst gaps in the knowledge of the other businesses, are filled in. A visit to the others' workplace is also desirable. Beware of those who only want to talk, and are not prepared to listen.

On first introduction, both parties form an opinion of the individual they're talking with, and of the business overviews presented to them. If the businesses have no connection and cannot be of use to each other, it does not necessarily mean that the individuals cannot be of use to each other in the future. Both have contacts that may prove useful to the other – whether or not they will refer each other will largely depend on how their relationship develops on a personal level.

All relationships begin with the ground work and will only flourish with continued effort. Effort that is rewarded when respect has been earned and not assumed. Successful networking and the building of worthwhile professional relationships, is down to the individuals to play a full and active part, both inside and outside of a networking meeting. Just turning-up at the meetings, is nowhere near enough.

And remember, above all, networking and the building of relationships is an on-going and integral part of building your own profile and of your personal development. The people you connect with will keep their eyes and ears open for business opportunities on your behalf. Bottom line, if you are not liked or respected by your networking partners then they will not refer their contacts in your direction.

Peter Hopkins is a Director of thebestof Newport and thebestof Torfaen, an online and off-line multi-level marketing platform, the principal activity of which is to raise the commercial profile of local business members to the business and public communities of South East Wales.

Twitter: @bestofnewport
www.facebook.com/bestofnewport

Peter Maynard: Prevention Is Better Than War

Agreeing your terms of business with both your customers and your suppliers is probably one of the most important things any business needs to do. And it is not something that should be considered an afterthought, to be looked at once the business is up and running. This is one of those things that should be in place before any business opens its doors.

Your terms of business are basically the contract between you and someone else. They should contain the most important things about how you will do business with each other.

Why? Well because the only time your business will really need them is if something goes wrong. At that point, if your terms and conditions were in place and contained the right information, then your chances of putting it right are greatly increased. Without any terms of business, it may be difficult to prove what the terms of the contract were. This could mean that you struggle to recover payment, or that the other party can argue that you haven't fulfilled your part of the bargain.

Although I have mentioned terms of business for both your customers and your suppliers, in reality, your suppliers will usually have their own terms that they will seek to impose on you. However, many suppliers may be willing to negotiate on one or two key terms, so don't be afraid to ask. What if you could get an extra thirty days credit? Or they accept payment by installments? Think what that could do for your cash flow.

Most people think that terms and conditions need to be long and complicated. Wrong!

In reality, your terms of business could simply encompass four things: what you will do; how much they will pay; when they will pay; and what happens if there are any disputes. Of course, you can add anything else that you think is important, but that will depend on your type of business, the nature of your customer, and whether this is a one-off transaction or one of many.

Don't get caught up in the basic trap of trying to make them sound overly legal. Plain English, clearly and unambiguously stated, is the order of the day. For example, why bother with "This agreement is between the parties hereinbefore stated," when a simple "This is an agreement between Joe Bloggs and John Smith." Don't bother with "The party of the first part will supply the goods and services delineated in the First Schedule," when you could say "John Smith agrees to supply to Joe Bloggs with 50 reams of 300g A4 white paper."

So, what can you include in your agreement? Well, the essentials are:

- The names of the parties
- The goods **and/or** services to be supplied (and remember to be as precise as possible here, as any ambiguity will probably be interpreted in favour of your opponent)
- The date by which the goods **and/or** services will be supplied
- When and how much will be paid
- What happens if there is any dispute.

For added clauses you might consider:

- When does ownership of the goods pass? Usually, this will be after delivery has been made and payment has been received, but if there is going to be a long period between delivery and payment, you may want to clearly state that ownership only passes upon payment. Then, if payment is not made, it should be easier to recover the goods, as technically they are still yours.
- Who is responsible for delivery? Again, this will often be obvious from the nature of the transaction, but if the goods are particularly large, then it may be that the customer should collect. You could then arrange delivery, if requested, but you would be entitled to raise an additional charge. Equally for some transactions, you may want to make delivery a separate item, so that you are not saddled with an additional overhead that could fluctuate if delivery prices go through the roof.
- Are there any trade or professional regulations you have to comply with? For example, as a solicitor, I am subject to money laundering regulations, and so all of my clients are notified of this from the outset. They are also told what this means which, in this case, means that they have to provide two types of identification evidence before I can start acting for them.
- Do the *Consumer Protection (Distance Selling) Regulations 2000* apply? For Internet businesses, in particular, it is vital that you now about these regulations and how they operate. In simple terms, they can allow your customer to withdraw from a contract within a certain time period at no cost. To a limited extent, you may be able to make the customer liable for any costs incurred by you before they withdraw, but it needs to be in your terms and you need to ensure that you don't incur substantial (and possibly irrecoverable) costs during that cooling off period.
- What payments will you be entitled to if the contract is cancelled part way through? If you are delivering some sort of office support services (like a virtual PA business), then you may be happy to just receive payment for the work done to date, if the contract is terminated three months into a six-month deal. But what about if you have cleared your diary of all other commitments to fit this client in? Perhaps you would then want to specify that the full contract price is payable in the event of early termination.

- Do you want to limit your liability in the event you get something wrong? Suppose you manufacture widgets that cost £1.20 each, and an order for 2,000 units is placed, but there is a manufacturing fault which makes the whole consignment useless. You might think that your maximum liability would be for the total contract price (i.e., 2,000 x £1.20), on the basis that your customer must now buy them from one of your competitors. But what about if each widget is an integral part of a hi-tech gadget retailing at £220 each, and the manufacturing defect results in the gadget catching fire, and the defect is only discovered when the gadgets have been assembled and are on the retailer shelves? Not only might you then be responsible for the costs of re-assembling new gadgets, there may also be a claim that your customer's reputation in the marketplace has been irretrievably scarred. Far better to insert a limitation of liability clause in your terms, which could, for example, limit your liability to the total contract price, or a maximum set figure. That way, if you are thinking of getting public liability insurance, you can be a lot more confident that the cover you have should protect you against all eventualities.
- What about if you do the work, but payment is not forthcoming? Off you go to your friendly, local debt collection agency, who manage to recover full payment for you. Good result, yes? Well, not really. If the debt collectors fees are 20% of the total sum recovered, and your profit margin was only 12% you have been working at a loss. Far better to have incorporated a condition into your terms of business that states that if payment is not received within the standard 30 days credit period, and you have to engage the services of an external debt collector, that debt collector's fees can be added to the total contract price.

The list could be endless, and it really is up to you to decide what is important. One way to get ideas is to look at what your competitors have in their terms. However, don't repeat the classic mistake of just copying everything. When they go under for having unsustainable payment terms, you want to be in a position to capitalise on the potential extra business! Equally, if you download a standard set of terms and conditions from the Internet for a tenner, then that is exactly what you will get: *standard* terms worth a tenner. You know your business best, so make sure you put in there what is important to you, not what might be important to tens of thousands of other businesses in totally unrelated sectors.

Next, in order for the terms of business to be binding, they need to be in place *before* the service is provided or goods delivered (i.e., in legal speak, before the contract is performed). You cannot impose terms of business retrospectively. That means that it is best to have them attached to all of your initial paperwork and even on your website.

If someone can purchase goods direct from your website, you need a tick box that they have to mark to agree that your terms of business apply. Equally, if a customer applies for some of your services and you write or e-mail them providing a quote, make sure that you state that the quote is subject to your terms of business, and enclose a copy.

So you've sent one copy of your terms to your customer. Now send another! That way, nobody can be in any doubt that they are to be incorporated into your contract. So, when the order is placed, add a copy of your terms to the confirmation. If you invoice before you dispatch, add a copy to the invoice.

It can also be helpful if you get a copy of the terms of business signed by both parties. That way, it would be difficult for either party to argue that they didn't realise they were bound by them. For some businesses, and in some transactions, this fits easily into the flow. With others, it may seem like a difficult thing to interject into the process.

For the avoidance of doubt, just because the terms aren't signed, does not make them invalid. If all of your documentation refers to them, and you have included copies from the very start of your dealings with the other party, then they find it very difficult to argue that those terms are not applicable.

Just because you have incorporated the terms into your contract, does not mean they can't be varied. For example, if your terms say that you will be paid within 30 days of delivery of the goods, but before the order was placed, you e-mailed the other side to say you would give them 60 days to pay, then 60 days it is. Any of the individual terms can be varied without jeopardising the remainder. This can be a good thing in that you have complete flexibility on each transaction to adapt your normal terms; but equally it does mean you need to be a little careful about throwaway comments in oral or written communications that could be deemed to have varied the standard terms.

So you have introduced the terms of business right at the start of your business relationship (and maybe even got both parties to sign them if appropriate). That means everyone is bound by them, right? Not necessarily. If you have had 50 transactions with the same customer, and on each of them your terms of business say the unit price is £50, but you have always accepted £40 per unit, then by custom and practice you could be deemed to have varied the terms. So the moral is, once you have agreed terms, stick to them.

You deliver on your side of the bargain (as far as you are concerned), but still there is trouble. A dispute is imminent. Well firstly, you will at least know what you are arguing about. If the terms of the contract are clear and binding, it should make it a lot easier to decide which side is at fault. This hopefully means that settling the dispute should be quicker and thereby cheaper than if one person thought they were buying 30 apples for £1 each, cash on delivery, with the delivery no later than 1 March; whilst the other was absolutely certain they had agreed to sell 400 pears, at £5 per unit, to be delivered in 4 batches on the 15th of each of the next four months, and credit terms agreed as 30 days after the final delivery.

No matter how well you do your job, mistakes are a simple fact of life. Therefore, having an additional provision in your terms of business about how any disputes will be settled, can often mean the difference between a minor blip in an otherwise successful long term business relationship, and all-out war.

Although lawyers and litigation may be the eventual result if the disagreement cannot be brokered, having a clause that commits both parties to mediation in the first instance can often assist. Mediation is a relatively low-cost and quick way to have a facilitated negotiation about what went wrong.

Whereas litigation can only result in a damages payment (and probably a fairly hefty costs bill for at least one of you), mediation means that simple things like apologies can be incorporated into the settlement agreement. In that way, it is often possible to preserve the business relationship, even when there has been a falling out.

So there it is then, a whistle-stop guide to getting your terms of business in place and in your business.

- Include everything that is important.
- Big is not always better.
- Get them to the other party as soon as you first make contact.
- Send them several times.
- If possible get a signature.
- Be careful not to vary them by careless throwaway comments or by consistently failing to abide by them.
- If a dispute occurs then you can rely on the terms of business as a framework of what was agreed.
- If you have a clause dealing with the settlement of disputes, try to make sure it gives you the best possible chance of resolving things amicably and allowing you to continue in your mutually profitable business relationship.

Peter Maynard is a Director at fwd Law Associates, offering a full range of legal services for businesses and individuals, with specialist expertise in business start-ups, employment, property and dispute resolution. As well as being a Partner and Director at a number of law firms, Peter has previously set up and developed his own small business.

01633 660440
peter@fwdlaw.com
www.fwdlaw.com

Peter Norrington: Take a Risk and Manage It

Your business is an opportunity and presumably you've got a plan to get it where you want it to be. Risks are the things that can upset your plan, and they can be more or less costly, and more or less likely. We rarely have perfect information or perfect reasoning, so opportunity and risk come as a package.

It's possible nobody has ever mentioned risk management to you. But with investors (in either money or other resources), you can be sure they'll give you plenty of advice, and probably some instructions. They only invest in something they think stands a good chance of succeeding. So do you, but your idea of a good chance can be different from theirs because of your personal attitudes to risk and reward.

Risk management will help you recognise what you can and can't control, and can also help to cut down worry.

When you talk to people or read more about risks, it's worth knowing that there are different ways of looking at risk, different definitions, and different ways of calculating what risks mean to a business. Find out more about how people perceive risk and what they do about it, and apply it to your own business.

What follows is a guide to what I wish I'd known, and practical examples of what I learnt during one venture.

When to do risk management

Risk management is best done while you're planning, *before* things happen. After the event it's crisis management! While you're planning, and after you've done each positive or optimistic component of your plan, ask yourself what-if questions.

Note all the questions you raise, even if you don't have an answer for them yet. If you plan in pictures or charts, put question marks next to the parts that have a challenge. If you've got people around that you can turn to for friendly, yet critical advice, ask them to help spot what you've missed.

You can get better at risk management with practice, and you'll almost certainly get the opportunity as your business progresses. Your plans can change for all sorts of reasons, and the environment around your business will change, bringing risks you couldn't foresee.

How to approach risk management

You're in business to provide services or goods to clients or customers to satisfy your goal in a way that matches your ethics. The difference between goods and services or clients and customers is important, but follow this through and replace my words with what describes your situation best. The lists here can't cover everything and boundaries can be fuzzy, so adapt to suit your situation. They are prompts, and hardly definitive.

You'll know what you need from suppliers to make your service or goods happen, such as: raw materials, components, equipment, premises, knowledge, skills, and other people. You know what you need to do, and how long it takes, to turn these into the actual services or goods your business offers. You also know what you need to get your potential customers to know about what you offer, and how to get your services and products into the hands of customers. Add to this mix your own abilities and shortcomings.

For risk management, you're looking for ways your plan can go off track. But this is to support and protect your plan, not to undermine it. If you have ideas about how to deal with a risk, make notes, but don't focus on getting solutions to everything immediately. Your initial ideas might be right, but there may be alternatives that, on reflection, or a second opinion, may prove better.

What to look for?

You may notice that I'm splitting things up into smaller parts. This is how you identify areas of risk, down to individual risks. You're in control here. Go through your plan (or a part of it as practice), and ask yourself, "What if...?"

- It arrives before or after you expected?
- It's the wrong quality, size, colour, etc?
- It's broken?
- There are too many or too few
- The price goes up or down?
- ... and other questions relevant to your specific business.

Then, ask yourself, "How much variation matters?" In other words, how much tolerance does your plan already have for these risks, without it affecting service or product quality? And how much variation needs risk management?

These questions work for products and services you get from other people (where you are their customer), for the products and services you give to your customers, and for the way in which you get your work done.

Which risks to focus on?

In the simplest terms, you start by estimating cost and likelihood.

Costs are often seen only in financial terms, but you may want to consider impact on your health, time, relationships, and even your reputation. You don't need exact costs; and they depend on so many things, so an estimate may be all you can reasonably get. Grade the cost implication in one of three ways and allocate points to it as follows:

(3) = very costly (2) = moderately costly (1) = little cost implication

Likelihood is also expected to be your best guess. Use another 3-level scoring system:

(3) = very likely (2) = moderately likely (1) = not very likely at all

That may be enough. Even multi-million pound companies may only use six levels on this scale.

Make a grid of cost against likelihood, using the three categories and the scores for each scale. Multiply the scores to give the level of risk for each box. For example, low likelihood with high cost would score 3 (1x3). Your greatest effort will go towards fixing the high cost and high likelihood risks; the least effort towards low cost and low likelihood risks. Don't get too obsessed with the numbers; this is not a science, even for the experts.

It is possible that you start with few risks, and that they're low cost and low likelihood. Or you may spot a high cost and high likelihood risk that you really need to pre-empt, a risk that you might never have taken precautions against without this process.

What can you do about a risk?

Plan! Some of the risks you can avoid. Can you do something a different way and cut the likelihood or cost implications completely? Some potential problems can be reduced before they happen, cutting likelihood or cost partially. Some you can make a plan B for. Some you can share or transfer to other people. Insurance is a good example of the latter, which cuts in after a risk has turned into an event. Don't just think about the policies you have a legal requirement for, as you may be able to mitigate one of your risks through additional insurance cover.

Some risks you may have to accept because you choose to, or because they're beyond your control (in which case there's no point worrying). Of course, some solutions carry other risks, but push on, or nothing will happen, and then your goal itself is at risk!

You're in control again. This is where your specialist knowledge of your product or service counts. It's where you can ask questions to find out more, through your networks, clubs, associations, societies, the web (although quality control on the information can be tricky), or libraries (they're still good at helping you find quality information).

What must you do about your risks?

Breaking laws is generally risky! You might want to fix those first. As for the others, do *something* or you've just wasted your time! You could keep some notes on how your risk management works out, and the things that took you by surprise. It's all practice.

A quick case study

Many years ago, I edited a non-profit community magazine, supported by advertising, backed by a local business that started in one city on two A4 pages, and over two years spread to several counties and cities on seven A3 pages. This expansion led to some profound changes to business operations and processes.

- I had to change production from a word processor to a publishing program for greater flexibility and control over content. This was necessary for improvement, and ultimately successful. I hadn't anticipated that the first program couldn't handle enough pages, and had to constantly develop workarounds which were time-consuming.
- An advertiser dropped out of one issue. I had to make up half a page of content the night before publication. I learnt not to give advertisers such late get-outs, to know who might step in at the last minute, and to keep some filler content.
- A competitor started up, taking some of our advertising. By then I could prove wider audience reach, more commitment and better quality. I communicated this to existing advertisers, and found new ones.
- I kept back-ups of templates and artwork in active use, and kept the back-ups in a safe place. Older material I archived onto the backer's computer. His son was told not to use it. He installed a game, and inadvertently destroyed the archive! At the time it was annoying, but the files were of limited value.
- The loss of the templates, however, was always high risk (cost and likelihood). Indeed, anyone with business critical files should back them up. Cloud storage (via an internet-accessible third party site) is a new, simple, and cheap method that solves this problem, sadly unavailable back then.
- I moved from all pages on coloured paper to coloured cover and white inside, cutting costs and improving readability.
- Later, I went for a full colour, glossy cover. It seemed right; it looked great! I had no idea. It required more time and skills (that I didn't have to start with) to design and make, and complicated each issue's production cost. I moved onto other things for other reasons. The next editor soon ditched the full colour. I don't blame them!

Some of the issues I encountered were predictable and avoidable with some prior thought and planning.

Hindsight is a cruel teacher, unless you can learn it from the mistakes of others. The time it takes to think about and pre-empt the possible risks is probably going to be rewarded many times over should any of them actually come to pass.

For my father, grandmother and grandfather

Peter Norrington is a Visiting Consultant at the University of Bedfordshire, and working on setting up his own business. Before this he was a Project Manager at the University, and has also worked extensively in education and publishing.

www.peternorrington.com

Phil Cheesman: Getting it All Done

Okay, if you've got this far in the book you must have some great advice to act on by now. If you've added anything to your to-do list, read on...

Getting it all done is simply about time management, right? So why can't most of us seem to do this? The simple answer is because *we can't manage time.* Time is a constant in our everyday world, unless of course, you are Doctor Who! All we mortals can do is manage what we do in the time we have available.

That's why we should think in terms of *task* management and not *time* management. You may think I'm splitting hairs, but there is a fundamental concept at work here and that is: if we do the right things at the right times, we will get far more done and make better use of our time.

A few people seem to sail through life, getting all the really important things done without any obvious process for achieving this. These few gifted individuals are the 'natural' task managers who intuitively know just what they should be doing at any given time, and have the self-discipline to get on and do it without distraction. The rest of us would love to be able to achieve similar results, wouldn't we? Well we can get the same results if we adopt the habits of natural task managers. So what do natural task managers do? Their habits for success are covered by four words

- They **analyse** each potential task to see how long it will take, what resources might be required, its importance, and urgency.
- They **prioritise** their chosen tasks, filtering out the unimportant ones and those they know they can't do.
- They **plan** each remaining task by scheduling when they are going to do it.
- They **act** by doing the task when they said they would.

They don't run to-do lists - if it's not in their diary, it doesn't get done. If you currently run to-do lists, ask yourself:

- How many items in your current to-do lists have been there for over a week? A month? Several months? So is it working? Be honest.
- How many times do you go to your to-do list and pick off the short, easy to do tasks, avoiding the big difficult ones?
- How many single-sentence tasks in your to-do list are actually large projects that need proper planning and scheduling?
- How often do you have to delete stuff that hasn't been done and never will be, because it's too late? Or do you rip up your old to-do list and start a new one?

To-do lists are toxic!

They set you up for failure, frustration, and a negative self-image. Why? Here are some of the reasons discovered by the *Harvard Business Review*:

- Choices of what to do in our massive to-do lists overwhelm us. Psychological research has shown that, if we have more than seven choices of action, we become unable to make any useful decisions. Psychologists call this "the paralysis of choice."
- We tend to pick off the easiest tasks first so that the bigger ones tend to get pushed to the back of the queue. Remember, all tasks on a to-do list tend to look the same—just one line of writing!
- Unscheduled tasks lack commitment. If you have just added something to your list without deciding how long it's going to take and exactly when you're going to do it, are you really committing to it? Or is your to-do list a simple dumping ground to avoid having to think about what the task really involves, and decide whether you will ever do it?
- We put all sorts of things on our to-do lists, including nice tasks. These are things that we like doing. When we have some time available, we turn to our to-do list and tend to choose the tasks that we like doing rather than the ones we *should* be doing. This is called a displacement activity and to-do lists are full of them.
- This is why to-do lists morph into what I call, "beat yourself up" lists, which end up with lots of tasks we don't like doing and feel guilty about because we haven't done them. All of this conspires to worsen our self-image and sap our confidence, which is why to-do lists really are toxic.

What's the alternative?

Live in your calendar! Try doing this:

- Take each task off your to-do list.
- Decide how long you will need and what resources you will need to do it.
- Schedule it in your calendar accordingly, making sure the resources will be available at that time.

But it doesn't all fit? Good! You have just proved that your current to-do list is truly toxic because you will never have the time to get it all done.

Learn to say "No." It's more honest to others and to yourself. When you live in your calendar, stuff that doesn't fit into it shouldn't be done by you. Either get someone else to do it, bin it, or take something less urgent and important out of your schedule to make space for it.

What if, by living in your calendar...

- You avoided over-commitment?
- People respected your honesty about your capacity?
- You suddenly had time to do everything that you committed to?
- You were on top of things and had time to work on your business instead of in it?
- You had a better work/life balance?

How would that feel?

Task management tips – DO...

- Plan your activities using your diary as a reality checker.
- Learn to say "No".
- Commit adequate resources to important tasks.
- Be prepared to modify your plan if it doesn't fit in your diary or you can't resource it.
- Schedule periods to deal with emails, and don't let them interrupt your time.
- Use your diary to ensure a balance of activities between:
    - Growth
    - Money-earning
    - Admin
    - Travel
    - Personal
- Schedule your time efficiently by:
    - Minimising dead time
    - Plan admin time efficiently
    - Schedule blocks of time for similar tasks (e.g., phone calls, email, etc.)
- Schedule recurring tasks at regular times, and set reminders and alerts.

Task management tips – DON'T...

- Ignore your diary
- Indulge in displacement activities
- Run separate to-do lists. If it's not diarised it doesn't get done!
- Forget to schedule preparation and travelling time
- Schedule chaotically.

Assessing how well you currently use your time

Evaluate how well you currently use your time by responding to the following questions. Mark the options that are closest to your experience. Use your answers to identify areas that could be improved.

Be as honest as you can, and use the following scale:

(0) – Never (1) – Occasionally (2) – Frequently (3) – Always

1. I schedule when I deal with e-mails and stick to it.
2. I use my calendar as a planning tool and reality check.
3. I commit resources to important tasks, including my time.
4. I modify my plan if it doesn't fit in my calendar or I can't resource it.
5. I use my calendar to ensure a balance of activities (money-earning, growth, administration, personal).
6. I don't ignore the things I've scheduled in my calendar.
7. I don't indulge in displacement activities.
8. I don't run to do lists; everything I plan to do is in my calendar.
9. I schedule preparation time, travelling time and the follow-up time for meetings.
10. I schedule things in my calendar efficiently to minimise dead time.

Add up your total score (0-30), and then check your performance by using the following evaluation:

0-10

You must learn to use your time efficiently, and reduce the time you spend working in chaotic and unproductive ways. Follow the above advice for a month and then mark the difference in your achievements.

11-20

You have some task management skills, but certain areas need improvement. Look at these areas and use the above advice to improve them.

21-30

You use your time efficiently; keep looking for new ways to streamline your work practices by referring to the above advice.

Phil is Managing Director at 4Words Management Improvement Ltd, helping SMEs with business strategy, planning, management, leadership, and project and systems management. Phil has lectured at UCL and Cranfield Universities and his main passion is to see companies grow through identifying what needs to be done and then ensuring that it happens.

07850 555307
phil.cheesman@4words.biz
www.4words.biz

Phil Terrett: Return on Experience

So, here's the thing, brought on by much thinking and much reading as I built my own appreciation marketing programmes (and with a tip of the hat to American marketer David Johnson) – it is not about *Return on Investment (ROI)*, it is about *ROE – Return On Experience.*

If you get a good return on the experience you create for your customers or contacts, then you are doing well. If they enjoy the experience of dealing with you, and the experience of being appreciated by you, then you will do well from them.

Let's define a tool to help improve ROE, called Appreciation Marketing. Appreciation can be defined as "Thankful Recognition." Appreciation Marketing is highly personalised marketing designed to increase your levels of business, by bringing your business to the forefront of your customers' minds and keeping it there. This increases business from existing customers, can recover past or lost customers, and increases referrals. How about some key points to get you started in thinking through how to do this.

Personalised marketing

Personalised *means* personalised. If you download a database, do a mail merge, and send out a standard letter, altered to reflect all of the names in the First Name column with a scanned signature, it is not personalised.

Why? Because what ends up on a database is often what is on people's business cards. Think about it for a moment. Is that what you actually call them? I recently received one such letter. It started "Dear Philip", and was signed "X.Y. Smith" (name changed to avoid embarrassment). The problem is that Phil is only ever called "Philip" by his mother when he is in trouble, and X.Y. Smith, who has known Phil for 9 years, is known to him as "Bert". Personalised means getting it right, and what better way to do this than handwriting Phil, and hand signing the letter?

Bringing you to the forefront of their mind

There is nothing quite as dull as the expected and unimaginative. If you send someone a Christmas card, or Valentine's Day card, yours will be one of many and will receive the appropriate level of attention. If you want to actively have someone's attention, you need to do the unexpected. Every day of the year is something day. September 19th, for example, is International Talk Like A Pirate Day – wouldn't that get someone's attention? This extends into the customer experience and is why we like ROE. Remember when we all used to read books about customer satisfaction? We're all satisfied with our water companies (we get water), but we don't ever refer them to anyone. Satisfaction and doing the expected in marketing terms is simply not enough.

...and keeping you there

Regular contact is the key to Appreciation Marketing. "Hello, I sent you a nice letter a year ago, please buy my widget" is not exactly compelling. The skill is in reaching people in different ways throughout a year without it becoming routine for them. Being systematically spontaneous is always a challenge. But if you want the experience to be good, and the message to be reinforced, and ROE to be achieved, that is exactly what is required.

Who should you be talking to?

Most of us know a lot of people, not many of us run a formal CRM system, and, for a lot of people, their "database" is the sum of the business cards they have received over the years. It will be un-sifted and unrefined. To get a better ROE, it is necessary to segment that database.

There are many different ways to segment a contact database, for example, by value of customer spend, by frequency of contact, by probability of a sale. What is rarely done is segmentation by the level of influence a contact can have over the growth of your business. One way to segment your databases (and to be clear this is contact databases, not just existing customer databases) is by the level of influence that person can bring to bear on future prospects of your business.

So let's get started. Dump your database into a spreadsheet. Open the spreadsheet and add an extra column, entitled A/B/C/D. Then, begin to go through every single entry in that database, and allocate a category against that person.

On what basis?

A – This person is a consistent advocate for your business. They are a cheerleader. They give referrals to you without being asked. They may or may not be a customer; however, if they are a customer they must be a good one, i.e., either high-value, or repeat purchasers, or great payers etc.

B – This person will always give a referral or introduction if asked. They are occasional advocates. They may be mid-level customers. They may be good loyal networking contacts.

C – People in the C category are the bulk of the database. They may be ex-customers, one-off customers, people you meet on the networking circuit, old contacts, and people you have not spoken to for a while.

D – People who you may have parted company with not on the best of terms, people you may not like; frankly, people who are on your database but you don't know why (admit it, we all have a few).

Finished?

We would suggest that you leave the list for a few days and then revisit it. You will find that optimism triumphed over realism in the first cut. Inevitably, you will have too many A's, too many B's, and not enough C's or D's.

This is the time to get harder in your choices. In my first cut, I had a gentleman in the A category who was a great friend; we used to run a company together. He had, however, recently taken a job overseas in a different industry. For the purpose of this exercise, he was a C.

Re-do the segmentation and you will probably conform to what is becoming a norm: 5% A's, 10% B's, 75% C's and 10% D's. These numbers will change as your appreciation marketing takes effect, but it is a good enough start.

What next?

Next, you will need to put in place contact programmes for each of the groups, to show them how important they are to you, and to make them feel appreciated.

The frequency and level of personalisation will vary depending on the group. If you have 1,000 people in your database, your A contacts will be around 50 people. Perhaps you should send him or her something every other month, for your B contacts every third month, and so on.

I spoke with a solicitor a while ago who thought of sending carriage clocks to his A contacts. I explained that the point was not the value of the item, but the thoughtfulness behind it. They would get a much better feeling of being appreciated by a hand-written post card from him than from an expensive gift.

So, think about what you can do. Contacts of ours have received ninja ducks, hand-written letters, information packs, worry dolls, and much more. What they do is remember the thought that goes behind the action, they remember us, and they then come back.

Can't we just send them an email, or tweet them?

Yes, of course, and we would not consider Appreciation Marketing to be a replacement for other forms of marketing; however, as an incremental approach, it can pay dividends.

By way of example, we sent a single appreciative hand-written letter to a contact last year after they had recommended a book to us. One week later, we got this response by email:

"What a great letter I received from you today. It really took me by surprise - no one bothers to write any more, so you are onto a winner here. Brilliant. I'm in the xxx from 9th to 17th. Let's get going as soon as I return".

Is it expensive?

Compared to what? Is the cost of a hand-written letter, carefully crafted, more expensive that a 2nd class franked, mail-merge letter? Yes, it is, but direct mail generally has a response rate of between 1 and 3%; we have had up to 50% response rates. So everything is relative.

Mother Theresa said, "There is more hunger in the world for love and appreciation than for bread." Appreciation Marketing is a way of showing your contacts that you appreciate them, and, through it, you can get a far better Return on Experience.

Phil Terrett is the founder of Philosophics and Regional Leader for 4Networking in South Wales. Philosophics offers done-for-you appreciation marketing services, destuckification programmes for small business owners and HootSuite Training.

07748 653990
phil@pholiospohics.com
www.philosophics.com

Picasso Griffiths: Delivering on Your Word

We all have to meet client deadlines at some point. There are very few businesses where they apply. My deadlines are for commissioned work, caricature, exhibition designs, brochures, magazine illustrations or animations. All of which require creative input, which can sometimes be very stifled by having a pressure to finish on time.

Whatever the job, my first magic question is always to ask *"What's the deadline?"* If they say it's open and that there's no rush I always insist on a deadline anyway.

More often than not, when I agree an end date, in my own diary I put the finish well before that, normally a week earlier.

I like to under-promise and over-deliver. In other words I'll promise only what I know I can deliver, and then try to deliver more wherever I can. I'm not happy with customer satisfaction, I want customer delight. By bringing it forward it makes me look professional when I deliver ahead of schedule. I don't do it for that reason but it does have that effect.

There are a number of reasons why it makes sense to me to finish well ahead of the agreed deadline. It gives me some breathing space; allows for illness; gives opportunities to change the concept or design; accommodates unexpected technical or computer problems.

Through experience I know how long a job will take and usually have a couple of jobs on the go at the same time. If something will take 3 days I always allow plenty of breathing space for myself so I can still do other jobs at the same time. For the way I work this is more interesting and I can jump from one to the other which I find more refreshing and challenging. The client does not need to know you have other work on as long as you deliver on time. If you don't deliver, that's when they notice, and it leaves a bad taste in their mouth – regardless of the quality of the finished product.

Never make a promise, if you know you can't keep it

Promise is another major word for me. I don't use this word often and if I do I spill blood to make sure I stick to it. This I carry on through to design work. If the work someone wants is not my style, or impossible to deliver because I have too much work already, then I will always say so, rather than make a promise just to get their business.

I will either say "No" but try to put them in touch with someone else who can do the job (and only recommend someone who I *know* is equally reliable) It's not good for me if they follow through my recommendation and are let down.

Alternatively I will say "Yes" but with a realistic deadline that I can achieve, even if that means weeks or months, rather than days.

Passing work onto people you might consider as competitors actually creates a win-win situation. Once you have passed work onto a friend, perhaps in return he or she will pass work back your way and a good healthy relationship is formed.

There is plenty of work out there, so there is no point pulling the shutters down. Saying *"Sorry can't help you"*, and *"I don't know anyone else who can"* is very negative. However, passing someone on leaves them with a good feeling about you as being a helpful and trustworthy person. I've found many times that this has led to further recommendations, even though they never bought from me initially.

Over the years I have done a lot of exhibition design work for *Steadtler*, a company that has a high reputation for quality. Recently I did a job that ended up taking three times longer than I had anticipated. But I still cracked on and delivered on time. The feedback was amazing to the point where the organiser of a large, prestigious exhibition event saw the design and asked if they could use it as part of their official brochure. Bingo!

As a result my client was even more thrilled. This is what my aim is, and it was facilitated by still allowing more time to complete the job than I had anticipated – by building slack into my schedule that allowed for the unexpected, so that really even though I hadn't anticipated it at first, I'd still accommodated the potential for disruption.

Don't do things you don't like doing

I had someone who promised me tons of work drawing icons for the web which they said would keep me busy for years to come. However it would mean drawing a door, a tree, a biscuit, a teapot, a lamppost, etc. Sorry, but I'm just not interested. If my only interest was in making money I'd do it, but that's not my main motivator.

I'd rather do something that stimulates me, even if there was no money involved and it was fun to do, or the client was fun. Life's too short – whatever you are doing you must make sure it is fun.

Prioritise your work if you want to deliver on time

I prioritise my work at all times, and I have a clear, colour-coded schedule on my computer that is regularly updated on the wall of my studio to keep me on track.

Expecting the unexpected

Reputation is of paramount importance to me. In twenty years I have only ever been late twice – once by just 5 minutes and the guests hadn't arrived; and once because my car was clamped.

I have friends who I work with and from experience they consider leaving at the last minute and arriving just before a booking as being fine. To me that's not good. There are so many ways a journey can be disrupted, and simply blaming it doesn't cut it with me. If you'd anticipated the problem in the first place, instead of leaving at the last possible moment there would be a buffer. If my reputation is dependent on arriving to an event with someone else, I'll want to leave early, and I'll soon stop working with people who are unreliable, as this will tarnish my reputation.

For me, arriving early allows me to prepare for the event calmly and it certainly impresses clients.

Even though I am consistently on time, I am always prepared in case of the unexpected. Whenever I'm out I'll have contact details of the person I'm seeing, even if my laptop were to crash on me I've always got a backup method of finding out where I'm meant to be.

A magician friend of mine had his laptop stolen in the foyer of a hotel, right from under his nose. The irony wasn't lost on either of us that it was funny him been a magician and it disappeared in front of his eyes. We can laugh about it now, but at the time it proved catastrophic to his business.

Learning is an active process

What I have learnt over the years is look at what your business friends are doing and never be afraid to adopt the good ideas they employ in your own business. Equally important is to listen to the stories of when things went wrong, and apply their error to your situation and see if you can learn from it as well.

When I first started I made reflective notes on what was good after every job, and what was not. This was an extremely good habit to get into, and I still do it to this day, but it's more in my head than on paper now. The process of reflection is so important to learning.

Reputation is built on rapport

It really costs nothing to be nice to everyone you encounter on a job. The receptionist is a person too, and just important as 'The Client'. So is the cleaner, or the waiter, or any of the people that somehow seem to become invisible when we are trying to impress the person paying our invoice.

But the impression we make with any one of the people might affect us in the future. Who knows, maybe the boss's wife was covering reception, or their son was doing some cleaning. Even if that's not the case, don't you think it's possible these people talk about you to each other when you've gone? Make conversation with them all, build some rapport and let the abiding memory of your visit be a good one.

The same applies when networking, or in any business situation. Don't get too hung up on trying to find and talk only to the movers and shakers. Try not to pigeonhole people as a waste of your time or write them off. First impressions take a few seconds to form, and they can often be so wrong. Talk to everyone (or as many as you can in the time you have), because you might do business with them at some time in the future if they have a good impression of you. You might even make some friends along the way.

Avoid “me, me, me” and “I this, I that”, and us the word “we”. Working as a team is mega important. Build teams with the people that you meet in business. Develop relationships that benefit all of you.

Quality comes from consistently doing things well, and on time. Reputation comes from consistently providing quality. That’s what I’ve built my business on, and it spills over into my family life as well.

“Thank you” is the cherry on the icing on the cake. It costs nothing, and conveys everything. Thank you for your business. Thank you for your work. Thank you for trusting me with your design. Thank you for reading this article. Thank you for buying this book.

Picasso Griffiths is a freelance Illustrator, Animator and Entertainer, working in numerous styles from caricature to corporate graphics. Soon to be published in his own right, he has helped numerous companies bring their annual reports, sales literature and events to life.

Twitter: @picassogrif
Facebook: www.facebook.com/picasso.griffiths
www.picassogriffiths.com

Rahim Mastafa: Why Every Business Needs a Corporate Video

Long gone are the days where a business could get by with just some text and photos on their website. Or hope that word of mouth and a good reputation would be enough to draw in new and repeat business. If a business is to stand out from the crowd, it needs to do this in such a way that will make an impact.

One of the best ways to make just such an impact and have others remember you, is with an impressive and memorable corporate video. I say 'memorable' deliberately, but memorable for the right reason. A lot of people think 'boring' when they think corporate videos. They link them with long, dull, videos with someone droning on about a particular subject they are not even interested in.

However, things have changed. We live in the age of HD and 3D! Your clients' expectations have changed. And you need to satisfy their expectations. Their attention spans have changed too. We live in the age of the instant download, live streaming, *Dropbox*, the Cloud and viral videos. A video can be a worldwide sensation in just a few days! People don't want to wait a long time to get what they want. So, getting your company's message out there, with the use of a memorable corporate video is vital to the future success of your business!

Choosing your message

What are you trying to say? What do you want your potential clients or customers to know about your business. Who is your client, your market? These are just some of the things you should consider when preparing a corporate video.

You should think of your video as an advert. If you think of TV adverts, they are short. Let's disregard for the moment American infomercials that go on for ages. Most TV adverts are under 30 seconds, and you can't deny their power. Really strip your message down to the least amount it can be, yet still give your client everything they need. Depending on the subject of course, your video can be anything from thirty seconds to about two minutes. As I said, people's attention span is short. Get your message in as soon as possible.

Think of a way to get your message across in a fun and informative way. People like humour, in most cases. So, if it's appropriate to your business, add some humour.

Also, you don't have to do the obvious. I hate to use the old cliché, but really try to think outside of the box. Can you tell your message in a way that isn't even related to your line of business? You'd be amazed at what works and what people remember. What does a gorilla playing the drums to a Phil Collins track have to do with chocolate? If you've seen the ad, you are likely to remember it because it is so extraordinary. Don't be ordinary, you'll be quickly forgotten.

What is your budget?

You might think that a corporate video will cost thousands of pounds, and you are right, they can. But, they don't have to. Really, the sky is the limit when it comes to how much a corporate video will cost, but it's up to you to set a budget and produce something to that amount.

You might want to use flashy graphics, commercial music, a celebrity and have 'the works'. But, is this really necessary? Think of a way of simplifying your video. Imagine trying to sell your product using a gorilla playing a Phil Collins track on the drums. No, don't do that exactly. *Cadbury's* won't be very happy.

Sometimes, it's the simple things that work the best. But, if you have the time and the money, by all means go for the works!

Who should make your corporate video?

This is an important decision. There are a lot of production companies out there offering their services. Depending on your budget, you will most likely want to choose a company with a solid track record and an impressive client list.

However, this can often wind up costing you more than you can afford. Sometimes, it can be worth your while to shop around. It's not always the best option to go for the more established, bigger production companies. You will find that there are freelancers out there who are more than able to produce a quality video for you, at a cost that may surprise you.

For instance, I personally know of someone who produced graphics for a TV show I worked on that was broadcast in America, simply by being discovered by some of his work he posted on *Youtube*. You might be surprised at what people can do, which can save you a lot of money.

Having said that, there are obvious benefits of going with bigger, more established companies: manpower, experience, contacts, insurance, etc.

There are many companies out there you can *Google*, but even placing a request on *Twitter* or *Facebook* can bring a lot of talent your way… there is a plenty out there.

Preparing your corporate video

So, let's say you've decided what your message is going to be, and you have found a company or person will produce your video, what other things should you consider? Well, one of the first things you'll want to think about is pre-production.

The longer you spend in pre-production, the smoother the shoot and edit of your video will be.

Have a plan. Perhaps create a storyboard of your video if it is going to be complex. Have structure in place.

Go through all the fine details. Are you going to film in a studio or on location? If on location, what if it rains? Do you have a back-up plan?

Have you settled on the duration of your video? Having a shorter video doesn't always mean a shorter shoot and edit, so make sure you agree with the production company how long they will take to produce it. Just one extra day of production, be that when filming or editing, can be very expensive. So try to eliminate any possible interruptions to your schedule.

Ask about any other hidden expenses, such as paying for travel expenses. Or perhaps when editing the video, will they charge you for storage space of the footage? Little things like this can cost a lot if you don't know about them in advance. Get the complete picture before you commit to production.

Pre-production is an important part of the process. So many times I have worked on a project and had the client change his mind about certain things after the shoot was finished and things had to be cobbled together in the edit, which can result in an inferior product. So, plan it all.

In conclusion

If you want to increase exposure to your business and attract new customers, a good corporate video is the way to go.

Plan it, think about the message, find a good person or company who can produce it and then use it in as many ways as possible. Get a version for the web, a version on DVD and/or *BluRay* for exhibitions, or to play on screens in the office or where customers may see it. There are lots of ways you can get people to see your video.

So, go and make one, and remember to keep it short, informative, fun and memorable.

Rahim Mastafa is a freelance editor and cameraman, with many years of experience in the corporate and broadcast sectors who has worked for ITV, S4C, MTV, Sky News, and currently the BBC. Corporate video clients include Sony, Nissan, The European Central Bank, The European Parliament, The Wales Tourist Board, npower, The Foreign Press Association, The European Commission, The Crown Prosecution Service, and The National Assembly for Wales.

@RahimMastafa
www.youtube.com/user/RMVideoeditor

Rebecca Parsley: Tips to Finding the Media Spotlight

"Publicity is absolutely critical. A good PR story is infinitely more effective than a front-page ad." So said Richard Branson – and he knows a thing or two about business.

But what is PR, and why do you need it? The CIPR – *Chartered Institute of Public Relations* – defines it thus: "The planned and sustained effort to establish and maintain goodwill and mutual understanding between an organisation and its publics." In other words, it's what you do and what you say and how others perceive you as a result.

PR isn't a direct sales tool, but it's essential for raising your profile, establishing your brand and getting your messages 'out there' – to the right people and in the right way. It's a way of shouting about your success, positioning yourself as an expert. Ultimately, it helps build a stronger and more successful business.

It would be impossible to cover PR in a single chapter, so I've focused on what is still a key area for many small businesses looking to build their own profile – getting yourself and/or your company into the media.

If you want coverage in newspapers, on the radio, or online, you're going to have to contact some journalists. Contrary to popular belief, they're all human (and most of them are jolly nice people). However, there are a few guidelines you'd do well to follow in order to maximise your chances of success and avoid getting their newshound's hackles up. Here are some of them...

Is it news?

Getting an independent third party to talk about you and your business is powerful. Saying how fantastic you are in an advert you've paid for doesn't have the same clout as someone without partiality saying it for you. Traditionally that's meant column inches or airtime and, while the digital revolution means the number of potential PR platforms has vastly increased, the rules have remained pretty much the same.

If you want to make the headlines, you need to offer a decent story. "Look at me...I'm brilliant at what I do" isn't one. Neither is "I've started a new business". What you need is a 'hook', something that will catch a journalist's eye and make them think you're worth talking about. "One of my clients is an Olympic gold medalist" or "I've just started a new business that's created 10 jobs for local people in a town where unemployment is well above average" is far more interesting.

Take a look at your business, at what's going on in it. Do you have new contracts to shout about, are you celebrating ten years of trading? Start small – you're not aiming straight for the nationals. That new staff appointment might only make a couple of paragraphs on the business page of your local paper – but it's still getting your name in front of people who might not have seen it otherwise.

Targeting

Here's a true story. I met someone recently who couldn't understand why nothing that happened at her business was deemed worthy of news coverage. Some months earlier the premises had undergone a massive, multi-million pound refurbishment - but nothing had appeared in the local or regional media, on or offline. I was surprised too - at first.

Her PR was, at that time, controlled by a parent organisation. They'd sent out a blanket press release with the headline "New Mayor enjoys cup of tea at ABC Business during first week in office."

Now I could tell her exactly why there'd been no coverage. Journalists are busy people. If you're on the news desk receiving a couple of hundred emails a day, you don't want to read to the bottom of each one to see if there's a story worth finding. You want the salient points to smack you in the face right from the start.

So the regional daily paper, whose business desk would have loved a piece about how the organisation was investing in the future of the region and helping the local economy (I know because I spoke to them) binned the release because all it saw was the mayor having a cuppa.

The local weekly paper found more photogenic appointments in the new mayor's diary than visiting an office block for no apparent reason, so they didn't bother either. It was a similar story for the town's radio station.

Targeting is essential for gaining media coverage. Yes, it means a bit more work to produce several versions of the same story – but you're going to get far better results.

"ABC Business marks 20 years of trading with £3.5 million refurb" would have got column inches in one paper, while a nicely composed photograph of the new mayor meeting the longest-serving members of staff or similar would have helped in another.

The moral – know your audience and tailor your PR efforts accordingly.

Spelling, grammar and jargon

This is my personal hobby-horse and I make no apologies for getting on it. I admit I'm more obsessed than most, but I have in my time decided against using a business or service provider due to the appalling quality of their literature or website copy.

This also applies to your media releases; journalists are a pretty pedantic lot who hate random apostrophes and badly-spelled text. They're pressed for time and will often spike something that might have made a couple of paragraphs, had it not needed an hour's editing to turn it into something readable.

There's no excuse for not spell-checking what you write. Granted, your brain reads what it expects to see and it's difficult to see mistakes in your own work... so get somebody else to read it too. If you can, hire a professional proof-reader / copy editor to make sure it's as good as it can be – or get them to write it in the first place.

The same goes for jargon. The same acronym can stand for different things to different people in different industries, and anyone on the outside is likely to be completely confused. Never assume people know what you mean.

One of the best tips I ever received was to write as though I was trying to make a child understand. You don't need to use long words to try and sound clever – keep it simple and straightforward. Say 'start' instead of 'commence'. And always, always check you know your *there's* from your *theirs*!

Attention to detail – in everything you write – is key.

A picture paints a thousand words

A real truism. In newspapers in particular, as resources decrease, a fantastic photograph can get an otherwise run-of-the-mill story star billing.

The best example I can recall was in the *Yorkshire Post* several years ago. The story was pretty dull; in fact, I can't remember exactly what it was, but it involved *The Deep* – a marine attraction in Hull – and some business event or other. It was the image that made it – taken through the shark tank, it looked as though the group of suited businessmen was inside it with them. Stunning. It got the best part of a broadsheet page – and even though the story is long-gone, at least one person (me) is still talking about *The Deep* as a result.

Just as everyone thinks they can write, they also think that – thanks to smartphones – they can take pictures. They can, after a fashion... but if you want true creativity, better quality and a stab at decent coverage, use a professional photographer.

There are some practicalities to remember, too. For print media, supply a jpeg image that's at least 400KB for newspapers, 750KB for magazines. For online, it can be much smaller – 100KB or less.

Try not to send the same picture to each outlet and if you can supply a choice of both vertical and horizontal, even better.

People sell, not buildings, so get some faces in there and don't forget a caption. A simple: "From left – local resident John Smith, store manager Jane Jones and driver Tom Thumb" is fine. Include first and last names, and mention titles/positions when relevant.

Distribution, deadlines and follow up

We've all done it. Sent an email into the ether and then fretted about whether it's been received. Should we call to check? Will they think we're a nuisance?

Let's start with sending out your release – to a named person if you can, and personalise the message. I'd recommend copying and pasting text into the body of an email rather than attaching a document. It cuts a step out for the journalist and, if they use industry-specific software, they can't necessarily access it. I freelanced for a newspaper where, until a couple of years ago, you had to forward documents to the one person with software to open them. Sometimes you might call before you send your release, to ascertain if they're interested or try and persuade them they are – whole separate chapter!

Either way, there's no harm in following up to check they've received it – but pick your moment. There's nothing more annoying than being on a deadline and someone ringing to say: "Did you get my press release? Are you going to use it?"

If the radio station has bulletins on the hour, don't call at two minutes to. If the paper comes out on Thursday, chances are Wednesday afternoons are pretty fraught. And remember they've received at least 50 other press releases that day and won't instantly recall yours.

If they're not interested, accept it. If it's a yes, thank them and check they have your contact details in case they need more information. If they do, make sure you respond to any deadline. If you don't, your story could get dropped and you'll be pegged as unreliable.

Don't pester them to tell you exactly when it will be used, and *never* demand to approve copy before it's printed / aired. That only happens when you're paying.

If your story doesn't appear, don't give them a hard time. Sometimes better or more important news happens, copy gets stripped out, and items get dropped. It's disappointing, but haranguing the reporter won't help. It's unlikely to be their fault and chances are you've got a better shot with your next story because you've been let down.

The other thing you shouldn't do is ask them to check if your story has been used and send you a copy/sound clip. Journalists aren't there to act as your personal cuttings agency – if you think it's going in the paper, buy a copy; if it's likely to be on the radio, listen in or 'listen again'.

Come here, there's more...

There are other areas of PR we haven't even touched on. How you communicate with your staff or suppliers, how you use social media and even the significance of branded vehicles are all areas that merit discussion. Not to mention crisis management and why "No comment" should never be an option. But that's another story...

Rebecca Parsley is a Partner at Montpellier Media Services, based in North Yorkshire – a creative, dynamic communications agency run by former journalists that offers strategic, multi-platform solutions to enhance and manage clients' reputations both on and offline

@MontpellMedia
www.montpelliermedia.co.uk

Robert Lang: Self-Employment: Rebuilding a Life

I suspect that it's true for many people who are self-employed that the option to take that route was in part, if not wholly, forced upon them by circumstance. Or, if that isn't completely the case, maybe as the result of a mixture of both circumstance and the realisation that enough was enough in the hard cruel world of being employed to do a job from which little real satisfaction was ever derived.

That was true for me and I know my case is not unusual. I had been recently divorced. My employer was sympathetic inasmuch as they had to be seen to be so, but utterly uncaring and thoroughly and uncompromisingly vicious when I returned to work after an enforced absence following a break down.

I recovered from the latter, ultimately, upon realising that I had now to take my life in to my own hands and make it work. The key point was the day I said, both to myself and to others – from now on I am going to live according to what I truly feel and believe I am good at and via that approach I will be a better and more fulfilled human being.

Eighteen months later I was able to leave my employment of 21 years, with some redundancy money, and having already established the framework of a business. Six months after that I registered as self-employed and I have been trading now for almost a full year. I'm looking forward to filling out a tax return – now that must mean it was the right decision!

It's worth looking back at that year as I wonder to what extent my experience is reflected in that of others'. I work from home, a situation I will comment further on, but I don't do so by choice. Like many fathers who have lost their home in a divorce settlement I rent accommodation and my flat is small. Fortunately my landlord and landlady are wonderful people who have allowed me to convert the flat as I see fit into a working environment and I should say that, despite the bijoux nature of the accommodation, I do live in a wonderful community where the support for my business and my long term aims with it has been tremendous. That is invaluable. I just don't have and can't afford any storage space.

I'm a poet. That's not an easy concept to sell as a business and I've shifted the emphasis where appropriate to "copy writer".

I set up a website (there are now two) and I went out networking, chiefly with *4Networking*. I was never very good at "mingling" let alone having to mingle and try to present a convincing business pitch at the same time. I went to my first meeting with another group, *Intro Biz* in Cardiff, to be roundly condemned as worthless by the first person I was introduced to – a chap subsequently discovered to be not very popular with very many people – he certainly succeeded in terrifying me and making me feel completely out of my depth.

However, surely the one key ingredient you must have when starting a business is perseverance. So I didn't give up. After six months getting to know people I renewed my networking membership with a plan – to be more pro-active and to travel a little to promote my business further afield. I have done both, though perhaps not as diligently as I planned and, I have to confess, I lack consistency in following up new contacts; which I accept is a short-coming I need to work on.

My perseverance has brought me a little business but not much. I am convinced that that is because my work and its value needs better explaining than can be achieved at such meetings, which are far too busy in their nature for me to a) properly explain what I do and b) have the time to also convince listeners of the quality of what I do. Also, although many who have met me might not believe it, I remain very uncomfortable explaining myself.

So, I've turned more to social media. I like *Twitter* and I've come to grips with *Facebook*. I'm working hard on *LinkedIn*. I paid for training on *Hootsuite* because I perceived that might be the most useful, but it was a waste of money. I wasn't informed that I needed to be using a certain level of membership and by the time that was set up for me on the day of the training I'd missed the key crucial instruction on how to use the site. But these things happen. I have been advised *Hootsuite* has a good "university" and there is nothing to stop me looking there.

In truth though the two biggest challenges I have had to overcome this last year have been: 1) Fear that *I'm* not good enough; and 2) Fear that the *business* isn't good enough. I'm sure many others have been through that.

My greatest support has come from two small children – mine of course – who enjoy my poetry and try very hard to understand my business. They even attended a networking meeting where my eldest introduced herself with the lines "I do school and I'm looking for people to give me sweets and toys".

My "office" is regularly shared by my visiting children, aged 9 and 7 who love to fight, dance, jump on the furniture and, their latest favourite, play a game called either "restaurants" or, as was the case a few days ago, and in its more dangerous version *Come Dine With Me*. This involves a total rearrangement of my flat and all the various piles of paper – which usually just go temporarily on the bed – in order to provide any number of clear surfaces which can be denoted "tables" for "diners". I do not stop these games because I have two wonderfully imaginative children and their interpretations and character creations (especially the kitchen rows between "chefs" and "front of house") leave me rolling in the aisles.

I also don't object because I am not permanently in their lives. It is essential that the time we have together is put to maximum use for their benefit and pleasure – even if that means the floor is covered with tiny shreds of paper of all colours, otherwise known as "restaurant meals".

So, I live with it all and after they have left I diligently return my home to a semblance of a working environment, with all the piles of paper stacked a bit more tidily and perhaps even with some put away. Then I sit down and I smile. Sometimes too, I look at my website with my eldest doing a testimonial on video. She certainly supports my work and both she and her sister continue to be its greatest inspiration.

I've written elsewhere about my problems with telecommunications in the last year. Everyone suffers it seems, so I will spare readers a further diatribe recounting that tragedy now. Ultimately, and I'm sure others will recognise this, the first year of being in business for myself has been a trial of resolve. I've made a large loss when costs are set against income, but I accept that that's normal and I did budget for it.

What I've gained is an ability to trust my own judgment more. It's not complete and I'll still make mistakes I'm sure, but it's a good feeling. I used to question everything I said and did and usually concluded that I must be wrong. Now I ask – was that right – and most times after thinking about it I'm able to say "Yes".

So I'm growing, just as I'd hoped. It's also true that in one year I've met more people whose company I really do enjoy and whose attitude is so obviously genuine and well meaning, than I did in 21 years in my previous employment. That's not so shocking though – I was a civil servant!

Self-employment came unexpectedly but necessarily into my life and I'm glad it did. People often say "I will succeed" as though just by saying it and believing it they will. I don't subscribe to that view. My perception is more that I *have* to succeed – both for myself and others around me – and there's no real reason that I shouldn't. It is up to me and it's about continued perseverance, patience and acknowledging that I'm capable of sound decision making that's fair and supportable.

In the film *Booze Cruise 2 – The Treasure Hunt*, an otherwise not very likeable successful businessman nonetheless delivers a terrific line when, remonstrating with another character, he says: *"...for you it's anything for a quiet life whereas for me it's anything for a better life".* I like that, taken as it stands and excluding any skullduggery, and take it as my mantra for the next year – it will be tougher than the first I suspect, but that doesn't mean it won't be better.

Robert Lang, a.k.a. The Modern Day Poet, writes poetry to commemorate special occasions, weddings, and for corporate commissions. He also writes copy for websites and advertising slogans, as well as offering writing workshops and recitals.

Twitter: @roberthepoet
www.themoderndaypoet.com

Sam O'Sullivan: Healthy Body, Healthy Business

People in business believe that, in order to be successful, they must put their business first. The business becomes the driving force, but people often forget that they are the business in many cases. I'm a huge believer in making yourself, as the person at the forefront of your business, the best you can possibly be. If you want to be successful you must invest in yourself, both physically and psychologically.

For me, being fit and healthy is the most critical factor in being successful in business. If you are fit and healthy you will be able to cope with the physical demands of building an expansive company far more successfully. It certainly isn't all rainbows and sunshine when starting out. From personal experience, I was working sixteen-hour days and putting my body under high levels of oxidative stress.

I combated the high levels of oxidative stress by ensuring I had healthy nutritional intake and participated in regular physical activity and exercise.

We get ill because of a build-up of free radicals in our system, caused by all sorts of things: long working hours, lack of sleep, bad food choices, emotional stress, alcohol, recreational drugs, cigarettes, plus many more. Too many free radicals in our system and bad things start to happen. These can include small things like lethargy, chronic fatigue, poor skin (acne), inflammation that can lead to lots of inflammatory problems within the body, illness (coughs, colds, fevers), or at a more severe level, disease. None of these things will help if you're in business.

What people don't realise is that simple, small changes, such as eating healthy food with balanced meals, can combat the free radicals and leave you feeling fit, healthy, and energised. This maximises your chance of being successful in business. At the end of the day, if your unable to look after yourself, why should potential customers believe you are capable of taking care of their needs?

Think of it like this:

Your body is your business, so look after it.

Your health is a direct reflection of your relationship with your body, so treat that relationship with maximum care, attention, and respect. You'll maximise your success in business and life if you do.

Healthy and fit people have energy and vitality. With increased energy, you can focus on your short and long-term goals both in business and in life to ensure you are successful.

Here are my top five tips to ensure you set yourself up for success:

1. Get exercise advice from a Personal Trainer to ensure you're not wasting any time with your exercise routine. Maximise your efficiency with your training so that you maximise the rewards in less time. If you have not got a spare hour in your day, you can get a 20-minute workout in before or after work. You could even squeeze one into your lunch hour. I see so many people wasting time with their exercise routines. If you're in business, time is money, so don't be that person.
2. Have breakfast every morning. Breakfast is the most important meal of the day and will set you up for success. Avoid sugary cereals and opt for nutrient rich foods. Fruit, natural yoghurt, oats, and eggs are all great options.
3. Drink 2-3 litres of fresh, filtered water each day. 70% of your body is made up of water. Dehydration can cause lethargy, a lack of concentration, and a lowering of the body's metabolism. Don't make this silly mistake.
4. Have 'you' time every day. Make sure it isn't all work, work, work. To be successful you must have a work life balance. Book out time in your diary to do things for *you*. It could be simply taking a walk in your lunch hour, or going to the cinema with friends. 'You' time is a chance for you to step out of the business and reflect on its success. If you're always in it, you can't have this outlook.
5. Maximise travelling time in the car by listening to audio CDs that work on you. As Jim Rohn says: *"For things to get better, you've got to get better. So don't waste this valuable time listening to the radio or you're favourite music. This is an ideal opportunity to have a self-help coach to improve your mind-set."*

If you can start following the five principles above, and do them consistently, you will change your life. The compound effect of the above principles will be enormous if they are done consistently for a long enough period. Don't expect to do these principles for a day, a week, or even a month and expect huge changes. However, if you do them for six months, and then a year, and then a decade you will maximise the way people see you. If people like you because you are fun, energetic, healthy, and give off a sense of confidence and vibrancy, people will want to do business with you.

Sam O'Sullivan is the Owner of SOS Executive Personal Training Company, and a qualifying National Marketing Director at NSA (Juice Plus+).

Twitter: @sam_sos_pt
Facebook: www.facebook.com/SamOSullivanPersonalTraining

Sian Bick:
Storage Tips for Small Business

For the small business, storage can be an issue. The challenge of getting the right space, at the right cost, can mean the difference between survival and failure, and almost every business needs storage, whether it is for stock, equipment or documentation. The good news is that business storage is evolving, with more flexible options opening up. Smaller businesses are also thinking more cleverly when it comes to the space they need. Here are five things to consider, to help you make the most of your storage space.

1. Security, security, security

Whatever you need to store for your business, you must ensure it will be securely stored. Not all self-storage companies are the same. Look out for

- individually alarmed rooms
- are accessed via your own PIN code
- 24 hour CCTV
- staff on site seven days a week
- secure perimeter fencing
- storage buildings are modern, clean, and equipped with smoke detectors and fire alarms
- good parking and access.

2. Plan for overspill

Whether you're an eBay seller or a traditional retailer, planning for the unplanned is vital. Most businesses don't consider overspill until it's too late, but by future-proofing your storage needs, you can make sure you have a cost effective solution. The main benefit of using self-storage facilities is flexibility. This means you use just the space you need for the time you need it. Whether you need it now or not, look for a self-storage facility that allows you to upsize or downsize your storage space without a penalty if your stock levels fluctuate.

3. Don't get tied into long contracts

No one knows what the future holds, and making sure your business isn't locked into long contracts will help you stay flexible. With warehouses you'll need to consider the necessary evils of business rates, service charges, utilities, maintenance, up-front deposits and contract lengths. This outlay can make it unappealing, especially for start-ups wanting low overheads. Self-storage companies may be a more cost effective and flexible solution, especially if they are 'all inclusive' and have security, utilities and maintenance all included in the price.

4. Create a distribution hub

Many businesses, from mail order sellers to large ecommerce sellers – add unnecessary extra steps when turning around stock by separating the storage and distribution processes. Working in the storage space can help streamline distribution - all your stock is in one place, so no need for additional transport.

The important factor is to have additional space to work in. Most people only think of storage in terms of the physical space they need for storage and not the room to manoeuvre. By ensuring there is space to unpack, repack and segment different types of stock, you can better harness your storage space without needing additional rooms for distribution.

5. Don't go off-grid

Location is vitally important when it comes to your storage space. Consider safe, brightly lit locations that have main road access, free parking and the ability to drive your vehicle right up to loading bays. You should also enquire if there is free use of trolleys and pallet trucks and if a forklift service is provided. Choose the right storage company and it will be like having an extra pair of hands. Some may also be happy to accept deliveries on your behalf, store them securely, and let you know when they have arrived. But if you don't ask for this, you might not get it.

Sian Bick can be found at Big Yellow Self Storage in Cardiff, who offer secure storage, flexible office space and packaging. Big Yellow Storage has 76 locations nationwide.

02920 729910
www.bigyellow.co.uk

Sibel McColm: From Hobby to Business

What woman doesn't like wearing a piece of jewellery of some kind? Whether it is motifs or buttons, brooches or sparkles attached to hats, shoes, or bags. The answer has got to be, for every woman, surely "yes!"

From a very young age, I have been very passionate about sparkly things, and this is how it all started for me as a hobby. As a child, I stopped outside every jewellery shop. I even read books about pirates so that I could read about all that jewellery they found.

A couple of years ago, I came across a tiny advert for a jewellery course. I attended the course for a year and I never looked back. Luckily, I came across a fantastic old-fashioned teacher who saw my potential, gently encouraging me, and my passion grew even more. I have attended many other courses since, and my expertise has grown quickly, from simple strung necklaces to complex bead embroidered jewellery.

I was originally just making jewellery for myself and friends, but, as people began to notice my work, they admired them and wanted me to make them the same style, but in a different colour. Following this, people began to ask if I had a website, and this is how my hobby turned into a business.

I learned just how hard it can be, moving from a hobby to a commercial enterprise. Be warned, it can be a bumpy ride, full of unexpected pitfalls, but also some exciting highs.

Getting started

You have to have enough start up funds in order to buy enough stock, materials, equipping your workspace, marketing materials, advertising, events, phone, travel, etc. It all adds up, and you need to budget realistically, and then double the amount you come up with.

- Decide on a name for your new company and stick with it.
- Advise *HMRC* that you are self-employed, which can be done online. They will ask you to complete a very short, simple form. This is so that you can pay tax on your earnings.
- Find a good accountant as soon as possible, so that s/he can advise you from the beginning what you need to do, what records to keep, and other financial implications.

Self-organisation

After working for many years for an international bank, I have found working for myself so completely different. As with any small business owner, I suddenly became the designer, artist, buyer, seller, market researcher, bookkeeper, whatever it took. I have learned that I needed to be a good multi-tasker, as sometimes it gets very busy, but loads of different things will need attention.

From day one, I set myself a target and working hours, because that's what I knew best from my corporate days. Monday to Friday, worked 8 am - 1 pm, lunch, gym, and then back to my home office and try to find inspiration by looking at famous beaders and artist's work, or from my own bead collection. Then get some ideas on paper and start beading, and try to create something which will be liked by some people.

It is important to have a space where you can work at home and keep all your items relating to your business. Keeping work and home separate was key for me to avoid working too far into the night too many times. You'll need to be not only self-motivated, but also organised when you move from your hobby to business. It's one thing playing at what you do, it's another making it pay. With a hobby, you don't have to do anything if you don't want to, however, when it's your livelihood, you do.

Working alone

At first I found it very lonely, but *Facebook* was my saviour, as I built up some very good connections and friends, and it has helped me learn and sell my items online. So, think about your support network: if you are having to spend more time doing your hobby (and all the other things associated with it being a business), who will you talk to, and how will you cope with this element of being self-employed?

I have learned that, on *Facebook*, it's give and take. I was able to give some tips, and in return I got some help when I needed it.

Looking the part

You need to have the right image, so you need to have business cards and the right equipment to do whatever you do on a more commercial scale. The equipment you used as a hobbyist may not cut the mustard when it comes to producing more, or higher quality products. You need to prepare yourself before you go public with your business. Every time you are out and about, every time you meet a potential supplier or customer, you are on show, and so is your business. You never get a second chance to make a first impression, so make sure it's good.

Defining your style

Initially, it was difficult to define my own style, but, after a while, I created a look that reflected what I wanted to create. Whatever it is that you make or do, you'll need to differentiate yourself from the crowd. I would, however, advise when moving from hobby to business to have a definite idea of their style, or whatever makes them different and memorable.

Finding buyers

When I first started selling my jewellery, I was still employed, and I used to do a craft fair once a month, where some of the profit was going to the chosen charity of the bank. This gave me confidence and prepared me for craft fairs. This was a limited success, as I knew most people when I was in the bank, but moving out into the wider world was not so successful. I went to a number of fairs, but didn't find them profitable, plus they were very tiring. At the end of the day, I found it cost me money to sell at these events.

I went to a few shops that sell jewellery, and I did sell through them quite a bit, but they slashed the prices because of their overheads, and it became a little scary at the time as I had to produce 25-30 pieces in the space of 3 months; that represented a big order, and a lot of hours to produce, but for a very thin profit. I produce one-off pieces rather than mass-produced, so I found this was not for me, and I didn't pursue this type of outlet to sell my products. I now have a shop on *www.Etsy.com*, along with other small businesses, who provide support for each other; everyone drives potential customers to one place, and I benefit from that.

When you are marketing your products or services, think carefully about where your buyers are. What do they look like? At first, I thought my potential customer was "anyone who likes jewellery." However, that view has changed as I've learned from my mistakes and found out the hard way, that making jewellery is one thing, and consistently selling it is a completely different matter.

Pricing

I found it very difficult to charge for my items, but recently, I joined a group discussion on a networking forum and found that other people who started in business also found it difficult, as I did. But it is so important to correctly price up your product or service to make a profit. If it is too low, it could be construed by your competition as price cutting, which could start a price war which nobody wins. It also demeans the quality of your work if you don't value it highly enough.

If you do insist on giving your stock away cheaply, or even for free, you need to ensure there's a business reason for doing it, not an emotional one. I fell for sob stories, and doing favours for friends. It might have made me look good, but it didn't really get me much business. I found people have got an idea as to how much they would like to pay for a piece, and if that item is below the figure in their minds, they think that item is cheaply made and not worth buying; therefore, you lose their custom anyway.

Since I have set the correct market price for my items, it has gained more interest and buyers. I have created a spreadsheet together with a friend with the correct formulas, which includes beads, time spent on making each type of item, and overheads etc. Now I get a more accurate cost price for every item I produce. It's not perfect, but it shows me in black and white how much it actually costs, and how much I really need to charge to have a business, instead of running a charity where I end up giving it away for free. As a result, I feel better about myself in the process. This is very important for anyone in any kind of business.

Conclusion

I have found that, if you treat your customers with respect, they come back time and time again; however, I find you need to keep up with the fashion and the times, all the while creating something different that cannot be found on the high street.

I have learned that online businesses are growing, and I am looking forward to growing my online business and doing less craft fairs. More importantly, I am looking now at publishing tutorials on how to make some of the creations I have produced. I've already done this a couple of times, and sold some. I can see this as being a potentially excellent use of my time. I can create something that can sell many times, instead of a single piece of jewelry that sells only once.

My journey so far has been interesting, sometimes costly, sometimes frustrating. But at the end of the working day I am in charge of my own destiny, something I could never say when I was just a small cog in a very big machine.

To all those who had the disease and won

Sibel McColm is the Owner of Bijoux Delights, who design and hand-make beaded jewellery. Sibel also creates original designs and sells tutorials for other beaders to use.

07986 017252
www.etsy.com/shop/BijouxDelights
Facebook: www.facebook.com/Bijoux-Delights

Steve Abel: Staying Focused

As someone who has now reached the point where I have a successful business, which largely operates without me needing to be there all day, every day, I was recently asked to write a book about my experiences. That became *Big Fish, Little Fish*, a book about how to stay focused on achieving what you really want. I'd like to think this could help with life, not just with business – and I've personally used these techniques, so I can recommend them.

Take your sunshine with you

On a scale of one to ten, one being bloody miserable and ten being ecstatically happy, what number are you right now? A number one is when everything is too bad to carry on, you can't get out of bed, you're burying your head in the sand. Picture a number ten – the striker of your favorite football team bouncing down the field with joy after scoring a goal.

Most of us wake up in the morning on a number five. We allow the rotten weather to dictate our mood for the day and drop to a four, but if we open the curtains and it's sunny we're up to a number six. Take control of your life and have more of an influence on the outcome of your day, and then repeat it every day.

Do you notice how we allow a phone call, or bad news on the TV, to affect the rest of our day, or the rest of our week? Do this and you are in no fit state to be making decisions. You're better off staying at home.

Conversely, you get that phone call with news you just got that promotion, you just won that contract or maybe you've just found out you're an uncle or auntie. Your number five on the scale has just shot up to a nine or a ten. You're feeling on top of the world and the rest of the day flies by. You are now in the best state to be working in and on your business. You are automatically becoming a key person of influence. Your passion is coming through, you're glowing and people notice it.

I'm no expert, but I read somewhere a while back, the reason women can remember everything is because they can take an event and then connect it to an emotion, that then burns in their memory and they can remember it forever. Men can do it too, but quite frankly, we're not very good at remembering everything, not unless it's got a strong emotion attached to it.

So, I closed my eyes and got all of my thoughts in front of me. Each thought has a little thumbnail picture, and they're all spread out like icons on my computer desktop. I'm now going to slowly start filing all of these thumbnail icons into two boxes. Keeping my eyes closed and using my hands, I'm taking all of the sad and unhappy thoughts and filing them in a little black box. This box is set down on the left hand side of my mind's eye. It's a very insignificant black box.

Now it's very important you don't forget about these sad thoughts; to be fair, it's not really possible due to the event and emotion that burnt it into your memory in the first place, but some of these sad memories have shaped and moulded you into the person you are today.

Then there's your gold box. All of the other memories and thoughts that you have not filed away in your black box should be happy and positive memories. Memories that when you think back to the day they happened, you can remember you were pushed above a six or a seven on your mood scale. It doesn't need to be gold, but something much more significant than the small black box.

Now wouldn't it be great if every morning we could take our gold box down from its shelf, crack open the lid and reflect on all of those successful memories, but reflect on them in the same way we did the day they happened?

Think yourself stronger

Time to force a new habit. For the next three months, commit to spending five minutes every morning reflecting on your happy memories. You'll feel a little stupid – it's just not deemed as socially acceptable, which is why we're not comfortable with it. After three or four weeks of forcing something, it naturally becomes a habit. Without reminding myself I'd find myself every morning around 6.30am reflecting on my happy memories and thoughts, and applying an anchor move too.

This is something Anthony Robbins taught me. The anchor move reinforces the exercise with physiology. It's similar to Usain Bolt's iconic pose, but when my hands are stretched out, I spring them back in and clap my hands. Once the hands clap and pass each other, I've programmed my mind to celebrate, which pushes me straight to a ten on the mood scale.

So once my hands clap and pass each other I am instantly in the zone, and experiencing the effects of being at a number ten on the mood scale. Remember what I said about the football player? He doesn't just score and walk slowly back down the field, he runs and jumps back down the field punching the air, acknowledging his achievement.

The fact is we're all using anchors right now; we all have a song or two, that when it's played on the radio it takes us straight back to the emotional experience attached to an event. This is the reason many couples have 'their song', it's probably because it was playing in the background the day they met, or when they first kissed. Every time thereafter when that song is played it just reinforces the anchor.

So, why not create our own event and apply an anchor to it? This where we gather all our successful memories and get ourselves into level ten state, and then apply an anchor move of our choice. Gradually bring yourself down from your level ten and then do it again. Eventually your brain will be able to recognise just the anchor instead of relying on you to gather your thoughts, to get you to a ten.

If you can tap into that feeling every time you want to perform at your best, then maybe this power move is the answer. It's not a 'fake it to make it' approach; I'm just mentally placing myself in the place I was when I was at a number ten.

Goals and rewards

When I set out to create a really successful business, I had to put a business plan together. Until this point, I had never done such a thing and to be honest it's not something I really wanted to do at the time. But it really helped – and I based my plan around a reward system.

Think of something you want, ideally it has to be something that costs money. Now what motivates you more, being asked to do something and getting it as a reward at the end, or being shown the reward and promised it if you do the work required to achieve it?

A lot of us operate like this, just that idea of getting away to that dream destination is enough to work for it and put the money aside so you can book it later in the year.

A child will tidy their room for the promise of a lollipop. Seeing *is* believing, and for me is a big key to my own motivation. I call it my 'Lollipop System'.

I got a pen and paper and wrote down a list of the things I wanted; like an *Aston Martin*, a *Sunseeker* yacht, a big house in the countryside with a gated drive, and so on. Dare to dream – and work out how much you'll need to be earning to achieve these things.

If you're thinking this sounds like a complete waste of time, think again. I'm not saying this is the best way to get rich or achieve your ambitions in life, but it's what I did. I was a million miles away from where I wanted to be, but I had point A on one piece of paper and point B on the other. Point A is where I was right at that time. This was easy, I just had to be honest and write down how my life looked right now. Once you have point A and point B, all you have to do now is work out the route and construct a realistic path.

I constructed bite-sized plans, which on paper I allowed three months to achieve each one. It had to be a reward that reflected the size of my company and what I could afford. I was quite flexible with my rewards in the early stages, but I always made sure I'd reward myself something and acknowledge it as a reward.

My three-month bite-sized plans were soon being reached within two months; the whole three-year plan was achieved in two years.

I went to an Anthony Robbins event in 2009, and met one gentleman who seemed to have lost his way and was attending the live seminar to give him a boost. It turned out he was hugely successful already but his own personal goal had not been met yet. He hadn't been keeping on top of his rewards and he had lost momentum, motivation and drive.

But what if the next bite-size chunk doesn't go to plan? What if three months turns out being five months? Plans need to be flexible, to allow for hitting them early, or behind schedule. Just get a reward system in place and stick to it. The thing is, our minds still work like this – but it's on a subconscious level so we're not aware of it. Become aware of it, apply this theory consciously and you'll reap the rewards and become motivated with great momentum.

Steve Abel is a serial entrepreneur, who established eight businesses before having his lightbulb moment, and founding his ninth – Parcels4Delivery. Success has enabled Steve to spend more time speaking, writing and mentoring others. His first book, Big Fish, Little Fish, was published in 2013.

www.steveabel.co.uk

Steve Tasker: The Accountant's Perspective

I made a bold (some may call it stupid) decision to set up my own practice in 2012 with the specific goal of helping and working with small business owners offering my services for anything from a few hours per month to days per week depending upon the needs of each individual business.

Most businesses are categorised by industry sectors and segments but even those operating in the same sector / segment have their own unique characteristics, be it the ambitions, philosophies and management styles of the owners, type of employees or staff, cultures and outlooks on life in general or systems and processes used. This is what makes my job so interesting, as you never know what sort of business you are dealing with until you really get to know its people and systems. In my opinion, producing figures and information without that knowledge results in very little job satisfaction.

My top 10 tips for starting up in business

1. Have a plan – talk to family and friends to gauge opinion and perspectives.
2. Speak to a good accountant – not just when it's time to do your accounts, but regularly to discuss your plans and their implications.
3. Consider carefully your trading structure – sole trader, partnership, limited company (your accountant can advise).
4. Let the tax man know – when you've decided your trading structure and when you are likely to start trading, let HMRC know. Speak to your accountant or the HMRC website is very helpful.
5. Open a bank account – again, when you've decided your trading structure, open a separate bank account for your business. This keeps business and personal transactions separate and 'uncluttered'.
6. Consider registering for VAT – speak to your accountant or go on the HMRC website. You can voluntarily register for VAT irrespective of whether or not you expect to reach the registration threshold (currently £77,000 pa).
7. Don't be afraid to ask for help – too many start-up businesses fail because their owners try to do everything rather than concentrating on what they're good at.
8. Set aside time to check progress and refine your plan – you can guarantee that your original plan will need amending and evolving as time moves on. Be prepared to evolve and keep your goals firmly in your sights.
9. Keep up to date – with technical and professional issues related to your products or services. You can be sure your competitors will be!
10. Keep all records and receipts – a small amount of your time per week keeping basic records and receipts will save time and money when your accountant reviews your figures (hopefully more than once a year!). HMRC also requires businesses to keep adequate records with penalties for failing to do so.

Growing pins – do you recognise any of these symptoms?

- Not enough hours in the day
- Regularly 'firefighting'
- Members of your team(s) unaware of what others are doing
- Members of your team(s) unsure of the direction the business is heading
- Not enough good managers
- 'If I want it done properly, I do it myself'
- Meetings are a waste of time.
- Plans not followed up, therefore nothing gets done
- Insecurity amongst staff
- Sales are increasing but profits are not.

According to Eric Flamholz, Ph.D., these are the 'Ten Most Common Organisational Growing Pains'. Many SMEs experience growing pains during periods of growth and following periods of relative stability. The business owners of those organisations often fail to realise that, rather than seeking help or having the confidence to delegate to or train staff to do many of the key tasks required to run the business, they try to do it all themselves.

All successful businesses have systems and processes which are well documented, with each role defined so that everyone knows what is expected of them and more importantly what impact that role has in producing the desired outcome for the business.

A good example of a desired outcome for any business is satisfied customers who keep returning and willingly recommending the business to others. Sounds simple doesn't it? However, too many fall into the trap of chasing the pot of gold (i.e. growth) without having the systems and structures to support it.

During my career so far, experience has taught me my four golden rules as follows:

Don't panic!

This is often easier said than done. Anyone who has worked for or with me knows that this is always Rule Number 1. I admit it was born out of the famous *Dads Army* quote now well marketed on posters, mugs, t-shirts and countless other items but the sentiment is truly serious.

Through the ages, the victors in battles and wars, key governmental issues, major sporting events etc. have succeeded by keeping their nerve through planning, practice, strength of resolve or faith and yes, sometimes a little luck, but rarely through panicking.

Remember that rational thought is not a natural consequence of panic.

Don't be afraid to make mistakes

Again, this is easier said than done but many of the most successful business people (e.g. Richard Branson) have tried and failed in previous ventures before they came up with a winning formula. Whilst managing individuals and teams, those making mistakes need to be made aware of what has happened. They then need to be asked what one or two things they are going to do to avoid it happening again. If the same mistake is being repeated, this should be resolved through training (or disciplinary action if it proves to be down to lack of concentration or negligence). We all make mistakes; it's how we learn from them that makes the difference.

Always have a plan

I'm well known in my family for constantly planning week by week, month by month, be it for business or personal reasons. Plans invariably change, but without an end result in mind, how are you going to achieve what you want or where you want to get to? As good as they are (and all the other technological advancements being made), sat navs have taken away one of my previous pleasures of planning a journey, so be careful entrusting all to technology alone.

Keep looking ahead

Very closely linked to planning is my mantra of looking ahead. One of the things Management Accountants are trained for is forecasting and anticipating the financial impact of multiple scenarios. Learning from what has already happened and building that into assumptions for future outcomes is an important part of what I try to impart to small business owners to help them grow their businesses and know where they are at any point on their journey.

Steve Tasker is a Chartered Management Accountant with more than 30 years of experience working in the SME sector (with turnovers ranging from £500,000 to £6m).

www.steve-tasker.co.uk

Steve White: Getting Paid is Not a Sin

As a small business owner I fully understand the stresses and strains of running your own company, and keeping on top of everything is hard work!

One of the biggest challenges, I believe, is juggling cash flow. After having made that crucial sale, how frustrating is it to wait... and wait... and wait even longer to get paid. Non-payment of your invoice could lead to pressure on your bank account, pressure on you to raise money personally, or even insolvency or bankruptcy.

Your credit control procedure

Credit control is a vital part of running any business. It sounds like a complex financial process but in reality it is just a set of simple steps taken to ensure you get paid on time. Every business, no matter how large or small, needs to have a credit control process and my top tips are as follows:

- Clearly set out your expectations
- Consider credit checking
- Make it easy to be paid
- Encourage prompt payment
- Have a clear procedure
- Think survival!
- Plan ahead
- Don't accept excuses
- Don't be afraid to take action
- Take control.

Most businesses have had to tighten their belts in the current economic climate and of course no-one wants to lose any hard-earned customers. However, you have worked hard to earn that sale and it is now time for you to get paid for that hard work.

How long do you wait for an invoice that is meant to be payable within 30 days? If it isn't paid in that time do you wait... one day, one week, one month, two months?

There is a fine line between antagonising your customers and showing them that you are on top of things. You will earn far more respect if they know that you have a strict credit control process.

If your customers have their own cashflow problems and can only afford to settle only some of their outstanding invoices, it is likely that your invoice will be one of those. After all, if the worst comes to the worst and their business fails, you don't want them to fail with your invoice unpaid!

Credit checks

For new customers, it is good business practice to carry out a company credit check to try to get some indication that the company with whom you will be dealing will be able to pay your invoices. Whilst such a check is no guarantee of payment, a company credit check with a good credit score provides some degree of comfort.

Even with existing customers, it is good practice to regularly check their credit worthiness as part of your credit control system. Diarising regular business credit checks is an important process for every business.

Even if the businesses that you are dealing with do not leave you with a bad debt, delayed payments can cause almost as many problems particularly in an environment of limited finance. Additionally, it can of course cost you time and money in chasing outstanding amounts.

Every business should have a clear system to deal with credit risk and should involve setting credit limits, procedures for chasing debts, all in line with your terms and conditions of business.

Company credit checks help build such a system.

Debt recovery

Surely your precious time is much better spent making money for your business rather than chasing your debts? Why not consider outsourcing your credit control functions to alleviate the worry of cashflow? By outsourcing this function you can detach yourself from appearing to be the bad guy.

When it comes to chasing bad debts, there's a perception that enforcement requires big men with hobnail boots and knuckle-dusters. This is neither the most effective method, nor the most likely to retain a customer after the debt is recovered.

While undoubtedly some debt recover companies do go in heavy-handedly, we wanted to do debt recovery in a different way to this stereotypical manner. That different way was a promise not to take sides, but to work with both parties to seek an amicable resolution. That ethos has stayed with us since we started, and is the cornerstone of our work. We now not only help our clients with their overdue invoices but also with all aspects of their cash flow.

Debt recovery is an art form and like anything else requires a specialist. Ask yourself what training have you had in this area?

The normal process can vary but in essence you must satisfy the court defined pre-action protocols and inform your debtor of your intentions through a (pre-action) letter. This letter must include certain details. The pre-action letter is also only valid for a certain period of time.

However, debt recovery, for us, is all about seeking a resolution before it ever gets to court. Presently you have 100% of nothing, so wouldn't something be better than nothing, plus getting that relationship back on track?

Cash flow is essential

Business finance is a topic that not everyone fully understands; neither the inner workings, nor the importance of a healthy cash flow. Any business can have a struggle at times with its cash flow, especially these days.

If you have a problem with your photocopier, you don't go and ask your bank manager to help fix it – you go to a specialist. If you need to improve your cash flow due to bad debts and / or late payments, and resurrect relationships with clients you thought were long over, you could consider outsourcing to a specialist.

After all, unless you are in the debt recovery business yourself, your skills lie elsewhere. Good time management is about maximising your opportunities to do what brings you an income. You don't have to be good at everything, and you particularly don't have to struggle with the less pleasant tasks all by yourself.

We all hear that the banks are not lending, or that their criteria are too stringent for you, so what is out there to ensure we stay financially healthy?

Factoring

In its simplest terms, factoring is the process of selling your invoices to a factoring company. This means that you get the cash quickly (sometimes the next day), and you don't have to collect or chase the debt. You also don't have to wait a month, two months or even longer to receive payment.

The factoring company then has to collect the payment. They make a profit by paying you less cash than the face value of the invoice, which is pre-agreed.

They will provide a professional and courteous service to collect the payment to ensure they don't upset your clients. In addition, as they also manage your sales ledger, this helps to cut down on your administration costs. You can use factoring in a number of ways:

- Get money quickly
- Avoid the hassle of chasing for payment
- Smooth your cash flow
- Borrow money, secured by your debt.

Invoice discounting

An invoice discounting company will buy the trade debts at an agreed funding rate. Discounters typically advance 80-85% of the face value of invoices and pay this immediately. The remaining 15-20%, less fees, is passed on to you when your customer pays.

The fundamental difference between invoice discounting and factoring is that you are responsible for the collection of cash from your debtors.

Where a Confidential Invoice Discounting (CID) facility is in place your customers are unaware that a discounter is funding your business.

The benefit of both factoring and invoice discounting is that once the facility is in place, there is no limit to the amount you can borrow as the level of finance is directly linked to the level of sales. So as your business grows so does the amount of funding available to you. This is in sharp contrast to bank overdrafts, which require regular re-negotiation and arrangement fees.

In addition, many discounting companies can provide a facility that will include bad debt insurance protection for additional security.

When should you write a debt off as bad?

You should only write a debt off if the debt is not valid or an expert has told you to. Don't assume that they won't pay and just write it off. Make sure you tell your accountant as there are further implications for businesses that are VAT registered.

Can you avoid ever having bad debts, or will there always be people who get away with it?

Good credit control will greatly help to avoid those problems and that includes good communication, but inevitably there will be a time when you get a bad debt. Dealing with it professionally and courteously is the way to approach it. All companies can pay late and have hundreds of reasons for doing so. As long as you're informed about it and happy then there's not a problem.

When emails start being unanswered, phone call diverted then the alarm bells should ring.

It's vital that you spend time on getting you terms and conditions and invoices correctly worded, out on time, to the right person, etc. Any company of any size that has poor cash flow will go bankrupt. The ultimate cost of poor credit control is therefore the loss of your business. So, whilst cashflow and debt management can seem like the elephant in the room for many people, it can also be very simple. Follow the advice above and get in touch if you have any further questions – this is what we do all day, every day!

Steve White is Managing Director of Thornbury Collections Ltd who help companies all sizes cash flow and debt recovery issues. Steve has been with Thornbury Collections since 2007, starting off as a Consultant and now as MD.

01443 224407
steve@thornburycollections.co.uk
www.thornburycollections.co.uk

Sue Worrall: Five Steps to Success

As small business owners we lead increasingly busy lives. The demands on our time, our physical resources, and our emotions sometimes appear never-ending. Rushing to see clients, going from meeting to meeting, or just slaving over the books for hours, all of these things take their toll over the long-term. If we don't take care of our body, how can we hope to maintain this pace?

Start with a healthy breakfast

I can't stress enough how important it is to eat breakfast. There are a few good reasons:

- You have been fasting for eight hours and at rest, but your body systems have been hard at work repairing, cleansing and detoxing. It's called *Break Fast* for a reason. Your body needs refuelling.
- Your brain can only use carbohydrates and needs some as you wake up in order to be alert for the day ahead.
- You also require a new supply of proteins to rebuild those sections the body has identified as needing further repair.
- Whether you are still in education, have a demanding job, or are responsible for your family and children, you need to be at your best at the start of each day in order to get the best out of it.

First thing in the day, you need to choose foods that keep your blood sugar level steady. You need to look for foods with a low *glycaemic index* or *glycaemic loading*. All carbohydrate foods are high in sugar but it's how *slowly* they are released into the blood stream that makes all the difference. There are good and bad sugars – the less refined and the more complex they are structurally, the better they are for you.

Exercise and rest

Exercise is really important for long and short term health. Our bodies were made to move, all our levers and pulleys need to be kept in good working order - it's use it or lose it. Also, our waste system has almost twice as much fluid as our cardiovascular system but it has no pump. It's movement alone that will help your lymphatic drainage system to move all the waste and toxins through and out of your body. The heart works to move blood around your body, but movement is the only way to get the toxins out.

So, people with sedentary jobs are at a greater risk of build-up of toxins and slower removal of waste products. If your job involves moving around a lot (and I don't mean sitting in a car for an hour), then you are doing your body a real favour. If you find yourself stuck in a chair for a while, then make sure you move around (get up, not just wriggle your toes) at least every hour.

Getting a good night's sleep is really important. That means quality sleep for 8-9 hours a night is optimum. Few people can really function on 4-5 hours of sleep, and while you might be able to do this occasionally, in the end it will catch up with you.

Have a strong reason

Why do you want to be healthy? It seems obvious, but if we simply think it's something we should do or it's others that want it for us more than we do for ourselves, it probably will not be sustained.

There are so many temptations to get into unhealthy habits and lifestyles. We need to really want good health more than the short term kick that bad foods or drinks provide. If we are to succeed and reap the rewards of great energy levels, fewer colds and viruses, looking younger, feeling more positive and gaining all round vitality, we need a strong reason why.

Supplement your nutritional intake

Our food is so depleted now that we can't get enough good nutrition from it unless we shop *very* carefully, or perhaps grow our own food. In the first years after the Second World War, we were underfed and well nourished. Now we are undernourished and overfed. The nutritional value of foods has been declining for years now, and even foods which might appear to be 'healthy', 'free range', 'organic', or 'something-free', are sometimes just a con. Food manufacturers appear to be consistently abusing the food chain, and as consumers it can feel overwhelming. While it might seem easier to just accept defeat and shovel anything in, in fact we are what we eat, and nobody else is ultimately responsible for what we become. Choosing to live in ignorance of what we eat is a choice. Sermon over. But in all seriousness, it's too easy to expect 'them' to sort it out for us, instead of taking personal responsibility.

Taking single vitamin supplements is a waste of time – the vast majority of the vitamin in a single dose ends up going straight through the body and into the toilet. You really could put it straight in there and cut out the middle-man. The body can only cope with a certain amount of each nutrient, and overloading it with any single one mean sit has to work extra-hard absorbing it, to the detriment of all others. Look instead for wide-spectrum nutritional supplements.

We all need good nutrition to live long healthy lives. If we enjoy exercise or have stressful jobs or situations we need more quality nutrition that will enable our body to recover and repair effectively. The food that is readily available to us is becoming more and more nutritionally depleted, and increasingly processed, and we need help to bridge that gap between what we would like to eat in an ideal world, and what we actually eat.

Anyone who remembers, or has seen, films and television from the 1950s onwards will recall futuristic views of the world that included taking in all our food as capsules. Our natural food supply isn't quite that bad yet, but we are well on the way to a world where the food we are able to buy just doesn't do the job is should. It may sell well, but it doesn't help our bodies.

Adopt a whole-food based diet

The *World Health Organization (WHO)* recommends a diet mainly based on fruits and vegetables and as part of their dietary advice promotes "5-a-Day". This means five daily portions of fruits and vegetables, preferably locally sourced. This equates to around 400-600g.

Furthermore, numerous scientific studies show that a good diet, based on fruits, vegetables and complex carbohydrates from starchy foods, linked with a good lifestyle, can help improve and maintain our health over time. We are so demanding on our mind and body nowadays that it has become necessary to adopt a diet that is as healthy and balanced as possible. Whilst the UK has adopted the "5-A-Day" recommended by the WHO, many other countries are now saying that we need more like 10-15 portions a day. Remember the adage, garbage in, garbage out? Well the same applies to your body. Mastering what we eat is one of the most basic ways we can also get the most from our business. Having the energy every day to face the challenges that business has to offer requires some self-discipline. Making the time to eat properly, hydrate regularly and rest properly will make all the difference.

Sue Worrall has been a nutritionist for over 20 years, working with business people, families, and sportspeople up to Olympic standard. Sue's an author, speaker and passionate advocate for healthy eating.

Twitter: @SueWorrallCom
www.sueworrall.com

Trish Fulford: *Three Little Words of Fear*

In business we live under a cloud of fear: fear that we may be prosecuted, fear that we may lose our business, fear that we may even lose our liberty. But ironically we also adopt a policy of complacency and contempt. What am I talking about? In three words, 'Health And Safety'.

These three little words seem to arouse so many emotions: fear, anger, contempt, and humour. So why has something that is as fundamental as you and your staff's welfare and safety become such a hated part of business life?

In a nutshell, we really have become victims of a Nanny state. We no longer appear to be trusted to make our own decisions about something as important as our own safety. So we have government funded quangos provide us with Codes of Practice which, whilst not telling us what we *must* do, advise us what we *should* do. However, if we choose to ignore these recommendations then we face prosecution. We are encouraged to have a paper trail for everything that we do so that we can exonerate ourselves in the event of a mishap.

We have all heard the "elf and safety police" stories. Like the headmaster that stopped his pupils playing conkers in the playground. Or the local council that would not erect summer flower baskets. Both of them too scared of people getting injured. This is Health and Safety gone mad. It's stories like these that have helped to create the contemptuous attitude people have towards such an important topic.

Health and Safety is important, and should never be treated flippantly. However, Health and Safety law is not black and white. It often uses phrases like "wherever practicably possible" rather than "you must do this", so is it little wonder that business owners are left wondering what they can and can't do in this arena of fifty-one shades of grey. Why fifty-one shades? Well, there are 51 Regulations that apply to general health and safety in the workplace. Most employers are unaware of most of them, and that's why they are scared into using the services of Health and Safety professionals. But Health and Safety is fundamentally just about common sense:

- Being aware of hazards
- Assessing the risks
- Using your common sense to control or remove the risks.

So when did it become necessary for the most intelligent and developed organisms on the planet (you) to need a manual the size of an encyclopaedia to be able to carry out our work safely? What happened to the common sense that we have learnt over the years?

The current government has acknowledged this state of lunacy, and that we are being strangled by legislation. They have determined that common sense must be allowed to prevail, at least some of the time. This is why David Cameron asked Lord Young of Graffham to commission a report called *Common Sense - Common Safety* in 2010. The purpose of the investigation was to take a long hard look at the legislation (Acts of Parliament) and the regulations that we are forced to abide by, and to apply a more common sense approach to how these rules are implemented.

The media, who have to take some responsibility for the anti-H&S hype, like to scare us further with press releases about issues like "Fees for intervention", which is where the Health and Safety Executive has the right to charge for intervening in your Health and Safety affairs prior to making a prosecution.

You must be aware that a breach of the *Health and Safety Act* is a *criminal* offence, and can result in large fines and/or imprisonment, apparently even more ammunition for having to use the services of Health and Safety professionals.

Because of these threats and also the litigious society that we live in, we have become obsessed with trying to follow the rules, often begrudgingly. But this often just involves undertaking paperwork exercises to satisfy our insurers, unions, or Local Authority.

This is not what Health and Safety is about! It is about ensuring that you and your staff are safe and well whilst in the work environment.

When regulations are passed, they have to take into consideration the worst-case scenarios. However, many that are applied to low-risk areas really do not warrant the level of protection that would be awarded in a high-risk activity or situation. For example, someone working off a ladder, erecting a satellite dish is at a much greater risk than someone using a stepladder in an office environment, and yet, since the removal of the 2-metre rule, exactly the same rules apply through the *Working at Height Regulations 2005*. Using a common sense approach here, a simplified risk assessment is the best course of action.

Actually, the perceived complicated undertaking of Risk Assessment is, in fact, really simple. For example, when you got in your car to go to work, or took the kids to school today you did a mental risk assessment. You checked your seat position, your mirror, you buckled up, you assessed the road conditions, checked your fuel, oil and water gauge, and if you were really vigilant you would have checked your water and oil.

We do this every day, without thinking about it, so why should it be made so mystical in a work environment?

You don't always need a severity and likelihood matrix to determine whether there is a risk or not, and you don't always need a qualified Health and Safety consultant to tell you what control measures you need to implement. Using common sense, you are able to cover most of the areas of risk in your business, and if you are unsure, then there is a mountain of information available through the Internet and the Health and Safety Executive (HSE).

The important thing to remember with Health and Safety is that everything we do in life has a risk; it's the control measures that we put in place that determine whether the risk is harmful or not. This may mean that we don't undertake the action at all, or it may mean that we have to change the way we do things, or we use some protective equipment.

The HSE devised a very simple approach to risk assessment called the *Five Steps*:

- Step 1 – Identify the hazards
- Step 2 – Decide who might be harmed and how
- Step 3 – Evaluate the risks and decide on precautions
- Step 4 – Record your findings and implement them
- Step 5 – Review your assessment and update if necessary.

You do not always need to apply the complicated approach of the professionals using Severity/Likelihood matrixes. This five-step system will allow you, with the help of your staff, to establish what the areas of concern are, and put the control measures in place to remove or reduce the risk.

You do *not* have to have a special form; you do not even *have* to document this if you have less than five employees. A word to the wise though. Whilst it is not a *requirement* in law to document, a paper trail will help your business in the event of a mishap. In the litigious society and the blame culture that we live in, it is in everyone's best interests to have a paper trail.

Let me clarify. If you are in business, you *must* adhere to Health and Safety Law, however, if you employ fewer than five members of staff (including yourself), you *do not* have to document it, unless you are in a high-risk occupation, such as construction.

Look for the hazards

Use your common sense. You can group hazards together if they have a common solution, or you can identify each one individually.

Look who might be harmed and how

Apply the same subconscious mentality that you used when you got in your car this morning. Think not just your workforce, but visitors, pedestrians, etc.

Think about the risks and use your common sense

Give people credit for not being stupid, whilst remembering that some people might be a little reckless. Knowing your staff and their behaviours can help here. Once you have evaluated the risks you can decide on how best to control them. For example, a risk may be removed or mitigated by someone being trained correctly on how to do something safely, so a control measure does not necessarily require you to spend loads of money.

Record your findings

We now know that the law does not require you to do this if you employ less than five people, unless you are in a particularly high-risk profession, such as construction.

Implementing measures to limit or remove risks

Unless you actually take the time to implement your measures, this has just been a wasted paperwork exercise.

Review

Personnel, environments, and circumstances change, so you need to regularly review for new hazards, and to check that the control measures you are using are effective. As a rule of thumb, your risk assessment should be revisited and every time there is:

- a change in staff
- a change in location
- a change in equipment
- a change in working practices.

View your risk assessments as a map to get you to where you want to be safely. They are something that everyone is able to undertake, and there is no need to be intimidated by them.

Trish Fulford is Managing Partner at HSC Partnership, developers of the Health and Safety Companion. This provides an online safety management solution for small to medium sized businesses. Trish has 21 years experience in the Health and Safety sector.

07861 718701
trish@healthandsafetycompanion.com
www.healthandsafetycompanion.com

Printed in Great Britain
by Amazon.co.uk, Ltd.,
Marston Gate.